Dean Datar,

HBS has played
such a pivotal
role in this book!
Thank you for all
that you do!
   Hemale '99
        H

Fundraising is one of the most crucial processes in alternative assets—and this book provides the frameworks to make it highly actionable, even for those with no prior fundraising experience. For experienced marketers, it provides fresh and insightful perspectives on an ever-evolving field.

—Frida Einarson,
Partner and Head of Investor Relations, Verdane

Marketing Alternative Investments takes a holistic and practical approach to fundraising. The book provides a very comprehensive guide to a challenging aspect of fund management and real-life tactical solutions—making it a must read for both fund managers and fundraisers.

—Daphne Dufresne,
Managing Partner, GenNx360

This book demystifies the arcane world of marketing to an immense but very nuanced pool of capital. Investors in alternatives are becoming ever more sophisticated, and selective about the managers they back going forward, especially with the steep and broad-based market selloff in the last 12 months. A must-read for not just first-time funds but also fund marketers with large IR teams who may need a refresher on latest trends in their customer base and sources of capital they may have overlooked.

—Sumit Pande,
former Head of Technology, Media & Telecom Investments,
Qatar Investment Authority Advisory, USA

Alternative investments, strictly speaking, are no longer "alternative." They are now mainstream. Two countercurrents are at play here. On the one hand, the industry is consolidating. On the other hand, new superstar managers are emerging. And investors are getting more demanding. If you have ambitions in this area, this book is a good guide on how to navigate fundraising.

—Gaurav Dalmia,
Chairman, Dalmia Group Holdings

SECTION 3
OTHER CONSIDERATIONS

CONTENTS

SECTION 1
FUNDAMENTALS

SECTION 2
FUNDRAISING IN PRACTICE

*Damyanti and Girdhari Dassani, aka Mom
and Dad, you have always encouraged me to
reach for the stars. Malaika McKee-Culpepper,
you believed in this book decades before it was
born, and planted the seed on those late-night
walks through Harvard Square. Thank you.*

Hemali

*Gratitude: My parents, Lalitha and Kuppuswamy,
and siblings for envisioning a future beyond our
circumstances. Dilip, Madan, and Vidya for helping
me realize that future. And my wife, Jyotsna, and
children, Amrutha and Aaditya, for their resolute
belief in me and for loving me despite myself.*

Nandu

1 2 3 4 5 6 7 8 9   LCR   27 26 25 24 23 22

ISBN   978-1-264-62764-6
MHID   1-264-62764-5

e-ISBN   978-1-264-63045-5
e-MHID   1-264-63045-X

This publication is designed to provide accurate and authoritative information in regard to the subject matter covered. It is sold with the understanding that neither the author nor the publisher is engaged in rendering legal, accounting, securities trading, or other professional services. If legal advice or other expert assistance is required, the services of a competent professional person should be sought.
> —*From a Declaration of Principles Jointly Adopted by a Committee of the American Bar Association and a Committee of Publishers and Associations*

Library of Congress Cataloging-in-Publication Data

Names: Dassani, Hemali, author.
Title: Marketing alternative investments / Hemali Dassani.
Description: New York, NY : McGraw Hill, [2022] | Includes bibliographical
  references and index.
Identifiers: LCCN 2022025939 (print) | LCCN 2022025940 (ebook) |
  ISBN 9781264627646 (hardcover) | ISBN 9781264630455 (ebook)
Subjects: LCSH: Investments. | Marketing—Cost effectiveness.
Classification: LCC HG4521 .D127 2022 (print) | LCC HG4521 (ebook) |
  DDC 332.6—dc23/eng/20220805
LC record available at https://lccn.loc.gov/2022025939
LC ebook record available at https://lccn.loc.gov/2022025940

McGraw Hill books are available at special quantity discounts to use as premiums and sales promotions or for use in corporate training programs. To contact a representative, please visit the Contact Us pages at www.mhprofessional.com.

McGraw Hill is committed to making our products accessible to all learners. To learn more about the available support and accommodations we offer, please contact us at accessibility@mheducation.com. We also participate in the Access Text Network (www.accesstext.org), and ATN members may submit requests through ATN.

MARKETING ALTERNATIVE INVESTMENTS

A COMPREHENSIVE GUIDE TO FUNDRAISING AND INVESTOR RELATIONS FOR PRIVATE EQUITY AND HEDGE FUNDS

HEMALI DASSANI
AND
NANDU KUPPUSWAMY, CFA

New York Chicago San Francisco Athens London Madrid
Mexico City Milan New Delhi Singapore Sydney Toronto

With unprecedented numbers of managers coming to market for re-ups as well as new managers competing for capital from the same investors, *Marketing Alternative Investments* is a timely and relevant book for any manager, large or small, looking to succeed in an overcrowded marketplace.

—Marvin S. Rosen,
shareholder, Greenberg Traurig, LLP

Marketing Alternatives Investments provides a detailed guide for private equity, venture capital, and hedge fund managers, marketers, and placement agents to successfully navigate the challenges and nuances of fundraising.

—Michael Oshiro,
CEO, CapLink Securities

Talent is at the core of any successful fund enterprise. That applies to a fund's investment team, their portfolio companies, and also to the operations and fundraising functions of an alternatives firm. *Marketing Alternative Investments* is an authoritative guide for alternative investment funds, especially as they address their senior talent requirements. The book discusses the process of fund marketing and ways to develop highly sought-after marketing talent. Highly recommended!

—Craig Buffkin,
Managing Partner Buffkin/Baker
(former Global Chairman, Panorama Search)

Hemali Dassani and Nandu Kuppuswamy have managed to make the complicated understandable. This book goes a long way to demystifying one of the foundational aspects of alternative investments.

—Steven Siegel,
Partner & Chief Operating Officer, KSL Capital Partners

Insightful, practical, and comprehensive. This thorough guide is an essential read for anyone looking to learn the state of the art in fundraising for alternative investments today.

—Martin Brand,
Head of North America Private Equity and Global
Co-Head of Technology Investing, Blackstone

Alternative asset fundraising has evolved considerably in the last few decades, and this book is a well written guide that explores the latest thinking. A valuable read for both experienced practitioners and fledgling marketers alike, whether while raising new money or better comprehending an important part of the fund life cycle.

—Sundip Murthy,
Partner, Norwest Equity Partners

Having been in private equity for over 25 years, this is one of the rare books that gives some clarity to the opaque world of fund raising. Anyone thinking about raising capital should read it—be it the investment professional who is looking to start a firm or the marketing person charged with fundraising. The field is getting more crowded, and going to market as smart as possible and with a plan can mean the difference in a successful fundraise or not.

—Ray Whiteman,
Co-Founder and Managing Partner, Stellex Capital Management

This practical guide offers invaluable advice in one of the most important aspects of fund success—earning investor confidence and building trust though effective communication and partnership. It's a unique and essential reference for anyone working in private equity and alternative investments.

—Laila Worrell,
CEO, Harvard Business Publishing,
private equity senior advisor and former portfolio company CEO

ACKNOWLEDGMENTS

I t has been almost two decades since we joined the alternatives investment industry. We made mistakes; we learned from thoughtful employers, meticulous and experienced investors, fellow marketers, and other industry professionals. We closed fundraising deals and learned how to write investor communications. We wished we had a guide—a compendium of what we needed to do, frameworks for how to think about our jobs, and mistakes to avoid. But we could not find a good guide, let alone one that was comprehensive. Three years ago, we began putting pen to paper to share our story, our view of the salient points of fundraising and investor relations.

This book is a passion project, a pay-it-forward effort from the two of us to give back to the industry that has benefited us so much. But that would not have been possible without the support of countless individuals: investors, fund managers and marketers, fund formation attorneys, placement agents, service providers, and many other intermediaries. In a secretive industry such as ours, many chose to be anonymous. But you know who you are. We are grateful for the hundreds of formal and informal conversations, breakfasts, rushed calls, and most important, the strong support throughout our three-year journey in writing this book. Additionally, we are thankful to our past employers, colleagues, investors, service providers, and other industry participants from whom we learned invaluable lessons. We acknowledge the ideas we captured emanated from a thousand wonderful minds. Any mistakes, unfortunately, are our own responsibility. We have tried our best to avoid them.

Additionally, we are really grateful to the experts that have helped us, and want to encourage readers to seek out the counsel of experts in a rapidly evolving regulatory landscape.

We are incredibly thankful to those who supported us in the development of this book. Mukul Pandya, your valuable insights and past experiences with Knowledge@Wharton, your countless introductions to thought leaders, and your daily encouragement made our book all the more special. Deborah Yao, our daily editor for five months, you were our saving grace. Sejal Goud, our Princeton University research assistant, you diligently scrubbed every data source and worked tirelessly during your holidays. Saira Dadlani, our University of Michigan research assistant, your tenacious work ethic helped us ensure the accuracy of data elements and create a robust marketing plan. We are very grateful to the numerous researchers and data aggregators who allowed us to reference or use their data for this book.

We also wish to thank Jeanne Glasser Levine, literary agent extraordinaire and founder of PubZone Consulting. We are grateful for your 30 years in the publishing industry that allowed you to make that warm introduction to McGraw Hill, which accelerated our journey to becoming published authors for the first time with one of the leading educational publishers in the world. And Judith Newlin, senior editor at McGraw Hill, for whom we have had the utmost respect since the moment we began these conversations and whose guidance, prompt responses, and unwavering support made it a true partnership. We thank you for believing in our book, championing us within your organization, and encouraging us to create the most valuable content we could offer to our diverse readers.

For all those who have contributed to this endeavor, we hope you enjoy reading this book as much as we did writing it.

With gratitude,
Hemali and Nandu

M onths before his death in the spring of 2021, David Swensen, the legendary chief investment officer of Yale University, sent a letter to the roughly 70 fund managers handling the university's more than $30 billion endowment.[1] He had been reflecting on the Black Lives Matter protests of the previous summer and decided that Yale would do its part in promoting diversity. Swensen's letter required fund managers to complete a survey on gender and racial diversity at their firms, with annual updates. Firms that did not show an improvement in hiring women and minorities over time would risk their allocations being taken away.[2]

Getting a foot in the door at institutions like Yale is much tougher today for fund managers than during the industry's heydays in the 1990s. Institutional investors no longer focus on having their portfolios managed by "star managers," whose investment acumen is expected to generate market-beating returns. Name recognition alone is not good enough to convince investors to allocate capital to the fund manager, and as Swensen's letter proves, neither is an excellent track record. Today, amid immense competition for investor capital, institutional investors look to the team, processes, strategy, and investment philosophy rather than rely on a single, brilliant individual.

GETTING AN EDGE

Successful marketing of alternative investments—often defined as assets that do not fall into conventional types like stocks, bonds, or cash—requires a specialized skill set that goes beyond traditional asset management sales. Many marketing books are too broad to address the needs of the industry, lacking contextual familiarity with investor wants, needs, sensitivities, and no-go areas. Overly broad customer relations paradigms are often impractical in an industry where significant risks and rewards abound, and the investor has little de facto control over the assets once the allocation is made to a manager.

Attracting deep-pocketed institutional investors is desirable, but few fund managers succeed in doing so. As such, most of the industry's marketing professionals learn "on the job" by trial and error—an expensive proposition few firms can afford. The success of an alternative investment firm relies not only on investment prowess but also on the ability to raise and maintain assets. This book is a practical guide to building an alternative investment marketing program, adaptable to big or small firms.

To be sure, in a crowded field of more than 10,000 hedge funds and at least 18,000 private equity managers globally,[3] investors may find it difficult to differentiate among similar funds. However, funds that are able to convey their "story" well will succeed in raising capital from investors.

To craft a highly effective marketing strategy for alternative investments, the key is to understand the investors' investment objectives, sensitivities, restrictions, and decision-making processes—prior to designing and embarking on a marketing campaign. While it is impractical for a fund marketer to know every investor's history and aspirations, some common threads exist based on the structure of the organization, as well as pertinent information that can be synthesized and acquired through research, and through public or commercial databases. Fund marketers need to design a thoughtful marketing and fundraising campaign based on the needs of their desired set of investors, instead of deploying a "spray and pray" approach.

PAYING IT FORWARD

For us, the authors, this book is a pay-it-forward, passion project. We are friends and industry colleagues, both of whom have spent over 15 years in the industry as investors and senior investor relations professionals. Much of our professional learning has been on the job, and we both have benefited from the coaching, mentoring, and advice received from friends, colleagues, and even LPs showing us the ropes. We have spent three years speaking with successful marketers, fund managers, allocators, service providers, and thought leaders in the industry to learn and collate best practices and standards of excellence in marketing alternative investments. Our objective is to share this collective wisdom with our readers.

We believe an investor-centric marketing and fundraising strategy is superior to product-guided fundraising, which is unfortunately the industry practice.

There are three major sections of the book:

1. **Fundamentals**

   Understanding your customer is the first and most important step in any marketing process. This section discusses the history, structure, decision process, stakeholders, investment expectations, regulations, and relevant information on major institutional investor groups.

2. **Fundraising in practice**

   This section gets into the tools, techniques, issues, regulations, skill sets, and processes required to complete a full marketing cycle from premarketing through investor relations. It covers a multitude of topics, techniques, and processes that fund managers need to build an efficient and effective marketing strategy and convert it into an actionable plan.

3. **Other considerations**

   The last section addresses key building blocks for a successful franchise in an evolving alternatives landscape. We talk about diversity, technology, and what we wished we had known when we began our careers in fundraising and investor relations.

We want our readers to:

- Gain an understanding of marketing alternative investments and the stakeholders involved
- Develop a process-oriented marketing plan that relies less on individual brilliance
- Build an investor-centric sales strategy that is suited to investor and stakeholder needs
- Improve marketing efficiency and effectiveness to add value at each interaction
- Follow a marketing process that is not burdensome on stakeholders (limited partners [LPs] and general partners [GPs] and service providers)

While speaking with various industry thought leaders, we made an early decision to not linger on terminology when there is variability in usage along with a wide acceptance of different words and phrases that all mean the same thing—"alternative investments," "alternative assets," "alternative investment class," and "alternatives" are all equally acceptable. Similarly, general partner (GP) and fund manager refer to the team or person who invests capital on behalf of a limited partner (LP), the asset allocator or investor who provides capital to a manager to invest on their behalf. We also have chosen to focus on two large sets of alternatives—private equity and hedge funds. However, note that most of the advice on private equity applies to a wide variety of closed-end fund structures with fixed terms in the private (not listed on an exchange) investments domain, including venture capital, buyouts, growth capital, and mezzanine finance. Similarly, in this book hedge funds refer to open-ended funds without a fixed term in the private investments domain. This is because:

1. The primary differentiator while marketing alternative funds is open- versus closed-end structures. Many of the other factors—liquidity, cash flows, return profiles, fund terms—are all neatly structured within this construct. The limitless variance around a common structure does not radically impact the marketing of these funds.

2. Other considerations that do impact marketing, such as regulations, are dependent on investment strategies that are too numerous for a single book to tackle. We aim to share best practices across alternatives, rather than offering guidelines specifically tailored for each and every strategy.

WHY ONLY ALTERNATIVES?

1. **Alternative investments are a large and rapidly expanding market.**[4]

   Total capital managed by private equity is around $5 trillion and is expected to grow to $9 trillion by 2025, which represents a 16 percent annual growth. For hedge funds, total assets under management were $4.3 trillion as of the second quarter of 2021. As the industry matures, there are new pools of capital around the world that are making significant allocations to alternatives for the first time. These range from large pension funds to smaller institutions and high-net-worth individuals. Furthermore, industry consolidation makes marketing an extremely critical component of success for midsize and small funds.

2. **Investors seek reassurance due to lack of transparency, control, and high dispersion of returns in alternatives.**

   a. Traditional assets (such as equity and debt mutual funds, ETFs, among others) are transparent. Investors in traditional assets know the actual investments they are in, even if that is likely to change later, based on either a benchmark change or through active management by the fund manager. When allocating to alternatives, however, investors are committing capital to a blind pool. The main constraint is what the managers can invest in and how they can manage the investment. Furthermore, as alternatives are considered the domain of "sophisticated" investors with high risk tolerance, there is limited active regulation to protect them as compared to traditional investments.

The bottom line is that investors back a specific investment when they invest in traditional assets, and they back a manager (including their investment strategy, acumen, and trustworthiness) when they invest in alternatives.

b. Alternatives are illiquid. Once investors make an investment, they have to wait until the lock-up expires (hedge funds) or there is an exit through a sale or liquidation from an investment (private equity) to get their money back, along with any returns. Further, the manager has complete autonomy regarding investment decisions within predetermined boundary conditions. This complete lack of control for investors means the cost of a choosing a wrong manager could be quite high.

c. While the average investment returns for alternatives are significantly higher than those of traditional securities—which drive high investor demand—there is great dispersion in returns between top quartile and bottom quartile managers in the same asset class as seen in Figure I.1. A great manager in an unfavorable subcategory could significantly outperform an average manager in a favorable subcategory. Traditional assets have a much narrower range (less than 2 percent for debt and 3 percent for equity) when measured over 10-year periods.

3. Marketing is limited by regulation in most jurisdictions.

In the United States, prior to September 2013, alternative funds were not allowed to advertise. Given alternatives' higher complexity, illiquidity, and risk profile, the restriction against advertising was to prevent fraud and to avoid solicitation of ineligible or inappropriate investors (nonaccredited). Even if funds attract investors without solicitation, managers have to confirm the accreditation or qualification status of the investor before engaging with them—adding to marketing friction when connecting with qualified investors. Similar restrictions are seen in Europe's

FIGURE I.1 Average annual manager returns by asset class, January 1, 2007–September 30, 2021

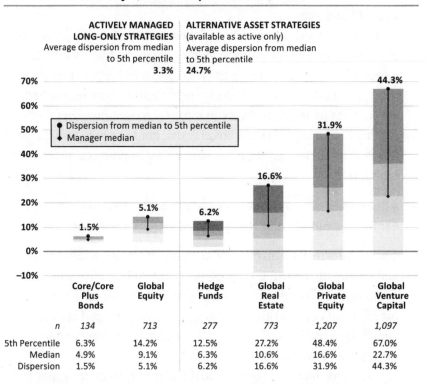

	ACTIVELY MANAGED LONG-ONLY STRATEGIES Average dispersion from median to 5th percentile 3.3%	ALTERNATIVE ASSET STRATEGIES (available as active only) Average dispersion from median to 5th percentile 24.7%

	Core/Core Plus Bonds	Global Equity	Hedge Funds	Global Real Estate	Global Private Equity	Global Venture Capital
n	134	713	277	773	1,207	1,097
5th Percentile	6.3%	14.2%	12.5%	27.2%	48.4%	67.0%
Median	4.9%	9.1%	6.3%	10.6%	16.6%	22.7%
Dispersion	1.5%	5.1%	6.2%	16.6%	31.9%	44.3%

Source: Cambridge Associates LLC.

Notes: Returns for bond, equity, and hedge fund managers are average annual compound returns (AACRs) for the fifteen years ended September 30th, 2021, and only managers with performance available for the entire period are included. Returns for private investment managers are horizon internal rates of return (IRRs) calculated since inception to September 30th, 2021. Time-weighted returns (AACRs) and money-weighted returns (IRRs) are not directly comparable. Cambridge Associates LLC's (CA) bond, equity, and hedge fund manager universe statistics are derived from CA's proprietary Investment Manager Database. Managers that do not report in US dollars, exclude cash reserves from reported total returns, or have less than $50 million in product assets are excluded. Performance of bond and public equity managers is generally reported gross of investment management fees. Hedge fund managers generally report performance net of investment management fees and performance fees. CA derives its private benchmarks from the financial information contained in its proprietary database of private investment funds. The pooled returns represent the net end-to-end rates of return calculated on the aggregate of all cash flows and market values as reported to Cambridge Associates by the funds' general partners in their quarterly and annual audited financial reports. These returns are net of management fees, expenses, and performance fees that take the form of a carried interest. Vintage years include 2007–2018.

Alternative Investment Fund Managers Directive (AIFMD) and in Section 21 of Financial Services and Markets Act (FSMA) in the United Kingdom.

Even after restrictions were relaxed as part of the JOBS Act in 2013, broadly advertising for investors would be like looking for a needle in a haystack, given the narrow qualifications, making this type of advertising extremely inefficient. Therefore, marketing alternatives requires an ability to attract the right investors without explicit marketing. No such broad restrictions apply to traditional assets that rely heavily on mass advertising to promote their products.

4. **Alternatives are complex financial products that may rely on esoteric securities and strategies, as well as a manager's skill set.**

These skills include investment acumen, expertise in taking over and managing a portfolio company, ability to influence a target company (activist investing), capability to leverage capital markets for financial engineering or exiting an investment, and talent for deploying a plethora of complex structures and technology to generate investment returns.

Investors, however sophisticated and experienced they may be, are not subject matter experts in these strategies and need to be educated to be confident in and comfortable with an investment. Marketers of alternatives must be able to explain the product in layman's terms, answer questions about the product and its associated risk profiles, while simultaneously making it appealing to investors. Part of connecting with the investor is building relationships and trust, part of it is pure salesmanship, and another is the ability to simplify extremely complex and risky products. The tools and techniques needed to succeed are vastly different from those of traditional assets.

In addition, an alternatives marketer relies on a direct relationship with a set of accredited investors and qualified purchasers who are highly sought after and constantly solicited by all kinds of fund managers (both traditional and alternative managers). To stand out in such a crowded market is a skill that few possess, but one that can be learned with experience and coaching.

5. **Most sales of traditional assets occur through distribution channels where the marketer is focused on intermediaries (like RIAs, retirement plans, and brokerages).**

The marketer of a traditional investment product would build a relationship with the distributor and push them to promote the firm's products. There is no real direct sales relationship to speak of between the fund manager and the investor, other than with intermediaries or large institutions. In contrast, the alternatives marketer relies on direct relationships with a set of accredited investors (including qualified purchasers) and institutions to sell their products and services.

A FINAL NOTE

There are plenty of reliable and well-researched books, guides, and journals addressing the investing function in alternatives. Yet there is a conspicuous absence of reliable books and guides addressing other functional areas that are necessary in a maturing alternatives industry—including marketing and fund operations. Our goal is to close the gap and provide a comprehensive and authoritative primer on alternatives marketing and capital formation that encompasses fundraising, investor relations, brand management, ethics, and public relations.

FUNDAMENTALS

CHAPTER 1

Endowments and Foundations

The foundation of any marketing strategy is to "know your customers." In the alternative investment marketspace, a few categories of investors are dominant. Endowments, foundations, pension funds, sovereign wealth funds, funds of funds, family offices, insurance companies, registered investment advisors, and high-net-worth individuals are all increasing their exposure to alternative investments. These groups of investors, within the same category, share common characteristics, face similar constraints, and often are governed by the same regulations. Given the growth and their dominance in the alternative investment space, it is important to understand each of the categories well before starting a fundraising campaign. This chapter, and the others in Section 1, focuses on "knowing your customer" for alternatives.

Endowments and foundations (E&Fs) are entities designed to meet a set of social objectives or "good" causes. A long history of American philanthropy, dating back to the nineteenth century, enabled the growth of these institutions. E&Fs are among the largest investors in alternatives, which are investments outside of traditional stocks and bonds. These institutional investors are often presumed to be perpetual entities and as such are long-term asset holders. This long view accords them the latitude to assume additional portfolio risks, such as investing in illiquid assets and exploring new asset classes, and still build a portfolio that meets their objectives, even if a particular investment or asset class in itself might be deemed risky.

There are distinct differences between endowments and foundations, although the alternatives industry generally groups them together.

In practice, while there is much overlap between them when it comes to their approach to investing in alternatives, there is also value in discussing them separately to better understand key but nuanced differences between the two.

ENDOWMENTS: A SHORT HISTORY

Roman Emperor Marcus Aurelius is credited with establishing the first endowment in the second century, when he personally funded chairs to head the four schools of philosophy in Athens: Platonism, Aristotelianism, Stoicism, and Epicureanism.[1] He set an example for others to follow, inspiring the practice of setting up endowments to fund the activities of educational, cultural, religious, medical, or other nonprofit entities. The practice of *glebe* (providing land within a parish to support a priest) in medieval Europe and *waqf* in the Middle East (donating assets for religious, educational, or charitable purposes) have similar purpose to the endowments of today, even if they differ in implementation.[2]

Initially, the assets of an endowment mostly consisted of agricultural land and other physical assets given by the donor or patron. That changed in the early 1900s, when English economist John Maynard Keynes was appointed bursar of Cambridge University's King's College right after World War I and he diversified the university's endowment portfolio by investing nearly 75 percent of the endowment in equities.[3] While his initial market-timing approach failed, in particular by not anticipating the stock market crash of 1929, his subsequent switch to a buy-and-hold strategy would lay the foundation of modern endowment management.

ENDOWMENTS COME IN ALL SIZES

Today, the word *endowment* might conjure up images of large, ivy-covered universities with multibillion-dollar funds, but this is an incomplete picture. There are a variety of endowments; essentially, they consist of a pool of investable assets, typically received as a donation, to be used for funding the operations of a nonprofit institution whose mission is consistent with the donor's wishes. Endowments are considered perpetual capital by which the original principal is meant to be kept intact, and earnings from the investment are used for funding or supporting the beneficiary entity's operations in accordance with the donor intent. While endowments themselves are often structured as nonprofits, they do not always qualify as public charities as they usually only have a single major source of funding.

There were 774 large endowments in the United States and Canada at the end of fiscal 2019, according to the participant count of the NACUBO-TIAA Study of Endowments.[4] But the actual number of endowments may be significantly larger, accounting for smaller entities not captured in the study. The market value of endowment funds in US colleges and universities in fiscal 2018 totaled $648 billion.[5] Of the total, $474 billion or 76.9 percent were held by the 104 largest endowments, those with at least $1 billion in assets.[6] The largest is Harvard University's endowment, with a market value of $53.2 billion.[7]

However, the median market value of endowments in the survey is far lower, at around $140 million. Most endowments do not invest on their own, but rather allocate chunks of capital to outside fund managers whose investment strategies and execution align with the endowment's investment objective. Endowment funds are more akin to a fund of funds, where the endowment's investment officer focuses on asset allocation, due diligence, portfolio management, and monitoring while external fund managers are responsible for security selection.

Endowments hold some of the largest pools of institutional capital available for investment in alternative assets. They were among the earliest large investors in alternatives such as hedge funds, private equity, and venture capital—particularly after David Swensen, the former chief investment officer of Yale University, shifted to the "Yale model" of endowment management in the mid-1980s with a higher allocation to alternative assets. As of June 2018, 28 percent of endowments had an allocation to alternatives in their portfolios.[8] But this average hides the true dispersion of exposure to alternatives: on a dollar-weighted basis, it is actually nearly double, at 52 percent.

The difference is due to the higher allocation to alternatives by larger endowments. Those with assets of more than \$1 billion allocated 58 percent of their capital to alternatives. As of June 2018, around \$321 billion was allocated to alternatives, of which \$275 billion came from just 104 endowments. The bottom line: there is a big pool of endowment-capital-seeking fund managers who can help them achieve their investment objectives, and there are managers who are seeking long-term capital for their funds, making them a great match for each other.

PLAYING THE LONG GAME

Today, an average endowment supports nearly 10 percent of the operating budget of the beneficiary institution. The challenge is to ensure they not only preserve the real (after inflation) purchasing power of principal and expected earnings, but also consistently support the institutions' spending needs. The following is the formula to calculate the long-term (LT) return of endowments:

$$\underset{(2\% \text{ to } 3\%)}{\underset{\text{LT Return}}{\text{Expected}}} = \underset{(2\% \text{ to } 3\%)}{\underset{\text{LT Inflation}}{\text{Expected}}} + \underset{(4\% \text{ to } 5\%)}{\underset{\text{for Institution}}{\text{Stable Support}}} + \underset{(50 \text{ to } 200 \text{ bps})}{\underset{\text{Growth}}{\text{Margin for}}}$$

The average expected long-term return for US endowments in fiscal year 2018 was 7.2 percent annually, but the actual return fell below expectations at 5.8 percent. However, given long investment horizons and holding periods for endowments, one advantage is they can play the time-horizon arbitrage game that few others can. What it means is that they can accept the illiquidity of investing in longer lock-up vehicles such as private equity, real assets, and hedge funds, as long as they can expect to be adequately compensated for the risk.

ENDOWMENT SPENDING BUDGETS AND IMPACT ON INVESTMENT POLICY

Endowments must set a Goldilocks spending budget for their nonprofits: not too much so as to preserve enough capital for the future, but not so little that it would curtail support sorely needed by beneficiaries who cannot function well when their budgets are uncertain. The situation gets more complicated when one considers economic and market conditions.

When the economy is weak and the market is in a decline, the demand for support typically increases from beneficiaries, so lowering funding in tough times is a nonstarter. However, giving more to beneficiaries in these times also brings risks. Raising spending incurs an excessive opportunity cost; the endowment could have invested these funds when the market is down and prices are low. By increasing the giving instead of investing the funds, the endowment is hurting its own future returns.

How do endowments balance the needs of beneficiaries and the need to generate adequate future returns? They choose spending policies based on what is mission-critical to them, which opens up a variety of methods. The simplest one is to set a fixed distribution over several years. This is either a fixed monetary amount adjusted for inflation or as a percentage of the endowment's market value. Others have more complex methods, including weighting for both stability (spending adjusted for inflation) and variability (percentage of the market value). The following is the formula for the MIT endowment's spending policy:[9]

$$\text{Distribution} = 80\% \times \begin{pmatrix} \text{Inflation} \\ \text{Adjusted Prior} \\ \text{Year Distribution} \end{pmatrix} + 20\% \times \left(5.1\% \times \begin{pmatrix} \text{Market} \\ \text{Value of} \\ \text{Endowment} \end{pmatrix}\right)$$

ENDOWMENT STRUCTURE AND STAFFING

Organizational and ownership structures at endowments are in the middle of a long-term evolution. Most endowments do not usually make direct investments, but invest the capital through external managers. The endowment staff is primarily responsible for asset allocation, manager search and selection, due diligence, performance monitoring, portfolio (endowment) risk management, and reporting.

Investment management at endowments generally are structured in one of three ways:

1. Asset allocation and portfolio management are undertaken by investment staff employed by the beneficiary (e.g., Yale).
2. An external investment management firm manages the entire endowment (e.g., MITCO, DUMAC, UVIMCO). This investment manager can be fully or partly owned by the beneficiary entity.
3. Investment functions are fully or partially outsourced, such as hiring an outsourced chief investment officer (e.g., Investure, Commonfund, Cambridge Associates, Makena), structuring fund of fund vehicles (e.g., Adams Street, Commonfund, Portfolio Advisors), or adding outside financial advisors.

No matter how the investment function is divided up by the institution, there will be oversight by a board of advisors, trustees, or an investment committee (IC). This is essential for ensuring compliance with the endowment's fiduciary responsibilities. The chief investment officer (CIO), whether internal or outsourced, reports to the board or investment committee and is accountable for day-to-day operations. An efficient and effective relationship between the board or investment committee and the endowment's CIO is one where the strategic direction and asset allocation policy are set together, but the individual investment decisions are made by the CIO. As Greenwich Associates founder Charles D. Ellis wrote in the foreword to David Swensen's *Pioneering Portfolio Management*: "One secret in Yale's success has been David Swensen's ability to *engage the committee in governance—and not in investment management.*"[10] [italic emphasis added]

UNDERSTANDING MOTIVATIONS

Endowments are perpetual pools of capital that are expected to go on indefinitely, but people in the investment management industry work with much shorter time frames and are compensated accordingly. While investment management firms often closely tie a fund manager's bonuses to performance to align incentives, it is not quite the same for the endowment's investment officer. The risk of a bad decision is a personal consequence for the employed investment staff. Given the size of investments, a single wrong investment decision could mean a demotion, lost bonus, or getting fired from the job.

Moreover, the same investment officer does not reap the benefits of superior returns from a great investment decision. In most cases, when the endowment earns amazing returns for an investment, the employee gets a small discretionary payout, if any. Fund marketers and general partners need to understand and appreciate the personal risks that play a conscious or subconscious role in the endowment staff evaluating your fund for an investment.[11]

It isn't uncommon to find several endowments gravitating toward the same fund manager, despite "sibling rivalry" among them, their objectives are similar and often face comparable constraints. There is safety in numbers and it is comforting for the endowment to choose someone familiar to the industry. Endowments are "patient" capital, seeking long-term relationships with managers; finding a new manager tends to be an arduous, laborious, resource-intensive and time-consuming task. Even if a fund has an excellent track record showing superior risk-adjusted returns and strong management teams, it does not guarantee the endowment will evaluate the fund, let alone consider it for an investment.

The decision to choose a fund manager, as with any investment decision, is made in the context of how that choice fits with the portfolio, and how it would help in achieving the endowment's investment objectives. Some questions they might consider: Is there diversification across sources of risks and returns including by asset class, liquidity, geography, reinvestment, duration, sociopolitical factors, and loss of purchasing power? Is there low correlation with existing investments and investment strategies? Are the targeted returns and risks assumed in line with portfolio objectives?

Furthermore, no matter how sound the investment is financially, institutions are particularly cautious of allocating capital to funds where there may be reputational risk. Institutions are dependent on donors who fund operations and contribute to endowments. Negative publicity alienates potential donors and adversely impacts donor fundraising efforts, whether the bad press is due to mismanagement of funds (as in the Bernie Madoff embezzlement case) or holding investments that are incompatible with the endowments' social goals (e.g., student protests during 2019 against endowments holding Puerto Rican debt).

ASSET ALLOCATION AND MANAGER SELECTION

While the process for a manager to receive an allocation varies from endowment to endowment, they do share common threads. Generally, endowments are flat and lean organizations. They are aware of the need for efficiency and the limitations lean staffing levels impose on them. For fund managers hoping to be selected, they are most interested in the investment officer's manager selection process. But the investment officer's day-to-day responsibilities go beyond; they include asset allocation, portfolio and manager monitoring, performance analysis, investment market research, risk management, due diligence, and other administrative tasks. With this context in mind, the investment officer will be efficiently sorting fund managers out of dozens of pitches they receive to determine who will likely add value to the portfolio. It is often a process of elimination.

Marketers should understand the differences between small and large endowments. The staffing and capabilities of endowments vary, but are associated closely with the size of its assets. Most endowments with more than $1 billion in assets have their own investment staff, and larger endowments like Harvard have the staffing and expertise to evaluate and allocate capital to primary investments. Smaller endowments do not have such resources, which constrains them in what investments to take up. They may circumvent the problem by outsourcing their investment operations to CIO firms and other asset managers.

THE MARKETER'S ROLE

As a marketer, you need to understand the thought process of an endowment's investment officer. These are some questions that go through their mind:

1. Is this an asset class the endowment should be invested in?
2. Is the manager's strategy the best way to achieve the goals of why we are investing in the asset class in the first place?
3. Do I trust this manager not only to deliver the results I want to achieve, but also to act in the investor's best interest at all times like a fiduciary?

A fund marketer should be able to address those essential questions completely and to the satisfaction of the investment officer before he or she will make an investment. Here is some context around those questions to help you craft the best answer:

1. **Is this an asset class the endowment should be invested in?**

   This is an internal decision of the endowment and there is very little a fund manager or any other external party can do to influence this choice. The decision is a strategic choice based on the needs, capabilities, and limitations of the organization. However, those needs can and do evolve over time; it is worth maintaining the relationship even if there is no imminent payoff—so long as you do so in an unobtrusive manner that is beneficial to the investor.

   One common mistake made by marketers is to add the investment officers to a broad mailing list and inundate them with communication that is not relevant or particularly interesting. This approach could result in your inclusion on a list of spammers and could cost you the relationship. The more effective method is to be respectful of the investors' needs and interests, and categorize investors into groups of similar interests and needs: immediate prospects willing to know as much as possible about the fund, long-term prospects who want to learn about the fund's thinking and execution over time, potential clients who are only interested in white papers and industry studies, and so on. This will help "mass customize" the content to be shared for efficiency and manage the frequency of communication. If the investment officer's thinking evolves and there is a potential for them to include your fund in their portfolio, you will be a point of call for them.

A simple time-saver is to have an initial screening discussion with an officer of the endowment. You can determine if what you are offering is in line with its needs, and direct the conversation to what is relevant to the investor—instead of conducting a pushy marketing session that leaves everyone disappointed. Endowments are generally very open to discussing the suitability of your offering, since it helps them allocate their time to relevant discussions. Some even publish detailed information on their investment philosophy, objectives, process, and must-haves from managers they would consider, which you will find useful as you learn more about how these endowments prioritize and operate.

2.　Is this manager's strategy and execution the best use of this asset class in achieving our goals?

Every fund manager has his or her own investment strategy, even if each is only a shade different from popular mainstream strategies. Most of the alternative managers do seek capital based on this nuance or interpretation—a "secret sauce" or "investment edge." Figuring out the best way to "ration" the available allocation to an asset class is a vital component of the decision-making process.

One of the reasons endowments build relationships with managers over time is because they can learn more about the manager's strategy, the evolution of that strategy, how well they execute the strategy, whether their strategy is drifting, and other shortcomings of the strategy or the team. As a marketer, you will start to realize the value of regular and consistent messaging with endowments to convince them why your approach is the best way to achieve their goals. Endowment investment officers are highly experienced and sophisticated investors who have honed their craft over years, learning from their own missteps. Long-term engagement helps them better understand the manager in ways that a few short meetings cannot reasonably achieve.

One of the most common complaints heard from endowments' investment staff is the lack of clarity about execution of the strategy in the funds' marketing materials. Too often, fund managers may be guilty of presuming their strategy is unique and do not want to share details broadly. However, shorn of all truly relevant information, the strategy will appear as generic as every other fund's pitch—and a sure path to rejection by the endowment. As fiduciaries, endowments need to ensure they can understand and determine the magnitude of the inherent risks and expected returns of the offering. They cannot, and should not, invest in a strategy they do not understand well enough to make a prudent decision—although in the case of black-box quantitative strategies, one can assess suitability through other means and limit overall portfolio exposure to such investments. It is frustrating for investors to spend hours on a potential investment only to discover they would have declined investing outright had they understood the strategy better at the beginning of the engagement.

3. **Do I trust this manager, not only to deliver the results I want to achieve, but also to act in the investor's best interest at all times like a fiduciary?**

Information asymmetry exists in investment management, as it does in most interactions in the world. Investors try to bridge that asymmetry and conduct comprehensive due diligence on managers, which is essential and critical to a functional asset allocation program that relies on external managers. No matter how extensive the efforts to obtain as much information as possible, the fund manager (seller) will always have more information than any investor (buyer) in the fund. Hence caveat emptor applies (or let the buyer beware).

Proper due diligence means the investor will ask necessary questions about the suitability and merits of the fund. However, scrutiny is only on past performance; it cannot foretell with absolute certainty how the fund manager will act in the future, especially when the investment has a negative outcome, when an unforeseen situation occurs, or if there is a conflict of interest where the fund manager has every legal right to act in their own favor but the ethical option is to act in the investor's interest. It is important for the investment officer and the endowment's decision makers to trust the fund manager with whom they are investing.

We use past experiences and judgment to decide who and what we want to trust and when to change our opinion. As the saying goes, "Trust, but verify."[12] While building trust with positive experiences over a period of time, especially with fund managers or their representatives, they must use sound judgment. Endowments generally look at newsletters, pitchbooks, fund documents, statements, and representations in meetings, comments, decisions, forecasts, and execution over time to ensure internal consistency between different pieces of information shared as well as consistency over time. They also compare statements versus track records, fund performances, external, public sources, and other information.

As a marketer, make sure you verify information and data before providing them to investors. Stay consistent, disciplined, and true to your investment philosophy and strategy. Learn to adapt to changes when they occur, whether in market conditions, regulations, or the strategy itself as it is improved by new information, technology, or other extrinsic changes. As Nobel Laureate Paul Samuelson said in a 1970 "Meet the Press" interview, "Well, when events change, I change my mind. What do you do?"[13]

A common catalyst for change typically relates to the size of the fund. As the fund becomes larger, the effectiveness of the original strategy shifts—larger checks are written, or the fund starts investing in bigger and more mature companies. During such transitions, it is important to document and communicate the changes to ensure the investor still feels the fund is meeting their needs and goals.

REGULATIONS GOVERNING ENDOWMENTS

In the United States, endowments with donor restrictions are governed under the Uniform Prudent Management of Institutional Funds Act (UPMIFA).[14] A key tenet of the act is that it requires the endowment's investing and spending to be at a rate that will preserve the purchasing power of the principal over the long term. The "prudent" part of UPMIFA requires the fiduciaries to use accepted tools and strategies to maximize the total return (e.g., interest, dividends, capital gains). Diversification, a cornerstone of Modern Portfolio Theory, is a necessary condition for all endowment investments as a result.

If a fund must support the charity forever, it needs to ensure that the amount of support to the beneficiary entity (the absolute value, not a percentage of the overall spending) is as valuable in the future as it is today—a concept termed *generational equity*. That means future generations get the same value of support from the endowment as the current generation, accounting for one of the basic concepts in finance—the time value of money. To meet that requirement, endowments generally have carefully crafted spending policies to ensure there is a fairly stable and consistent appropriation and allocation of the earnings toward (1) spending on current institutional expenses, and (2) retained earnings that not only preserve purchasing power, but also ensure the support is stable irrespective of market conditions.[15]

FOUNDATIONS

While endowments are meant to support specific organizations, such as a college, foundations focus on supporting a cause and will allocate their spending to multiple organizations that support this mission. They are charitable organizations set up for the sole purpose of giving to philanthropic causes. Private foundations derive most of their funding from a single source (e.g., individual, family, group, corporation, or any other legal entity), whereas public charities or foundations depend on funds from the general public. Contributions to foundations are tax-deductible to the entity (or individual) that establishes the foundation and funds its activities.

Private foundations are usually established with a large initial corpus and do not rely on public fundraising to support causes the foundation promotes. However, since these organizations are typically established as perpetual entities, contributions from donors can continue for the life of the private foundation. Some foundations can have a time limit or finite life. Given the reliance on the donor for funding, private foundations are typically controlled by the donor, who decides on the structure of the organization, staffing levels and board representatives, investment management policies, and grant distribution guidelines within the broad requirements of governing regulations.

Private foundations typically focus on making grants to other nonprofits and seldom directly engage in the operations of a charity. Beneficiaries of a private foundation can also be other public or private foundations. They are exempt from restrictions placed by the Internal Revenue Service (IRS) to show funding support from the general public to receive privileges accorded to tax-exempt entities.

FOUNDATIONS: A SHORT HISTORY

Charitable foundations can trace their roots to the tenets and preachings of various religions. Charitable giving, *dāna*, is an important part of one's duty, *dharma*, per Indo-centric religions (i.e., Hinduism, Jainism, Sikhism, and Buddhism). Abrahamic religions have similar expectations: *tzedakah* or *sedaqah* of Judaism (Hebrews 13:16, Proverbs 19:17), and *sakat* or *sadaka*, which is the third pillar of Islam.

Modern foundations can trace their origins to the establishment of charitable legal structures in common law jurisdictions, such as the Charitable Uses Act of 1601. Steel magnate Andrew Carnegie is considered the pioneer of modern charitable giving and the establishment of foundations to accomplish certain goals. His 1889 article "Gospel of Wealth" called upon the ultra-wealthy of his times to address the ills of economic inequality through philanthropy.[16] Donors and volunteer trustees were given the responsibility of directing and managing the investments. With no specific laws or regulations governing them, trustees invested cautiously and focused on individual investment prudence, rather than using portfolio measures to assess if the investment was sound within the context of portfolio goals and long-term investment horizons.

However, professional management of foundation assets is generally credited to the Ford Foundation and its then-president McGeorge Bundy. McGeorge Bundy commissioned two studies, released as "Reports to the Foundation" in 1969, challenging the legal principles governing endowment and foundation investing and recommending changes to investment processes.[17] The result was the Uniform Management of Institutional Funds Act of 1972 that provided statutory guidelines and standards of prudence to maximize their resources.[18]

At the end of 2020, the largest foundation in the world was the Novo Nordisk Foundation in Denmark, with a corpus of more than $73 billion. In the United States, the Bill & Melinda Gates Foundation is the largest foundation by assets ($47 billion in 2020). Most modern foundations are based in North America and Europe, with the notable exceptions of Azim Premji Foundation in India ($21 billion in 2020),

Al Maktoum Knowledge Foundation in Dubai ($10 billion in 2020), and Li Kashing Foundation in Hong Kong ($8 billion in 2020). As of January 2022, there were more than 140,000 private foundations and nearly 3,000 corporate foundations in the United States, of which nearly 3,000 qualify as accredited investors with assets exceeding $5 million.[19] The average asset size of the top 100 largest foundations in the United States is approximately $3 billion.

INVESTMENT OBJECTIVE

Since foundations must adhere to minimum spending/grant require-ments of the IRS to be considered a tax-exempt entity, their investment objective is slightly different from that of an endowment to preserve the real purchasing power of the principal. The long-term (LT) returns objective can be simplified as:

$$\begin{array}{ccccccc} \text{Expected} \\ \text{LT Return} \end{array} = \begin{array}{c} \text{Expected} \\ \text{LT Inflation} \end{array} + \begin{array}{c} \text{5\% Minimum} \\ \text{Spending} \end{array} + \begin{array}{c} \text{Incremental} \\ \text{Spend} \end{array} + \begin{array}{c} \text{Growth} \\ \text{Margin} \end{array}$$

$$(2\% \text{ to } 3\%) \quad + \quad (5\%) \quad + (50 \text{ to } 200 \text{ bps}) + \quad (1\text{-}3\%)$$

Basically, this is a similar formula to the one for endowments, with the addition of a minimum threshold of 5 percent for spending. How-ever, the long-term orientation of a foundation's asset allocation would be similar to endowments, which is why much of the industry groups E&Fs together, even though they are two different investor categories.

FOUNDATION STRUCTURE AND STAFFING

Most foundations invest their capital through external managers. Internal staff are responsible for asset allocation, manager search and selection, due diligence, performance monitoring, portfolio risk man-agement, and reporting.

Oversight of the foundation, including investment management, is a responsibility undertaken by the board of trustees or the governing body of the foundation. While an overwhelming majority of trustees are not compensated, nearly a quarter are, according to GMA Foundations.[20] Particular attention must be paid to the compensation structure to ensure it is reasonable and not perceived as self-dealing. As the case with endowments, individual investment decisions are best delegated to professional investment staff after the board sets the strategic asset allocation policy and an investment framework.[21]

REGULATIONS GOVERNING FOUNDATIONS

In the United States, foundations are regulated at both the federal and state levels. First, foundations need to be formed under state law in their usual place of business, and then must apply to the IRS at the federal level to be recognized as a charity or foundation. The IRS adjudicates the recognition of the applicant under Section 501(c)(3) of the Internal Revenue Code. IRS will also classify the organization as a private foundation under 509(a), if eligible. Any cross-border philanthropy in the United States must adhere to antiterrorism compliance in accordance with the USA Patriot Act of 2001[22] and comply with the regulations and policies under the US Treasury Department's Office of Foreign Assets Control (OFAC).

Internationally, cross-border philanthropy is mired in a myriad of laws, regulations, policies, and structural impediments. One major regulatory entity is the Financial Action Task Force (FATF). FATF is an intergovernmental policymaking body, a global money-laundering and terrorist-financing watchdog of 39 member countries. FATF's stated goal is to "establish international standards, and to develop and promote policies, both at national and international levels, to combat money laundering and the financing of terrorism."[23] Foundations with international grant-making or direct operations have suffered the unintended consequences of the FATF standards, which has impacted fund flows in international philanthropy.[24]

As for investment-related regulations, the standard fiduciary laws such as the Uniform Prudent Investor Act (UPIA) apply. Investment income from passive investments such as rents, interest, dividends, and capital gains are exempt from federal income tax, although the excise tax of 1 or 2 percent of net interest income may apply.[25] However, unrelated business income tax (UBIT) applies according to Internal Revenue Code (IRC) Section 511 for any income that is generated from any active, regularly carried on "trade or business," which is unrelated to the charitable purposes of the foundation.

UBIT is a serious concern for foundations when they are making investment decisions as it reduces the net return (after UBIT) to the foundation. In addition, foundations are subject to IRC Section 4943 (excess business holding, typically pegged at any economic interest that exceeds 20 percent of a business enterprise). Severe tax liabilities can result from noncompliance. Further, some investments can jeopardize the tax exemption enjoyed by foundations, which, per IRC Section 4944, include imprudent investments and taking unnecessary risks (e.g., trading on margins, futures, derivatives, insufficient diversification, or any action that can put significant charitable assets at risk).

Foundations will be examined by the IRS for activities that jeopardize their tax-exempt status. The IRS categorically states that production of income or appreciation of property is not a significant purpose of the investment, but accomplishing one or more of the foundation's exempt purpose is a relevant metric.[26] Non-compliant investments also impose penalties on decision makers who approve such allocations, in addition to penalties levied on the foundation itself. Any investment that might be considered self-dealing, irrespective of whether the terms were favorable to the foundation, will be subject to IRC Section 4941. The taxes on self-dealing amounts are meant to be punitive to both the decision maker and the recipient.

CONCLUSION

E&Fs are a coveted group of investors for alternative fund managers due to their higher allocation to alternatives, large check sizes, and long-term capital allocation. The same characteristics make the process of marketing to E&Fs longer, involved, and iterative as a wrong decision will be costly for the E&F and the decision maker. Fund managers and marketers will benefit from being sensitive to the constraints and risks of the decision makers and invest time to understand the decision process, criteria, and objectives before soliciting them for an allocation.

CHAPTER 2

Pension Funds

Pensions are pools of funds that provide periodic payments to individuals to support them in retirement, and are usually provided by an employer or a government. But this seemingly generous program has a much craftier origin. In the first century BCE, Roman Emperor Augustus Caesar worried that idle, retired soldiers presented a risk of revolt against the empire, given their skills and organization.[1] To earn their enduring loyalty—as well as keep them in the army ranks longer—he rationalized that a bounty payment would keep them content and less likely to rebel against their benefactor. His proposal was to pay the soldiers a bounty of nearly 13 times a legionnaire's annual salary, after 20 years in a legion and 5 years in the military reserves.

In the United States, pensions can be traced back to the eighteenth century, when the Continental Congress rewarded soldiers who survived the American Revolution with a monthly income for life. This practice continued for other wars that followed, including the Civil War, World Wars I and II, and other US-led conflicts. The first nonmilitary pension plans appeared in the mid-1800s, when some cities and municipalities started offering pensions to municipal employees such as teachers, firemen, and police officers. The American Express Company offered the first corporate pension plan in 1875, to "create a stable, career-oriented workforce."[2]

The growth of pension coverage is attributed to employers' desire to attract workers, reduce labor turnover, and "more [humanely] remove older, less productive employees."[3] Most of the plans started with an eligibility criterion of long employment, typically with a requirement of at least 20 years of service and a retirement age threshold of at least 60 years to ensure those employees stayed with the company for many years. The earliest adopters of pensions were companies that were flourishing at that time—those in banking and railroads.

There were regulatory and sociopolitical changes that also helped the propagation of pension plans. Prominent among them were the Revenue Acts of 1921 and 1926, and the Stabilization Act of 1942. The two Revenue Acts exempted an employee's pension income from federal taxes making them attractive to both employers and employees. The 1940s witnessed the confluence of two major events that dovetailed to form a fertile ground for pension plan propagation—the rise of powerful labor unions and the inflationary environment sparked by World War II.

While the labor unions were pushing for more wages and benefits, the Stabilization Act of 1942 froze wages to contain wartime inflation. However, since fringe benefits were exempt from the freeze, the act prompted employers to offer pension, health and welfare benefits as an alternative means to attract workers.[4]

With the rise in the number of pensions, there were also a few that failed. This prompted the government to enact the Employee Retirement Income Security Act (ERISA) in 1974. ERISA's goal is to minimize pension fund failures by establishing a framework that protects beneficiaries through legal, participatory, accountability, and disclosure requirements. Furthermore, if a pension should fail despite the guardrails provided by ERISA, the Pension Benefit Guaranty Corporation insures the employee benefits.[5]

Since then, pensions have come a long way. While the twentieth century mostly saw the flourishing of fixed pension payments (also called defined-benefit [DB] plans); in recent decades they have been replaced by defined-contribution (DC) plans such as 401(k)s and 403(b)s. Since the employer assumes liability and investment risk on behalf of all beneficiaries, DB plan assets are pooled together for investments. Participants of DC plans own their account, contribute pre- or post-tax income, and assume investment risk. The employer typically matches the contributions up to a ceiling, usually a percentage of wages. Employers set up the plans, set policies (such as vesting schedule, loan conditions, and rollovers) in compliance with ERISA and other regulations, hire administrators, and often subsidize organizational costs.

As of 2019, there were 733,678 private pension plans in the United States, with 93.6 percent being DC plans.[6] Aggregate assets at the end of 2019 across pension plans were $10.7 trillion. Geographically, North America accounted for nearly 41.7 percent of global pension assets under management (AUM) in 2020, with Europe and Asia-Pacific tied at 27.5 percent each.[7]

PUBLIC AND PRIVATE PENSIONS

Pension funds are broadly subcategorized into *public pension funds* (also called publics and public funds) and *private pension funds* (corporates or private funds). Public pensions are retirement funds for public-sector employees. These include municipal, city, state, federal, and military pension plans. Private pensions are retirement assets of private-sector plans intended for a company's employees. Each differs in applicable laws, policies, or restrictions, and the nature of these laws may also differ by geography.

The largest public pension in the world is Japan's Government Pension Investment Fund, which has more than $1.4 trillion in AUM. The largest public pension in the United States is the Federal Retirement Thrift Investment Board with assets of $443 billion. Corporate pensions are much smaller but still behemoths in themselves, such as the IBM Retirement Fund with $98 billion in assets and the BT Pension Scheme in the United Kingdom, with $66 billion in assets.[8]

GOALS OF PENSION PLANS

Although both DB and DC plans aim to provide periodic income over a retiree's lifetime, their fund management goals diverge since their constraints are different. A DB plan promises a specific payout amount where the fund sponsor administers the fund and assumes the investment risk. Any shortfall must be covered by the sponsor, such as a corporation, which has a legal obligation to do so irrespective of investment returns.

A DC plan does not promise a specific payment to the retiree. Instead, both the employer and employee contribute funds, usually as a percentage of the employee's earnings, towards retirement benefits. How much the employee gets at retirement will be dependent on both the contribution amount as well as the investment returns on those contributions. Thus, the onus for investment decisions and the assumption of investment risk rest entirely with individuals. This absolves companies from the uncertainty of future retiree pension payments and the financial impact of that uncertainty on the valuation of the company.

Almost all DB plans use a specified formula to calculate the monthly pension benefit, although some plans allow for a lump sum payment as well. Typically, the formula incorporates three factors: (1) the years of employment, (2) the average salary over a certain number of years (i.e., the final 3 to 5 years of service or 3 to 5 highest earning years) and (3) a benefit multiplier. Pension payouts from a DB plan can be deduced from this formula:[9]

$$\begin{array}{c}\text{Expected} \\ \text{Payment}\end{array} = \begin{array}{c}\text{Effective} \\ \text{Annual Salary}\end{array} \times \begin{array}{c}\text{Years of} \\ \text{Service}\end{array} \times \begin{array}{c}\text{Benefits} \\ \text{Multiplier}\end{array}$$

Since employee benefits cannot be curtailed or reduced, in situations where investment returns fall below assumptions, either the fund has to tap into the principal—which dampens future returns—or the sponsor has to make additional cash contributions to compensate for the pension deficit. According to a 2021 report by The Pew Charitable Trusts, state plans ended fiscal 2019 with an estimated liability of $4.35 trillion but only $3.1 trillion in assets—a shortfall of $1.25 trillion (see Figures 2.1 and 2.2).

DIFFERENCES IN ASSUMPTIONS

Pension plans use a set of factors called *actuarial assumptions* to project future expected income and liabilities to determine pension funding

FIGURE 2.1 Funding gap of US public pensions

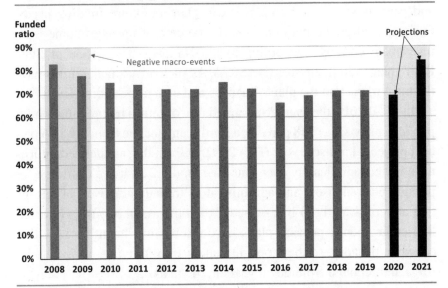

Source: https://www.pewtrusts.org/en/research-and-analysis/issue-briefs/2021/09/the-state-pension
-funding-gap-plans-have-stabilized-in-wake-of-pandemic

FIGURE 2.2 US states by pension funded ratio, 2019; state pension funding in 2019

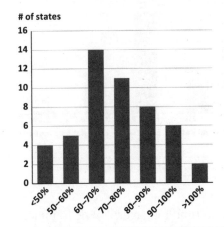

Below 60%	CT, HI, IL, KY, NJ, PA, RI, SC
60%–69%	AL, AK, AZ, CO, IN, KS, LA, MA, MI, MS, ND, NH, NM, TX, VT
70%–79%	AR, CA, FL, GA, MD, MO, MT, NV, OH, VA, WY
80–79%	DE, IA, ME, MN, NC, OK, OR, WV
90%–100%+	ID, NC, NE, NY, SD, TN, UT, WA, WI

Source: https://www.pewtrusts.org/en/research-and-analysis/issue-briefs/2021/09/the-state-pension
-funding-gap-plans-have-stabilized-in-wake-of-pandemic

requirements. These assumptions include projecting likely returns and payouts so that the employer can plan for future funding needs. For a typical public pension fund, 62 percent of revenues come from investment earnings, according to the National Association of State Retirement Administrators (NASRA). As such, investment returns have the most impact on the plan's finances and actuarial funding levels.[10]

In fiscal 2019, the average assumed rate of return before inflation for public pensions was 7.18 percent, a significant decline from the 8.05 percent projected in fiscal year (FY) 2002.[11] Given that annualized returns have varied significantly over time (see Figure 2.3), it is a challenge for pension plan sponsors and administrators to maintain levels of returns that are consistently in line or better than the assumptions.[12] However, like endowments, pension plans have a long investment horizon that can span decades, so they too can benefit from the *time-horizon arbitrage* and rebound from down years in the market.

FIGURE 2.3   Median annualized returns for US public pensions; distribution of expected investment returns

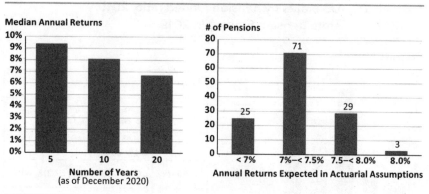

Source: https://www.nasra.org/files/Issue%20Briefs/NASRAInvReturnAssumptBrief.pdf

One of the most relevant issues for a fund manager, or GP, to understand is the significant dispersion in pension assumptions. Given that assumptions must adhere to Actuarial Standards Board guidelines, the dispersion can be attributed to their investment allocations, specifically the proportion allocated to alternatives.

While the bulk of pensions' portfolios consist of traditional equity and fixed-income assets, they are increasingly growing their allocation to alternative investments, primarily private equity (PE), as they seek higher returns and investments that allow for longer-term planning. Private equity accounted for 27 percent of *new* allocations made by US and UK pension funds in 2018, an uptick from 25 percent in the prior year, according to eVestment.[13] Public funds have a significantly higher allocation to alternatives than private plans: 22 percent versus 18 percent from 2009–2015.[14] This translates to between $1.5 trillion and $2 trillion available to alternatives out of $8.6 trillion in total US pension assets at the end of 2018, among largest pools for alternatives.[15]

PENSION FUND STRUCTURE AND STAFFING

Unlike endowments, many pension funds deploy a mixed strategy of both managing their assets themselves and hiring outside GPs. This is especially true of public pensions, which are usually large organizations that perform complicated functions, including actuarial analysis, investing, operations, and providing customer service to beneficiaries. Investments are managed by the investment office, which reports to a board of administration and perhaps also an executive office. In addition, there usually are supervisory or oversight committees that provide external supervision of operations and make strategic decisions. Typically, the investment staff at large pension funds are segmented by asset class and investment mandate.

To meet their pension liabilities, most pension funds need higher returns than what can be expected from the traditional mix of large-cap equities, treasuries, and investment-grade corporate fixed-income securities. The trend has been to increase allocation to alternatives. In recent years, the size of pension teams overseeing alternatives has been increasing, especially those focusing on private equity. The push to lower fees and boost portfolio transparency have led to the rise of co-investments and secondaries. Accordingly, the size of pension teams focusing on those strategies have increased as well.

The search for above-market returns has also led to pensions making direct investments, such as buying a company instead of investing in a private equity fund that acquires the business. This means the pension may either compete or partner with alternatives firms for direct investments. Canadian pensions have forged ahead along the direct investment path through their subsidiaries, but recently larger pensions worldwide have been following suit. This helps rein in the high fees paid to external GPs, responding to public demand to lower total fees, including management fees, performance incentives, consulting costs, and other charges. For example, the California Public Employees' Retirement System (CalPERS) spent $722 million in 2020–2021 on performance and management fees alone,[16] and there is growing demand by stakeholders to reduce these fees through direct investments.

As highly regulated entities, pension funds are held accountable for managing assets prudently to ensure eligible retirees will receive the benefits they are promised. Consider that $11.3 trillion of $37.4 trillion in total retirement AUM in the United States (end of Q3, 2021) are DB assets,[17] and the investment officers managing these assets are fiduciaries of the plan who are bound to act on the demands of their beneficiaries.

INVESTMENT DECISION PROCESS

The process for decision-making at pensions bears several similarities to endowments; this section will focus on nuances and differences.

At pensions, oversight responsibilities can be held by a variety of people. For example, the composition of the board can be as diverse as the pension's beneficiaries: they include elected officials and political appointees as well as representation from beneficiaries.

With a large stakeholder base, especially those in public service and government, pensions must keep focus on their fiduciary responsibility of providing retirement income to beneficiaries while managing multiple priorities. These priorities include social initiatives such as socially responsible investments (SRI); environmental, social, and governance

(ESG) issues; and advocacy of minority- and women-owned enterprises. These goals, however, remain secondary to their role as a fiduciary.

While it might appear that pension boards are much more active than those in endowments, most pensions actually co-opt the board to be effective. The role of boards is to set guardrails for investment decisions, to deliberate issues, approve exemptions, confirm pension compliance with guidelines, and approve the recommended decisions.

As public entities, public pension funds are under heavy scrutiny for their decisions, and cost and operations management because they are ultimately funded by taxpayer dollars and serve public sector employees. Transparency is a requirement for most public pension funds and in many cases mandated by laws and regulations. Indeed, pension funds are often the target of The Freedom of Information Act (FOIA) requests seeking investment information otherwise not available to the general public.

That is not to say they are giving away their secret or that they disclose proprietary information shared with them by their GPs. Pensions recognize that their "information edge," or "information asymmetry," drives superior returns for most of their actively managed investments. Therefore, they have created sandboxes of information that comply with transparency regulations, yet protect proprietary investment information and the personal data of its managers and other functionaries.

SELECTING A FUND MANAGER

The process of selecting a GP is quite extensive, starting from the request for proposal (RFP) elicited by most public pensions. Completing RFPs requires a considerable investment of time and resources from a GP to comply with all of the requirements. But this is an effort that most GPs arguably would make because of the large payoff: big checks from the pension to start and the potential for future investments in the firm's other funds. The win is also sticky. Given the extensive selection process, once a pension chooses a GP, the pension tends to stay with the firm unless serious problems arise with the fund's performance, strategy, or team.

Like other institutional investors, a pension's investment staff bears the risk of poor investment performance (getting fired) but does not participate in the gains beyond a token show of appreciation or a relatively small bonus for doing well. The risk tolerance of pensions also differs. Well-funded Canadian pensions are willing to take higher levels of risk by making significant direct investments and co-investments. On the other hand, many pensions have yet to make significant investments in alternative assets.

It is important that GPs understand a pension's current asset allocation and future plans while making a pitch. It is unlikely you could persuade a pension to change an investment allocation without going through careful deliberation. However, it is beneficial to keep communication lines open with prospective pension officials, as some of the largest initial allocations to alternatives come from pension funds.

QUESTIONS PENSIONS ASK WHEN CONSIDERING AN INVESTMENT

GPs must prepare satisfactory answers to the following questions:[18]

1. Is this an asset class the pension fund should be invested in?
2. Is the GP's strategy the best way to achieve our investment goals pertaining to this asset class?
3. Do I trust this manager not only to deliver the results I am seeking to achieve, but also to act in the investor's best interest like a fiduciary?

Fund managers also need to be able to address other concerns:

1. Reputational issues are a prominent source of discussion among pension funds and other stakeholders. These could relate to issues of fraud or breach of trust by a manager (e.g., Bernie Madoff, Galleon Group, Pequot Capital Management), large

losses due to poor risk controls, performance reversion to the mean (Amaranth Advisors), ESG issues (Satyam Computer Services, fossil fuels, tobacco, human rights violations), and more that could hurt the brand value of the corporate or government sponsor of the pension fund.

2. Perception issues can exist, especially as some prominent public funds have been entangled in pay-to-play scandals. The one involving New York state pensions in 2016[19] led to the arrest of some fiduciaries, managers and brokers facilitating the transactions.

3. Consultant approval is a factor in investment decisions as most pension funds seek opinions from an objective and informed third party (pension or investment consultants) to confirm the appropriateness of the investment.

4. Given the high investment fees of alternatives, there is stakeholder resistance to paying fees and other investment costs. Mediocre performance by some highly compensated managers strengthens this aversion and can be unfairly used against GPs who have delivered results in line with or better than expectations.

5. Pension funds are subject to information requests from stakeholders and in the case of public pensions, also from the general public in compliance with FOIA regulations. Pensions request extensive information from GPs, who in turn want to maintain their investment edge and are hesitant to share proprietary information. In most cases, the solution is to sandbox information under FOIA to be restricted to nonproprietary information. However, pensions do bear a compliance burden and GPs do risk that more information would be disclosed than they wish.

While the sole goal of pension investments should be to deliver returns that will fully fund the retirement of pensioners, there may be ancillary issues that also weigh on the investment officers or trustees. For example, it will be hard for an oil and gas pension to justify an investment in an

ESG fund that is at loggerheads with the parent company, because the fund will be actively undermining the valuation of the company.

REGULATIONS

Both public and private pensions are highly regulated entities, whether they are under actual laws such as ERISA or must conform to the *OECD Guidelines for Pension Fund Governance*. ERISA is a federal law that sets minimum standards for most voluntarily established retirement and health plans in private industry to provide protection for individuals in these plans.[20] ERISA ensures beneficiaries know their rights and sets minimum standards for who can participate and how benefits will accrue. In addition, it also sets responsibilities for those charged with operating a plan, including grievance and recourse mechanisms for participants.

In case a plan is terminated (company goes bankrupt or any other exigent reason), it guarantees payment of benefits through the Pension Benefit Guaranty Corporation (PBGC).

However, ERISA generally does not apply to retirement plans established or maintained by government entities or churches, or those made solely to comply with applicable workers compensation, unemployment, or disability laws. ERISA also does not cover plans that exist outside the United States for the benefit of nonresident aliens, or unfunded excess benefit plans.

The primary purpose of ERISA is the protection of plan assets and prevention of their misuse by fiduciaries. Responsibility for the interpretation and enforcement of ERISA is divided among the US Department of Labor, the US Department of the Treasury (particularly the IRS), and the PBGC. ERISA does not mandate that employers offer a pension plan or provide certain benefits; it merely requires that the operations of the pension plan be compliant with the regulation if they do. ERISA preempts all state laws that relate to any employee benefit plan, although there are specific exceptions. The most important exceptions, even when they relate to employee benefits, are state insurance, banking, securities, criminal, and domestic relations laws and regulations.

Most public pension funds are exempt from standard state procurement processes for hiring investment managers and investment consultants. However, other purchases that are not directly investment related, such as IT and compliance infrastructure, typically must comply with existing state procurement regulations and processes, hindering the ability of pensions to adapt to evolving technologies and stay competitive.

PRACTICAL APPLICATION

Marketing to public pension plans can be an especially complex, multifaceted process. To be successful takes a lot of hard work, patience, and dedication. When Hemali entered the business more than 15 years ago while working for a hedge fund manager and focusing on securing large allocations from pension funds, she had to look for practical, and sometimes creative, ways to make connections with pensions. She recommends these strategies:

1. **Enhance your targeting.** Broaden your reach by using the existing network. Any stakeholder can be the conduit: CIO and staff members, trustee, treasurer, local state senators, and gatekeepers (consultants and advisors).
2. **Find the right avenues.** Look for localized events. For example, your chances of connecting with a pension in some states are greater if you are the only marketer attending their open-to-the-public state senate meetings with pension CIOs. Pension and regional conferences are also good options.
3. **Be prepared.** Connecting with decision makers without first doing the necessary preparation will yield few results and unproductive meetings. The quarterly newsletters and meeting minutes of trustee sessions are great resources to understand the developments of each fund and its strategic direction.

4. **Find creative options.** Organize events such as lunch-and-learn sessions to build a community. This also raises your profile among prospective investors.
5. **Co-opt others.** Ask others in the industry, including other fundraisers, to make personal introductions. Warm introductions yield better results than cold calling. However, remember to return the favor when it's your turn to introduce LPs to your network.

CONCLUSION

Pension funds are the largest investors in alternatives. They are also among the most highly regulated investors. Their structures and decision processes typically take longer than that of family offices, endowments, or foundations and pose an additional compliance burden with ERISA and strict pay-to-play rules. Since many pensions work with investment consultants, otherwise known as gatekeepers, it would be important for a fundraiser to also build relationships with consultants. To successfully secure a meaningful investment from a pension, fundraisers for alternative funds need patience, perseverance, and some creative thinking. Given the long investment horizons and large check sizes, pension funds are a natural fit and are coveted by alternative fund managers.

CHAPTER 3

Family Offices

A family office is a wealth management entity established by or for an ultra-high net worth (UHNW) individual or family to cater to their investment and financial management needs. Family offices come in different sizes, shapes, and forms, but they typically have several features in common:

- Their clients are members of a family or group of families.
- Traditionally, they do not offer their services to the general public or to anyone beyond the family or group of families who might also own the entity.
- They may also offer bookkeeping, secretarial, travel, legal, tax planning, and estate planning services, financial management of the family's philanthropic and charitable ventures, as well as payroll and HR services for the household staff.
- Many have mission statements that help manage intergenerational developments and objectives of the family, which often include family unity, harmony, and financial prosperity.

Beyond these commonalities, family offices can be very bespoke. Some provide a very broad set of services, while others may be focused only on wealth management and investment services—all depending on what would meet a family's specific needs. However, not all services a family office offers must be provided in-house.

A common practice is to outsource services in which expertise is necessary, but the size of the family office may not justify a full-time employee. Typically, the wealthier a family is, the more services are offered by its family office, ranging from wealth and lifestyle management to supporting the family's financial, legal, and taxation needs.

FIGURE 3.1 **Distribution of global wealth**

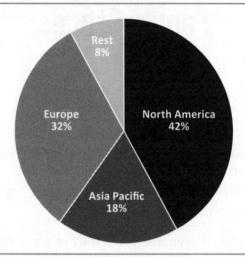

Source: The Global Family Office Report, 2019, UBS and Campden Research

Globally, there were approximately 7,300 single family offices, managing about \$5.9 trillion in assets in 2019, an increase of 38 percent from 2017.[1] Geographically, 42 percent were in North America, 32 percent in Europe, 18 percent in Asia Pacific and 8 percent in emerging markets (see Figure 3.1).

After the 2008 global financial crisis revealed the fault lines around counterparty risks, high net worth individuals realized that highly compensated private banks and wealth managers were not always able to protect their assets. They sought improved wealth management, leading to faster growth in the number of family offices in the following decade. However, the operating cost of running a family office constrained growth. Given the high cost of a professionally run home office—operating expenses can exceed \$1 million a year—an estimated \$100 million AUM is needed to justify opening up a shop. UBS and Campden Research estimate 80 percent of family offices are single family offices.[2]

FAMILY OFFICES: A BRIEF HISTORY

While some attribute the origins of the family office to the medieval concept of majordomo, a trusted manager of the affairs of a wealthy family, it is not quite equivalent to the family offices of today. The roots of the modern family office date from the nineteenth-century formations of the House of Morgan, by the family of banker J. P. Morgan, and the family office of the Rockefellers, oil and banking magnates, in subsequent decades. However, UBS estimates that 68 percent of family offices it surveyed were founded a century later, in 2000 and beyond.[3]

Some reasons for this rather late growth include fund managers returning outside capital and converting to family offices to avoid Dodd-Frank regulations after the financial crisis, the rise in successful tech startups that created massive wealth in a short span of time, an economic boom in Asia and Latin America, and the entry of large private banks into the family office business.

COMMON STRUCTURES OF FAMILY OFFICES

1. **Single family office (SFO):** This entity is generally 100 percent owned by the family whose wealth and finances it manages. While the majority of SFOs are professionally run, there are many cases where a family member manages the family office for the rest of the family. There is usually a multigenerational involvement in the operations of the SFO by design so that future generations are educated on financial and investment matters.
2. **Private multifamily office (MFO):** Similar to an SFO, this entity is 100 percent owned by the group of families whose wealth it manages. Owners usually are people who have built their wealth, worked together, or been well acquainted for a long time. The private MFO usually is managed by a professional team with active involvement from some family members.

However, the professional management does not have an ownership stake in the entity.

Since the assets of individual families are combined in the private MFO, the minimum AUM threshold per family is much lower than that for an SFO. These MFOs can be formed from the merger of two SFOs, or an SFO opening its doors to select outside UHNW individuals. Some alternative investment firms have even created private MFOs as a perk for senior partners who are not wealthy enough to open their own family office.

Private MFOs offer at least two benefits: they spread operating costs among several families and enable multiple people to share the responsibility of oversight, thereby freeing up time for the owners.

3. **Professional MFO:** This is an organization that shares many similarities with the private MFO, except that its services are all outsourced. It is owned by professionals and operated as a profit-seeking business. Many of these entities are subsidiaries of larger financial institutions. The staff of MFOs often possess varied and complementary areas of expertise—such as in wealth management, tax planning, estate planning, and legal— to ensure the holistic management of the assets.

4. **Hybrid family office (HFO):** This entity has characteristics of both the SFO and MFO; some critical functions are managed by the owners, while others are outsourced with a low-touch approach akin to a "build some, rent some" approach.

BENEFITS OF A FAMILY OFFICE

1. Confidentiality and privacy for all matters related to the family
2. Centralized decision-making and information-sharing among members
3. One-stop shop for all their financial and wealth management needs
4. Cost management by combining multiple outsourced services

COMMON CHARACTERISTICS OF FAMILY OFFICES

Family offices tend to be secretive. Generally, only family members are apprised of the AUM's investment performance and related activities. While they prefer to stay private, family offices are also eager to discover what other family offices are doing and learn from each other about opportunities and investments. As such, they exemplify the adage, "birds of a feather flock together." It is not unusual to find a group of family offices using the same fund managers and engaging in similar direct investments, as permitted by their liquidity status and investment objectives.

MFOs, however, tend to be more independent from their owners than SFOs in that their process for investment decisions is similar to that of an institution or wealth manager. Much like other institutional investors, they handle in-house activities they consider critical, such as maintaining control over investments or allocation, and outsource other functions if the cost of these services does not justify a full-time employee.

SFOs tend to have actively engaged owners. This is not surprising given the time, effort, and money that the owners invested to start the entity in the first place. They also meet regularly with staff, unlike fund managers who provide an annual update. For example, according to the "2020 UBS Global Family Office Report"[4] more than 56 percent of the families are actively involved in strategic asset allocation.

Many family offices are still led by individuals, founders who created the vast fortunes being managed, and they have a higher propensity for risk-taking and an affinity for direct operational control of physical or business assets.[5] These traits give rise to a preference for investing in private equity and real estate over financial assets, since these founders are confident in their ability to add value to the investments and generate superior returns. They also are willing to take a long-term view and accept illiquidity for the potential of higher returns, especially since these family offices are meant for multigenerational wealth transfers. The 2021 edition of the UBS report noted that 75 percent of family

offices viewed private equity as a key driver of returns and had allocated 40 percent of their portfolio to alternative assets (see Figure 3.2).[6]
Private equity is a favored option due to (1) an expectation of higher
returns than public markets, (2) diversification benefits, (3) broader
investment opportunities, and (4) the ability to exercise influence and
control over the business.

FIGURE 3.2 **Asset allocation of family offices—2020**

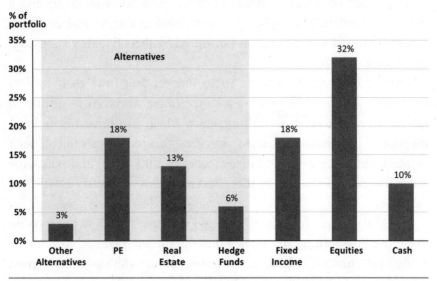

Source: The Global Family Office Report, 2021, UBS and Campden Research

Furthermore, 54 percent of private equity investments were direct
and only 46 percent through private equity funds. Not surprisingly,
many owners prefer investing in an industry or sector in which they
have created their wealth. This penchant for the familiar is almost an
extension of the entrepreneur's career; he or she may invest directly in
a venture or co-invest with a partner.[7] Owners tend to be proactive in
looking for investment deals; the staff research business opportunities
instead of waiting for an offer to arrive. An emerging trend is investing
in assets that promote ESG causes, with a third of family offices having
done so as of 2020.[8]

The family office must be closely attuned to the interests, norms, legacy, objectives, and passions of the family whose wealth it manages. This gets trickier in MFOs since the staff oversees needs of several families across generations. It is important to ensure families' priorities and interests are clarified at the outset and any changes are communicated to and documented by the staff.

Note that there is potential for intergenerational differences in objectives and outlook. The family office should play an impartial role in getting all stakeholders to agree on a common set of goals and find ways to manage any differences adeptly.

REGULATIONS

In the United States, MFOs are regulated as *registered investment advisors*, although some exemptions exist for trust companies, law firms, and accounting firms that operate these entities. Historically, family offices have not been regulated, although some aspects of their operations did fall under the purview of laws not intended for them in the first place. This changed under the Dodd-Frank Act, enacted after the 2008 financial crisis, which now requires the US Securities and Exchange Commission (SEC) registration and regulation for advisors, even if they have fewer than 15 clients. That means family offices must comply with the regulations if they provide securities-related advice to others for compensation, which includes reimbursement of salaries, payment of management fees, or sharing of profits (carried interest). If an advisor manages only private funds and does not exceed an AUM of $150 million, they are still exempt. However, in an acknowledgment that the new law was not meant to regulate family offices, the SEC adopted a rule where SFOs (but not MFOs) can qualify for an exemption under certain conditions.

CHALLENGES

Startup Costs

Setting up a family office requires arduous effort by an owner, and the costs can be considerable. As such, the family might be better served by being part of an MFO or by retaining the services of a wealth management firm. The larger the assets of the family, the better the odds of creating a bespoke office that more closely reflects the owners' interests and investment choices.

Recruitment

One of the biggest challenges for family offices is recruiting the right people, who are both capable and willing to give up careers in alternatives or wealth management. Hiring the wrong people can have long-term consequences for the family and the family office.

Typically, family office senior leadership are compensated in line with wealth management executives and can receive an additional 40 to 80 percent of their base salary in bonus compensation. Some families have created an incentive structure that aligns the interests of staff and owners. For example, an investment pool that invests alongside the family office could be funded by an owner for the benefit of staff. The principal is returned to the owner and the returns flow to the staff. This benefit is meant to attract the best people in the industry, the same rationale behind the private equity fund carried interest, though it is structured differently. Offering competitive compensation is key, since family offices do compete with wealth management and alternative investment firms for the same talented staff. However, with such arrangements, risk management is critical to prevent investment staff from undertaking excess risk in hopes of higher payouts.

Operating Costs

Annual operating costs typically range from 0.75 to 1.5 percent of AUM, which includes paying for services of external providers such as custodians, lawyers, accountants, estate planners, investment managers, and auditors. These costs can put pressure on a family office to ensure investments bring in superior performance to justify the overhead.

For some, it might be more feasible to outsource the entire functions of a family office to an MFO, private bank, or wealth manager. However, the loss of control must be weighed against cost savings, lessened efforts, and assumed risks of running a family office. Most family offices, given their relatively modest assets, cannot benefit from economies of scale enjoyed by asset managers with a greater than billion-dollar AUM, such as private equity and hedge funds. They also do not have the same pull with deal sources or investment banks. On the other hand, some of this is offset by their affinity for personalized and high-touch service.

Investment Conflicts

Many SFOs and MFOs make direct investments, but also allocate capital to outside GPs for investment. At times, this can create a conflict of interest. One of the proprietary deal sources for a GP are LPs and their networks. If SFOs are going to invest directly in an asset or business, conflicts might arise with a GP's fiduciary duty and personal interests. It is natural to wonder whether family offices are partners or competitors for GPs.

Fortunately, both GPs and family offices have created sandboxes to ensure there is proper and legitimate use of information shared, and there are no investment conflicts that would jeopardize mutual interest. The same is true for public market or hedge fund investments. Both players recognize the reputational and legal risks presented and strive to handle them appropriately. However, GPs and family offices must ensure that the delineation is clear and there is compliance with the policy.

Succession Issues or Continuity Risk

The investment horizon of a family office is presumed to be long term for multigenerational wealth management. However, that is not always the case; family disputes can lead to a breakup of the family office and division of assets. Most family offices recognize risks of breakups—as has happened to a few well-known families—and take great care to ensure there is a clear succession plan, such that future generations (and any spouses) are educated about asset management and family office operations.

Reputational Risk

Family offices prefer to stay out of the public eye, because publicity can be a two-edged sword. Wealthy families generally do not benefit much from or even need publicity. The Panama Papers scandal, where financial information about offshore accounts of the elite were leaked, demonstrated that disclosures can lead to reputational and political harm, even if activities were legal and appropriate. At the very least, families care about their standing in society, especially within their own circles, after years and even generations of carefully crafting their image. Most would be wary of investment choices and associations that would not show them in a good light, should these become public knowledge.

Communicating the Family's Vision to Staff

A family needs to be clear about what they want from their SFO. Most family offices are established when there is a sudden inflow of investable cash—typically after a liquidity event like the sale of a family business. Since the family can make its family office as bespoke as it wants, it must ensure that its vision is fully communicated to the staff and codified. To minimize crossed signals, the family should first assess their needs and then find the right people with appropriate qualifications and experience. Without that clarity, the vision and objectives of the family may be lost in translation and lead to a less than acceptable outcome.

Disproportionate Costs Incurred by Members

In a private MFO, there is bound to be a disproportionate use of resources by one or some family members. One solution is to provide a base level of essential services, paid for by a percentage of the wealth managed by the MFO—the rest would be à la carte options for which families pay extra. This would ensure that the common goal is met, while individual usage is charged as it is incurred.

Investing Versus Monitoring

It is difficult for families to effectively diversify through direct investing alone, especially when they seek exposure to alternative assets. Some families are comfortable with the lack of diversification and seek to entirely focus on direct investments. Others outsource investment management to outside managers, focusing on monitoring these managers, and rebalancing assets according to strategic asset allocation choices made by the family.

HOW TO MARKET TO FAMILY OFFICES

Family offices are high-touch, high-involvement organizations. Marketing efforts should aim to build a strong relationship with principal decision makers. A model that is a true partnership will work better than a client-advisor relationship, but building these relationships requires consistent effort over a long period of time.

Family offices are concentrated in certain geographies, many in large cities. However, the top destinations for family offices globally are countries with favorable tax regimes. It would help to have boots on the ground by approaching them directly, by connecting with third-party marketers, or by building strong relationships with consultants, advisors, and wealth managers in these geographies. It is also important to note that while a lot of concerted marketing effort is aimed at the locations where family offices tend to congregate, a large portion of the investable family office capital lies outside these regions: they're in the suburbs, exurbs, and remote areas around the world. These "underserved" family office regions are likely to be more receptive to overtures from an alternative assets firm.

A wise investment of resources is for GPs to get a toehold into a regional family office or even different family networks. Since family offices tend to be curious and hunt in packs, breaking into a family office network will open up many more doors through word-of-mouth and network effects. To succeed, asset managers looking to serve family offices should also consider smaller cities where influential attorneys, accountants, and other service providers are likely to have outsized influence in opening doors to wealthy families with whom they have longstanding relationships.

Family offices controlled by founders who built their wealth are more likely to take an entrepreneurial view and accept the risks of backing an emerging GP, before institutions are willing to make a commitment. However, this comes at a cost. Typically, the economics are attractive for the earliest investors, and preferential terms such as co-investment rights that are a requisite condition for an early investment from a family office. Some funds proactively offer founders shares to entice risk-taking investors into investing early.

Family offices value reputation by association. It is easier for a fund manager with a recognizable name to raise capital than someone with a better track record but without name recognition. This has parallels to art auctions; uber-rich individuals purchase art at record prices because they do not have to explain who the masters—Picasso, Monet, Chagall, or Rembrandt—are to their friends. It could also work for budding star managers. Years ago, the CEO of a multibillion-AUM family office said to a team pitching its fund that while the sizable check he was writing was miniscule relative to the family's overall portfolio, the investment would give them bragging rights in their social circles about the amazing returns they received by backing the yet-to-be-discovered star manager.

Obviously, there is no sure-fire formula to developing a strong brand. GPs should still invest the time to create name recognition and be seen as leaders prior to engaging with a family office. For example, they can make appearances on television, be interviewed in newspaper articles, speak at conferences, and serve in leadership positions at well-known public and not-for-profit organizations.

MARKETING STRATEGIES

1. Let Them Try Before They Buy

Family offices like to make direct investments. GPs who have difficulty raising capital from a family office can introduce the possibility of direct investment through the fundless sponsor route, or as a co-investment opportunity—such as participation in an investment round they lead. This way, LPs get to try the GP before buying. Once the family office has a successful venture with the GP, the relationship is more likely to mature into a long-term partnership.

Why would family offices invest directly? Most wealthy families have earned their fortunes through successful entrepreneurship. As such, they are more apt to back entrepreneurs and get involved in a business rather than be passive investors who merely collect a return from the GP.

2. Establish That You Understand Their Sensitivities and Interests

Most family office assets are held within taxable entities—though the proportion of assets for philanthropic initiatives is increasing—and family offices would be looking for ways to decrease their tax burden. By ensuring that your fund and its operations are structured to be tax efficient (e.g., infrequent trading, longer holding periods for lower capital gains, among other practices), you send a strong signal to the family office that your fund is aligned with their needs.

Another way to show that you understand their needs: Increase the emphasis on co-investments and involve them in deal sourcing and due diligence. In some instances, the authors have encouraged GPs to take LPs who are interested in co-investment on due diligence trips before making an investment. LPs can provide a tremendous amount of insight into the process, and they can see firsthand how the manager works. This engagement tactic is both marketing-efficient and functionally superior.

3. Tap into Prominent Networks

Family offices find comfort in obtaining and learning from the input of other like-minded family offices. Since family offices are usually lean organizations with limited staff, some often congregate into groups that collectively consider a GP and share analysis and due diligence. This network of peers is especially attractive to smaller and even midsized family offices. If an SFO finds early successes from joining this network, it will determine how strong the network's influence will be on future endeavors. Emerging fund managers would also find a more receptive audience among these networks.

4. Tap into "Conference Water Coolers"

Join conferences that are popular with family offices. GPs can interact with family office professionals and owners at these events; they also can build or expand their co-investor network and strengthen relationships. This also is a time when family office executives are away from the daily grind and have a more receptive frame of mind when it comes to new manager relationships. For GPs, going to a conference would be an efficient way to reach a larger family office audience than one-on-one meetings. Reputed conferences such as the Milken Institute Global Conference are good avenues for connecting with family offices.

CONCLUSION

Given the multiplicity of structure, size, and scope of a family office, it is important to understand the history, staffing, and investment objectives of each family office as early in the process as possible, even years before a fundraise begins. The biggest challenge to marketers is in finding family offices. Many want to shield themselves from the public eye, but actively seek out similar offices to exchange ideas and find the right opportunities. This propensity to run in packs provides an opportunity for the right manager to leverage connections and warm referrals that greatly benefit fundraising efforts.

CHAPTER 4

Sovereign Wealth Funds

Sovereign wealth funds (SWFs), especially those from smaller or emerging nations, can be enigmas to many fund managers. SWFs are large pools of investment capital that are owned, managed, or supervised by a state for its own interest, as well as for its citizens' benefit. Usually, these vehicles are created to invest fiscal surpluses, excess capital from its balance of payments, proceeds from the sale of state assets, or income from commodity exports. Some participants also include state-owned pension funds, enterprises, and development banks in this category.

The Organisation for Economic Co-operation and Development (OECD) defines sovereign wealth funds rather broadly as "pools of assets owned and managed directly or indirectly by governments to achieve national objectives."[1] The US Department of Treasury's definition is narrower: it is "a government investment vehicle which is funded by foreign exchange assets, and which manages those assets separately from the official reserves of the monetary authorities (the Central Bank and reserve-related functions of the Finance Ministry)."[2] Regardless how one defines SWFs, they are among the largest investors in alternatives and on their way to becoming the biggest (see Figures 4.1 and 4.2).

Not all SWFs invest in alternatives. State-owned enterprises and state-owned development banks by their nature generally do not. We will focus on other SWF entities that do, differentiating among the various types of SWFs, their investment objectives, processes, investment considerations, the strategic roles they play nationally, and how these fit in with their investment mandates. We also will discuss the specific

FIGURE 4.1 **$1 billion club investors: capital-weighted breakdown by investor type**

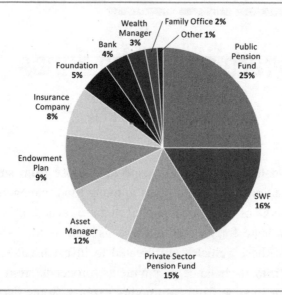

Source: The $1bn Club: Largest Investors in Hedge Funds, May 2015

FIGURE 4.2 **Allocation to alternatives by SWFs**

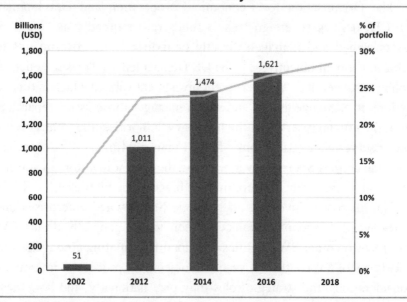

Source: SSGA Research, using data from the Sovereign Wealth Center, and SWFC and SSGA data

risks and the regulatory treatment of SWFs, including differentiating them from other government holdings such as central bank assets.

A BRIEF HISTORY

Before the formation of modern SWFs, government surpluses were exclusively invested in gold and short-term debt instruments. That changed in 1953 with the establishment of the first SWF: the Kuwait Investment Authority (KIA).[3] It was tasked to provide a stabilizing mechanism to cushion against the fluctuating prices of oil (a commodity whose revenues Kuwait was dependent on), invest the surplus and reduce its reliance on a finite commodity. In 1956, the Republic of Kiribati would be the second to create a SWF, for the investment of phosphate mining revenues.[4]

In the United States, the first SWF was established by New Mexico in 1957.[5] The New Mexico State Investment Council managed the state's permanent funds for the benefit of its citizens by maximizing distributions to the state's operating budget while preserving the real value of the funds for future generations. The funding originally came from minerals and natural resources on public lands first granted to New Mexico upon reaching statehood. Later, funding would encompass other sources such as tax surpluses, tobacco litigation settlements, and other government revenues and wealth proceeds.

After a lull in activity for a few decades, the 1970s saw the start of a proliferation of SWFs that continues to this day. While some question the categorization of Temasek Holdings (1971) of Singapore as a SWF, other large SWFs like the Permanent Wyoming Mineral Trust Fund, Abu Dhabi Investment Authority (ADIA), Alaska Permanent Fund Corporation, Alberta Heritage Saving Trust Fund, Oman State General Reserve, and Brunei Investment Agency were all formed during the 1970s and 1980s, coinciding with a spike in energy prices. The majority of the SWFs can trace their funding to revenues from commodities.

The first non-commodity SWF was established by Singapore in 1981 with the formation of the Government of Singapore Investment Corporation (now called GIC Private Limited) to manage its surplus foreign reserves with a mandate to preserve and enhance the country's international purchasing power over the long term.[6] Today, the number of non-commodity SWFs remain dwarfed by commodity SWFs; nonetheless, they still characterize most of the Asian SWFs, which are funded by national and balance-of-payment surpluses. Indeed, 5 of the top 10 SWFs globally are non-commodity.

As of 2020, 155 SWFs worldwide managed $9.1 trillion in assets, according to the "2021 Global SWF Annual Report."[7] Most SWFs are based in Asia (41.7 percent) or the Middle East (32.8 percent).[8] The only major funds outside of the region are in Norway, Russia, Canada, Australia, and New Zealand. The primary catalyst for SWF growth was the exponential increase of crude oil prices from $11.22 per barrel in 1998 to $140 per barrel in 2008[9] that created a surplus for oil-exporting nations and the need to manage that wealth. The second was the strong GDP growth among export-driven economies such as China and South Korea. One silver lining: proliferation of SWFs in the years leading up to the financial crisis in 2008–2009 enabled many countries not only to mitigate the economic impact of the Great Recession, but also deploy excess capital as "shareholders of last resort" to companies trapped in a liquidity and credit crunch.[10]

The sources of funding, reasons for inception, and investment objectives can vary widely. Some countries might have more than one SWF—such as Singapore's Temasek and GIC, and Abu Dhabi's ADIA and Mubadala. The purpose of a country having multiple SWFs is either to have a specific mandate for each entity or to encourage competition among them. Some SWFs are exclusively focused on foreign investments (KIA, Government Pension Fund Global of Norway), others are restricted to domestic investments (1Malaysia Development Berhad, FSI of Italy), or have no geographic limits (Khazanah Nasional Berhad of Malaysia).

SWF GOALS

Unlike other institutional investors, SWFs have very little in common with each other when it comes to investment and existential goals. Such heterogeneity, which sometimes can come across as incongruent within the same SWF, make this investor type among the most difficult to generalize. We recommend that marketers take a bespoke approach specifically tailored to each individual SWF. Hemali found it beneficial to utilize regional placement agents (PAs) with deep, long-term relationships to specific SWFs. Such PAs are well versed in the nuances and needs of these funds and are at times able to provide unique access that a marketer new to the region may not be able to get.

SWFs do share some common objectives. The International Monetary Fund grouped them into the following five categories based on their principal goals:[11]

1. **Stabilization funds**
   Purpose: To insulate economies from volatility in prices of commodities whose revenue the countries depend on

2. **Savings funds**
   Purpose: Intergenerational wealth transfer

3. **Reserve investment funds**
   Purpose: Invest surplus reserves in pursuit of higher returns

4. **Development funds**
   Purpose: Allocate resources to socioeconomic projects, such as infrastructure

5. **Contingent pension funds**
   Purpose: Funding the pension or other contingent liabilities of the nation

While this categorization is a good starting point, most funds have a mix of these objectives. Furthermore, objectives change over time due to policy considerations or accumulation of capital beyond what is necessary for achieving the objective.

It follows that an SWF's purpose largely determines its investment objectives, investment horizon, risk tolerance, and asset allocation (see Figure 4.3). Stabilization funds, for one, will need to have sufficient resources invested in assets that are inversely correlated with the economic risk they intend to mitigate—and must be liquid enough to fund the need when it arises. Therefore, it is prudent for them to consider lower-risk investments, often with shorter holding periods. One example is the Russian Oil Stabilization Fund, which invests mostly in fixed-income assets in US dollar, euro, and the British pound denominations. Given its aversion to higher-risk options, this and other such SWFs will not be good prospects for alternative investments.

Savings funds are better suited for longer-term investments, and by extension, alternative assets. They capitalize on market disruptions by investing in and increasing exposures to depressed assets during turbulent times, with the full expectation that they can wait for the conditions to return to normal over time.

FIGURE 4.3 **Asset allocations at sovereign wealth fund, by type of fund**

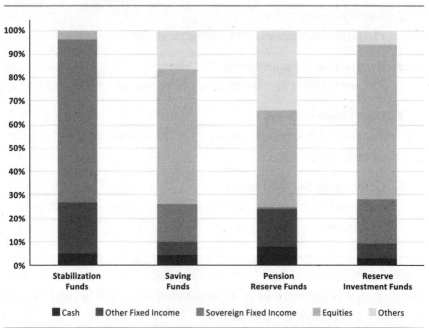

Source: IMF, Global Financial Stability Report (April 2012)

Given the multiplicity of SWF objectives, there is significant dispersion of asset allocation among these funds. As such, GPs and fundraisers should avoid a "birds of a feather" approach when soliciting SWFs, customizing their marketing pitch to specifically address the needs of each fund.

While you could say this about any institutional investor, there are two main differences: (1) SWFs' investment objectives and mandates are the most dispersed among institutional investors, and (2) SWFs have extremely large AUM; so there is a larger return on investment to the GP in creating bespoke strategies.

The average SWF allocation to alternatives is skewed toward private equity, but remains below the target allocation. As such, SWFs present a promising opportunity for GPs that can display their prowess in helping these funds reach their portfolio objectives.

SWF SPENDING POLICY AND ITS INVESTMENT IMPLICATIONS

Unlike endowments, foundations, and pension funds, SWFs do not have a predictable spending pattern. Their expenditures are usually quite volatile. This unpredictability and volatility might be a problem for any institutional investor's strategic asset allocation and liquidity management, but extremely large SWFs can handle it. Given their size, they can afford to keep a portion of their assets liquid.

Therefore, even in severe market declines (such as during the 2008 financial crisis and the Covid-19-induced bear market in 2020), SWFs have the wherewithal to opportunistically invest in distressed assets, often as a "white knight" for companies in financial distress. Some notable examples are ADIA's investment in Barclays, Kuwait Investment Authority and GIC's investment in Citigroup during the financial crisis, and the Saudi Arabia Public Investment Fund's investment in cruise operator Carnival during the Covid-19 pandemic.

However, most SWFs have clear guidelines, if not explicit rules, for the transfer of funds between the SWF and the ownership entity. Such clarity is essential for the SWF to practice and adhere to an effective strategic asset allocation.

SWF PERFORMANCE

Annual returns for SWF portfolios from 2016 to 2020 have ranged from 4 to 9.4 percent. Since most savings and development SWFs are not pressured to meet spending requirements, they can afford to take a very long-term view compared to other investors—to their great advantage. SWFs have been more than willing to take the illiquidity of long lock-up investment vehicles such as private equity, real assets, and hedge funds, so long as they are adequately compensated for the risk. A large asset base also gives SWFs the freedom, and perhaps even the necessity, to make direct investments, more than any other institutional investor.

SWF STRUCTURE AND STAFFING

There are very few SWFs worldwide, which makes this terrain more navigable for marketers. This is not an easy mission, by any means, because SWFs have the most disparate objectives and operations among institutional investors. Their organizational structures are dispersed and constantly evolving. While some of that evolution is due to the nascency of SWFs, the rest is intrinsic to any organization that has an outsized influence in the marketplace.

Broadly speaking, there are three main legal structures for SWFs:

1. **Separate legal entity (e.g., GIC, KIA, ADIA)**
    These structures usually invest through a mix of direct investments and allocations to external managers. They may occasionally act as an outsourced CIO to manage assets for other entities of the sovereign.

2. **State-owned corporations (e.g., Temasek)**
    This structure is similar to a holding company setup, where the SWF takes an active role in the company in which it has an investment; these SWFs tend to have a very concentrated portfolio.

3. **As an account of the central bank or other sovereign entity (e.g., Chile, Botswana)**
   Typically, the investment mandate is carried out by multiple external managers or funds to implement its portfolio objectives.

Many large direct investments come from SWFs that are structured as separate legal entities or as state-owned investment corporations. They generally have dedicated staff responsible for asset allocation, manager search, due diligence, performance monitoring, portfolio risk management, and reporting. Some of them also have internal fund managers—which makes them a multimanager fund. The bottom line: it is important for a fundraiser to understand the SWF's investment strategy to see if the manager's fund will compete with internal fund managers or complement their activities. In this case, marketing efforts should center around the parameters of value proposition and negotiations.

Most SWFs have asset-class-based team structures: private equity, venture capital, real estate, real assets, infrastructure, or public equities, and so on. Those that are private-equity-like with fixed-time structures may be grouped together. Sometimes, there are geographically focused teams, especially among the Middle East SWFs that have large allocations to specific regions. These teams often operate with relative autonomy within the boundaries of the asset allocation policy limits.

These asset-class-based teams also have an operational management group responsible for implementing strategic asset allocation, as set by the fiduciary board of trustees (or an equivalent entity). Operational management is responsible for administration functions, in addition to portfolio management. Investment decisions flow through in a similar fashion to other institutional investors—with investment staff researching and recommending an investment within their teams, which is then rolled up to an operational management group.

While it is common for an investment team and operational management to make investment decisions, in many cases these can be vetoed by the board. The board is usually composed of representatives of the ruling affiliation and sovereign powers, who are aligned with the dispensation of the nation's rulers and their strategic and political objectives.

Governance, supervision, and operating structures of SWFs are complex. The structural construct underpinning the SWF might seem similar to any large institutional investor, given that decisions appear to be made at the lower levels with approvals sought at higher rungs of management. Reporting structures can be rigid and are subject to heavy bureaucracy. Practically all fundraisers and a large proportion of current and former employees of SWFs voice concerns about red tape they encounter in the asset allocation and investment management processes.

Decisions can be vetted and challenged throughout the process, and the interests and concerns of different actors can be as varied as the number of people associated with it. Given this robust, laborious, and time-consuming process, decisions are usually not swift, nor are they changed once finalized. Therefore, SWFs take relationships with GPs very seriously, and these relationships tend to be long term. GPs and marketers must have patience and perseverance. They should also understand an SWF's decision constraints before allocating significant fundraising resources behind the effort.

ASSET ALLOCATION AND MANAGER SELECTION

As with other institutional investors, SWFs' criteria for manager selection follow a similar track of finding a portfolio fit, alignment with the strategic asset allocation, and risk allocation. Given the diversity of SWFs and multiplicity of complex and intermingled objectives, it is difficult to generalize asset allocation considerations or processes. However, larger SWFs do share common factors in allocating to GPs.

The underlying questions during manager selection are: Why this asset class? Why this strategy? Why this manager? SWFs are public entities and national assets. It is important, as with political decisions, to ensure there is broad consensus—allowing no unilateral or unchallenged decisions by the participants in the decision process. Every decision needs to be *seen* as thoroughly vetted. This starts from the setting of an investment policy and strategic asset allocation.

SWFs set investment policies with input from the board. During this process, they may speak to domestic stakeholders, external consultants, multinational bodies like the IMF, and even other SWFs from friendly countries to get their perspective and learn from their experience. The fund's objective and ruling affiliation's risk tolerance determine investment policy and strategic asset allocation. Implementation of strategic asset allocation is delegated from the board to operational management and the investment teams. Typically, a benchmark portfolio is established at the onset of implementing a strategic asset allocation for both compliance and performance measurement.

Historically, before SWFs were established, countries needed to invest "temporary" surplus to preserve the purchasing power and shield the domestic economy from the so-called Dutch disease or resource curse—the notion that abundant resources may be a curse rather than a blessing.[12] There was a bias toward liquid, fixed-income investments. That changed with the formal establishment of SWFs and delegation of investment activities to professional investors. Today, most SWFs are global investors with a strategic asset allocation weighted toward equities and alternatives, with allocation to alternatives increasing since the beginning of the twenty-first century.

Between 2002 and 2016, SWF allocation to private markets increased from $61 billion to $1.66 trillion.[13] However, since then, asset allocation has not increased and remains significantly below their own target allocation. Fund size is a good predictor of asset allocation, with larger funds allocating more to private markets, given that they can endure illiquidity for longer periods in search of higher returns.

One clear trend among SWFs is that the incremental capital they received has gone disproportionately to alternatives, especially private markets, after the fund has reached a threshold liquidity through their fixed-income allocation. This means allocation to private markets has come at the cost of that for fixed income.

Similarly, 34 percent of SWFs globally are actively investing in hedge funds.[14] Average allocation of SWFs to hedge funds increased from 7 percent of AUM in 2016 to 8.2 percent in 2017. Not only are they direct investors in hedge funds, but they also invest through funds of hedge funds—tapping into existing relationships and expertise of the fund of hedge funds during the SWF's initial foray into hedge-fund investing, and later to concentrate on relationships with fewer outsourced managers.

SWFs have been active direct investors in domestic companies, sometimes as a lender or stockholder of last resort—as seen during the 2008 financial crisis when the Chinese SWF (especially Central Huijin Investment) injected liquidity into three of the largest Chinese banks (ICBC, Bank of China, and China Construction Bank) to stabilize the Chinese banking system during a challenging time. SWFs also can act as a holding company for domestic investments of government-owned or linked companies such as Temasek's stake in Singaporean companies like SingTel, DBS, Singapore Airlines, and CapitaLand. However, such investments will not necessarily be of interest to GPs and fundraisers, except to understand the competition they face for a SWF's investment dollars and to recognize the impact of SWFs in markets where they operate.

FIGURE 4.4 **SWF direct investments by number of transaction and type of partner**

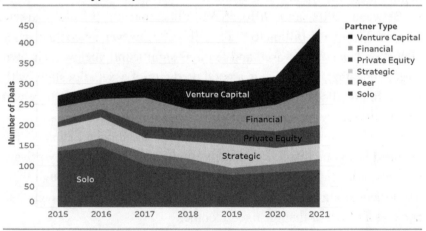

Source: https://ifswfreview.org/long-term-trends.html

SWFs have shown a higher affinity for co-investments and direct investments compared to other institutional investors (see Figure 4.4). While private equity managers have customarily offered co-investments, it is becoming common for hedge fund managers to offer co-investments as well to entice reluctant large institutional investors, including large SWFs, to allocate significant capital to them. SWFs are not only able to invest copious amounts of capital on a low-fee or no-fee basis, which reduces their investment costs, but they are also able to selectively allocate capital to deals that are expected to generate higher returns without being restricted by the limitations of the fund's terms.

As the population of senior citizens rises globally, SWFs will need to allocate more assets to alternatives in search of better returns to sustain wealth across generations. They are also cautious about not overallocating to alternatives, which can result in unintended consequences, such as not having enough liquidity to cash in on market disruptions.

With SWFs' increased allocation to private investments globally, one question they grapple with is whether this asset class's superior returns are sustainable, especially in an inflationary environment where yields on lower risk and liquid traditional assets (fixed income and listed equities) are extremely low. While these concerns have some basis, we do not see that as an impediment, much less a deterrent, to sustained higher allocations to alternatives—primarily infrastructure, real estate (including land banks in some cases), and private equity. Given the scale of capital to be invested and the sustained long-term returns needed by SWFs, alternatives are among their best options for the foreseeable future.

However, despite increasing allocation to alternatives, the SWF median allocation remains below their own strategic asset allocation target. "Preqin Sovereign Wealth Funds in Motion" report of May 2021 shows a shortfall of 4.1 percent in private equity, 3.3 percent for real estate, and 3.1 percent for infrastructure. Hedge funds saw median target allocations decreasing from a high of 8 percent in 2016 to 6.1 percent in 2020.[15]

There are several SWFs with an active and growing private equity allocation, but no hedge fund allocation. Lack of transparency is the primary impediment for state-sponsored funds adhering to specific policy restrictions. However, owing to pressure from SWFs, the Hedge Fund Standards Board and the International Forum of Sovereign Wealth Funds (IFSWF) signed an agreement in 2016 to ensure transparency and mutual exchange of information, which is expected to result in increased hedge fund allocations from SWFs.

Given the large checks SWFs write, they favor separately managed accounts for more control and flexibility. These accounts—in addition to offering negotiated fees (significantly far from the usual 2/20 model), offer full portfolio transparency, an ability to adapt the manager's strategy to adhere to a specific mandate (e.g., ESG, Sharia-compliance), and place limitations on using leverage. They also let SWFs avoid co-investor risks on fund liquidity during difficult times, and allow allocation to a smaller but high-performing GP without running afoul of internal policy controls around maximum exposures to a commingled pool.

One key trend for fundraisers to note: like most other institutional investors, SWFs are increasingly paring down the number of GP relationships. This increases the inclination to deepen relationships with fewer managers, concentrating investments among multiple offerings of the same manager—which one could argue is itself a risk. Already, larger asset managers were favored to win SWF mandates due to their ability to absorb and invest the capital without affecting investment performance. This trend makes it more difficult for smaller and emerging managers.

SWFs are more willing to underwrite concentration risk, especially in allocations to emerging markets and alternatives, compared to other investors. Also, they view an inability to meet its investment objectives (such as stabilization, transfer of wealth to future generations) as a worse outcome than being weighed down by traditional investment risk metrics such as volatility and concentration. In fact, savings funds have a higher affinity for short-term volatility. They are able to hold on to investments for a longer duration and mitigate the impact of such volatility, while simultaneously generating higher returns as a compensation for assuming greater risk.

Another recent trend among SWFs is a focus on ESG policies. The heightened interest has resulted in SWFs excluding entire sectors, such as tobacco and polluting industries, from their universe of investments; instead, they are directing investments to poorer countries to aid in their development (e.g., Temasek and Qatar Investment Authority's Africa-focused allocation) and favoring sectors viewed as beneficial to the country's strategic and political objectives (renewable energy and healthcare). With their size, ability to take an activist role, and patient capital, SWFs can significantly influence companies, industries, and countries to improve their sustainability standards and shore up the governance of companies.

WHY DO SWFS PREFER TO INVEST ABROAD?

One characteristic of most major SWFs is their preferential allocation to foreign assets compared to home-country investments (see Figure 4.5). Primary reasons driving the preference include:

- Most commodity-rich countries are overreliant on commodity revenues. They lack sufficient domestic investment options to adequately diversify risk away from commodity price fluctuation.
- During periods of elevated commodity prices, increased foreign currency receipts cause real currency appreciation. Appreciation hurts other domestic producers and exporters. Allocating to foreign assets helps mitigate the impact of commodity price-fueled currency appreciation. For commodity producers, establishing a SWF is a way to ward off the Dutch disease or resource curse.[16]
- The return on investment will fall when the domestic economy is shocked with a large infusion from surpluses. Foreign assets can be gradually and systematically repatriated to avoid such shocks.
- They are not limited to domestic options for risk allocation. SWFs can choose to invest in the best options globally, instead

of being tied to the limitations of potentially suboptimal domestic risk/return trade-offs.

- SWFs seeking stable longer-term returns are predisposed to higher real estate and infrastructure allocations. The number of projects that can absorb large capital allocation without impacting stable returns or causing inflation at home is limited for any single nation. A global allocation mandate opens a wider and deeper pool of options.
- Investing in businesses whose risk factors differ from those of the domestic economy is a good diversification play.

FIGURE 4.5 **SWF direct investments by value ($bn): local versus overseas**

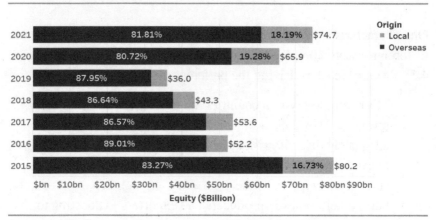

Source: https://ifswfreview.org/long-term-trends.html, IFSWF Database 2021

DIRECT INVESTMENTS: COMPETITION OR COOPERATION?

Direct investments are an important part of the SWF investment strategy. They become as much a partner as they are a competitor to GPs on some of the larger deals worldwide, especially in real estate and infrastructure. Sometimes they syndicate with other managers and bid for the deals in consortium. However, much of the competition comes from larger SWFs, who have internal teams that function like any fund manager. While SWFs might appear as competitors for the same deals, GPs who can show superior investment acumen and generate excess returns will compel SWFs to channel their allocation to them instead.

REGULATIONS GOVERNING SWFS

SWFs are generally established by a legal or legislative mandate in their home countries and are governed by that specific regulation. However, the regulatory situation in the country being targeted for investment depends on several factors. SWFs that are structured as an account of the country's central bank or other sovereign entity will be treated as sovereign entities by other countries and will enjoy the tax and immunity privileges they command. On the other hand, the tax treatment of SWFs not structured as an account of the central bank or another sovereign entity will depend on the bilateral tax treaties between the countries and are not accorded any immunity by foreign nations. Another issue is the ever-changing political disposition toward foreign investors, especially sovereign entities that are not transparent.

Despite the sometimes-negative response to foreign entities, SWF participation in equity and fixed-income markets brings benefits: SWFs increase that country's market liquidity and reduce short-term volatility due to their comparatively long-term investment horizons. Indeed, when a foreign SWF announces an investment in a company, the company's stock price typically reacts positively. Foreign SWFs have sometimes been viewed with concern, since they are presumed to be less transparent, their objectives are unclear, or they run afoul of a country's FDI restrictions.

The widely used Linaburg-Maduell transparency index (LMTI)— used to rate the transparency of SWFs—and the accountability and transparency scorecard from the Peterson Institute of International Economics indicate that many of the large SWFs score poorly on their accountability and reporting transparency, especially in the Middle

East.[17] This lack of transparency may be a cause for concern for some recipient countries. The fear is that the governments controlling these SWFs might pursue political or economic power in the target nation through their investments (especially stakes in strategic and security-related companies).

The Santiago Principles are 24 generally accepted principles and practices—voluntarily endorsed by IFSWF members—that promote transparency, good governance, accountability and prudent investment practices among SWFs.[18] The IMF has been a supporter of the Santiago Principles, which aim to maintain a stable global financial system, regulatory compliance in the nation targeted for investment, adequate risk management, and a transparent and sound governance structure.

In 2021, 34 full members and 6 associate members were part of the agreement. The idea is to demonstrate to recipient countries that such investments are carried out under strict economic and financial criteria. Despite the Santiago Principles' voluntary compliance and lack of an enforcement mechanism, they are a step toward encouraging recipient countries to welcome SWF investment, and not to set up roadblocks under the cloak of national interest or national security considerations.

TARGETING SWF ALLOCATIONS

Fund marketers should understand some SWF-specific issues while seeking an allocation:

1. Check sizes are large. You should have the ability to absorb an allocation without an impact on investment performance. We have seen instances where a fund has had to turn away capital or pare the allocation to a SWF.
2. SWF marketing takes time. You need both patience and perseverance.
3. Location is a constraint. While SWFs are establishing offices globally in locations like New York City and San Francisco, to better understand opportunities worldwide, a GP might still

have to gain the confidence of the final decision makers in their home countries. Some funds have opened satellite offices in Asia and the Middle East, where there is a concentration of SWFs.

4. In regions where high touch and personal connections are cultural expectations, local PAs can play a strong role in opening doors to potential SWF investors. While it is rare for PAs to act as advisors to SWFs, they might greatly assist in helping you get access to family offices and other investors in the same region that have similar expectations.

5. Using a regional specialist PA is also beneficial for teams not large enough to dedicate staff to a specific region, as they can serve as an extension of your team in the area and provide you with an assessment of the competitive landscape.

6. Each SWF has a unique set of needs and requirements. Separately managed accounts and bespoke investment strategies offer an avenue to cater to such differences, while also creating a stickiness to the relationship, given the investment of time, resources, and effort to build both the operating infrastructure and the professional trust necessary to succeed in such ventures.

7. Managers who are able to accept and appreciate large check sizes—through preferential terms and as true partners in the SWFs overall investment strategy—will forge better partnerships. Co-investments, facilitating direct investments as a syndicate, creating deal flows for direct investments—all of these will help strengthen relationships between GPs and SWFs.

More than a decade ago, a large SWF said this to the GP pitching for an allocation:

I don't like funds telling me they treat all investors the same. That may sound catchy to the rest, but for me, I expect to be treated differently, as I have more invested in the fund than any other. The risk and trust I am placing by allocating $200 million to you should never be the same as the $2 million from someone else. So, if it requires you to put in 100 times more effort to service my account, it should be reasonable, and you should be happy to. I expect better terms and conditions for my investment than the rest. It is an absolutely fair expectation.

We agree with that assessment, although not all SWFs or even teams within the same SWF would share that attitude.

CONCLUSION

Given the heterogeneity of objectives, investment horizon, risk tolerance, and asset allocation, marketing to SWFs does confound and challenge fund managers and marketers. But the value of securing an allocation from an investor with deep pockets and longer-term orientation cannot be underestimated. The marketing process can be long and can run into bureaucratic delays even when there is an intent to invest; marketers should account for this in their fundraising plans. Thus far, SWF allocations tend to be skewed toward private equity, but that could change over time. If you understand the specific nuances of each SWF early in the marketing process and possess the necessary persistence and patience, you could potentially see a large payoff at the end of the process.

CHAPTER 5

Other Major Investor Categories and Gatekeepers

The preceding chapters covered groups of investors that form a majority of the investment capital allocated to alternatives. This chapter focuses on other very large groups of investors, who together have as significant an allocation of capital to alternatives as the ones we have explored up to now. This group includes insurance companies, funds of funds, registered investment advisors and wealth managers, and feeder funds.

1. INSURANCE COMPANIES

Insurance companies are among the largest holders of assets globally, with more than $33 trillion in assets at the end of 2020, making them an important investor group for fund managers to target.[1] However, this market is quite fragmented. There were nearly 6,000 insurance companies in the United States alone in 2019, according to the Insurance Information Institute.[2]

Insurance companies assume investment risk on behalf of their policy holders in return for premiums collected. Traditionally, the premiums collected were allocated to near-risk free assets—US Treasury bills, notes, and bonds. In 2020, bonds and other debt instruments accounted for nearly 77 percent of all investments by insurance companies worldwide.[3] However, the ultra-low interest rates over the past two decades, especially after the 2008 financial crisis, pushed insurance company investment managers to look elsewhere for allocation of their risk capital. Nearly 75 percent of insurance companies considered interest rates *the* primary risk to their portfolios.[4] One solution was to increase allocation to alternative investments in search of better returns in a low-yield environment (see Figures 5.1 and 5.2).

FIGURE 5.1 **Nontraditional investments have gained market share in recent years**

Asset Allocation, 2017 vs. 2021			
	2017	2021	Change +/−
Total Liquid Equities	9.1%	5.5%	−3.6%
Domestic Equities	7.2%	4.2%	−3.0%
International Equities	1.9%	1.4%	−0.5%
Total Liquid Fixed Income	66.8%	56.3%	−10.5%
IG Fixed Income	60.7%	48.5%	−12.2%
Non-IG Fix Inc (Bank Loans & HY)	6.1%	7.8%	1.7%
Total Nontraditional Investments	20.3%	31.8%	11.4%
Structured Credit (CLO, CBO, etc.)	5.9%	9.2%	3.4%
Private Credit	5.6%	7.7%	2.1%
Private Equity	2.4%	3.2%	0.8%
Hedge Funds	0.5%	0.5%	0.0%
Real Estate Equity	1.5%	2.7%	1.2%
Real Estate Credit	3.7%	5.9%	2.2%
Commodities/Energy	0.4%	0.1%	−0.3%
Infrastructure	0.4%	2.4%	2.0%
Total Cash/Other	3.8%	6.4%	2.6%
Cash	2.7%	4.9%	2.2%
Other	1.1%	1.5%	0.4%

Source: KKR Global Macro & Asset Allocation.
Note: May not equal 100 due to rounding. Data as of August 31, 2021.

FIGURE 5.2 **Insurers have had to shift their asset allocations in recent years to protect returns—with private credit, real estate credit, infrastructure, and private equity benefiting mightily**

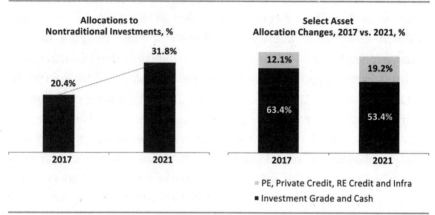

Source: : KKR Global Macro & Asset Allocation.
Note: Data as of August 31, 2021.

In the United States, approximately 22 percent of insurance portfolios were allocated to alternatives and structured notes in 2020.[5] However, the allocation within alternatives is skewed toward private equity (PE) and private debt, and insurance companies in the United States and Europe have been increasing their geographical diversification in recent years.

Complicating matters is that insurance is a heavily regulated industry across the globe. In the United States, they are regulated at both the federal and local levels. The primary goal of regulation is to ensure that insurers stay solvent. Ironically, this strict oversight can hamper the ability of insurers to invest in higher risk assets such as alternatives, whose potentially higher returns could help them meaningfully cover their liabilities over time. In addition, the inertia from regulatory constraints often leads to the slower allocation of resources—for example, in matters such as recruiting experienced staff to build and manage an effective alternatives strategy—further slowing their path to alternatives.

For fund managers or GPs, it would help to look at insurance companies in a similar fashion as pension funds, but with a much stricter regulatory environment that impedes their allocation to alternative assets. While the allocation may be smaller compared to their size, there are still trillions of available investment dollars for GPs to seek an allocation. Some insurance companies also have in-house fund management teams that GPs are competing against for allocation. Outsourcing is common for their alternatives allocation, with emerging market, high-yield, and structured debt allocation going to external managers.

Insurance companies not only want their managers to have an excellent track record but also to be cognizant of the regulatory environment in which they operate and the constraints they face. The necessary conditions include a track record of generating superior returns across market conditions, diversification benefits, defined investment philosophy and strategy, investment discipline, strong controls and governance, team capability and working relationships, stability of the team (low attrition or churn), and a focus on superior returns.

In most firms, the strategic asset allocation decisions are made by the portfolio management group, which is separate from teams that focus on asset classes and that make investment decisions. Before a deal closes, the decision must be approved by a pricing committee (or equivalent supervisory structure) at the insurance company. Most larger insurance companies have dedicated teams for each asset class. Insurance companies, similar to institutional investors, do not seek to time the market in alternatives. While capital allocation can increase or decrease as a function of various factors, including internal constraints and external investment environment (risk/reward proposition), there is a steady flow of investment dollars from insurance companies to alternative investments irrespective of the conditions.

It is difficult for larger companies with a substantial amount of investment dollars to implement tactical asset allocation decisions quickly. Therefore, they are more likely to keep up a steady flow, even as they move toward longer-term desirable allocations. Given the importance of capital adequacy ratios to protect against insolvency as a result of inadequate risk controls (e.g., AIG during 2008), there is a bias toward assets that have a lower equity requirement. While some insurance companies are comfortable working with a placement

agent, others avoid them in favor of internal deal sourcing and due diligence. RFPs are not a common occurrence in the insurance industry
for finding new managers or for making a substantial outsourced asset
allocation for alternative investments.

Offering a co-investment opportunity, even before an investment is
made into the manager's fund, is a favorable way for GPs to get the
attention of insurance companies in the alternatives bucket. Insurance
companies find that such "date before you marry" processes give the
investment team great insight into the workings of a GP, and the ability
to assess quality of deals and depth of their due diligence and value
addition to the company before making a substantial allocation to the
manager's fund(s). Some of the primary reasons for declining a manager include lack of transparency, dishonesty, performance volatility in
the track record, sizing of deals not commensurate with the opportunity set, self-dealing, and conflicts of interest.

As insurance is a highly regulated industry, insurers rate GP transparency quite high on their list of IR requirements. The composition
of Limited Partner Advisory Committees (LPACs) and ensuring that
members execute their responsibilities—such as assessing GP conflicts of interests, compliance with LPA provisions, LPAC consent and
approval, regulatory awareness, and access to appropriate professional
assistance, among others—are extremely important for insurance
companies.

Industry insiders expect a trend toward separately managed accounts
for larger investments. These would provide transparency and improve
control over assets. However, these accounts are only viable for larger
insurance companies with expansive assets, due to the need for better
infrastructure and back-office support, and allowance for incremental
accounting overhead.

Another trend is consolidation among asset managers. Midsize
insurance companies that are able to allocate capital to GPs who are not
"front page names" will find it challenging, as consolidation results in
larger GPs and propensity for bigger checks. In addition, if consolidation
involves an existing manager, the resulting culture and process evolution
will require a reassessment of the manager and a need to find new GPs

similar to the one that was consolidated. Consolidation also results in the crowding out of smaller and midsize LPs in favor of larger checks. This opens opportunities for managers of alternatives funds who want to establish or expand their relationships among insurance companies.

2. FUND OF FUNDS

Fund of funds (FoFs) are commingled pools of capital that invest in other funds (usually around 15 to 20 other private equity or hedge funds). FoFs are essentially portfolios of other funds. There are primarily three different types of FoFs based on their portfolio—fund of mutual funds, fund of hedge funds (FoHF), and private equity fund of funds (PE FoF). We will focus on FoHFs and PE FoFs in this chapter. While some FoFs have a mixed asset portfolio, their importance is largely insignificant to most managers. The need for FoFs is amply substantiated by some of the larger asset managers and wealth management firms, who are responsible for allocating client assets to GPs, as they set up in-house FoFs that cater to the needs of their clients.

The value FoFs bring to the alternative assets industry include gaining access to top-tier GPs, diversification, due diligence capability, entry into nascent markets where information or expertise is scarce (such as frontier markets investments), or exposure to niche or specialist strategies (such as secondaries). They serve as an outsourced allocator for investors who lack internal resources to build and manage a portfolio in a noncore asset class.

Access is extremely important, since many funds have capacity constraints but will accept money from existing investors even if they are "closed," including from FoFs that have contributed to their earlier funds. In many cases, investors can shorten the time frame required for a new alternatives program (PE or HF) to mature by investing in an FoF that provides access to the underlying GPs at once, instead of having to cultivate these relationships over several years.

LPs eventually migrate to direct investing as their program matures. One other value addition, specifically for illiquid strategies such as private equity or venture capital through a secondaries FoF, is to shorten investment duration. The greatest disadvantage is the double layer of fees—paying underlying funds and the FoF. Furthermore, since allocation is outsourced to the FoF manager, the underlying portfolio construction depends on the manager's decision. This is less than ideal for portfolio management and risk control by larger LPs who could have had direct access to underlying funds. The investment term is extended beyond the longest duration offered by the underlying funds, since additional time is needed for the FoF to raise capital and source and select managers to make the investment.

According to Preqin's PE FoFs report, aggregate AUM of the PE FoFs was $381 billion as of 2017.[6] By far the largest number of PE FoFs are based in the United States, followed by Europe and China. The popularity of FoFs has been waning over the past decade (capital raised fell from $55 billion in 2007 to $26 billion in 2016), due to investor concerns about double-layered fees. FoFs make up less than 5 percent of the capital raised by private equity worldwide—but that could be a skewed number.

Many emerging managers benefit from FoF allocations. In addition, a larger portion of alternatives allocation from smaller LPs flow through FoFs. For most midsize institutions, the allure of FoFs is due to their access to top-quartile managers who are selective about their investor composition. Given the average size of PE FoFs is $250 million to $300 million, it is easy to see why midsize managers will have better success getting an allocation from FoFs, compared to larger managers for whom checks from FoFs are not meaningful.

PE FoFs also have a longer fundraising cycle, about 1.6 times the time taken by direct private equity funds. Since FoFs must ultimately market their portfolio of underlying managers to end investors, fund managers seeking an allocation from FoFs will find better success by accommodating terms that in turn make the FoF more attractive to the FoF's investors. These include guaranteed access to successor funds, increased portfolio transparency, fee accommodation for larger checks, and acknowledging the FoF as a conduit for absorbing larger investors from the FoF's investor base.

On the investor side, FoFs will have better success with smaller investors (lower than $1 billion AUM) who form the bulk of the potential market for FoFs (47 percent of FoF investors have lower than $1 billion AUM) (see Figure 5.3).

FIGURE 5.3 **Investors with a preference for PE FoF by assets under management versus all investors in private equity**

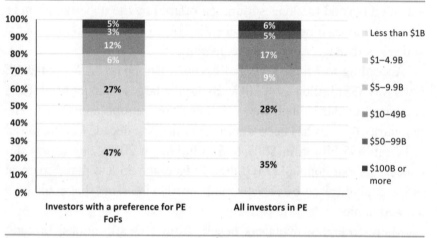

Source: https://docs.preqin.com/reports/Preqin-Special-Report-Private-Equity-Funds-of-Funds
-November-2017.pdf

Some FoFs have a lower minimum investment requirement compared to the underlying funds, which helps smaller investors diversify their exposure across asset classes and provides better liquidity terms than underlying investments (although at times it ends up hurting FoF performance, due to a focus on liquidity as opposed to performance potential).

Given the large number of private equity and hedge funds globally, it is difficult for most investors (LPs) to have the resources to fully cover the market on their own. FoFs can act as the outsourced arm in sourcing, selecting, and monitoring investments for resource-constrained investment offices or high-net-worth individual (HNI) investors. The cost of outsourcing is weighed against developing an internal program, considering both direct costs (FoF fees versus staffing costs) and indirect expenses (e.g., opportunity cost of denied access to managers, a steep learning curve, and cost of missteps).

FoFs have begun to address the cost obstacle by lowering their fees (from 1.2 percent in 2020 to 0.8 percent in 2017), and carry. They further add value by seeking a fee rebate from underlying managers for larger checks they write, compared to their own investor pool. FoFs have also succeeded in backing emerging managers more amenable to lower fees and gaining access to successor funds, provided strong investment performance by the manager.

Venture capital (VC) FoFs should emphasize that in a sector dogged by "performance persistence" and "high dispersion of returns," the ability of FoFs to provide continued access to strong managers more than compensates for the additional fee layer with superior portfolio returns in excess of the fee paid.[7] Similarly, FoFs seeking an allocation from LPs will find better success by reducing the additional FoF layer fee, increasing transparency, involving FoF LPs in broader decision-making, and providing bespoke portfolio solutions for larger LPs.

3. REGISTERED INVESTMENT ADVISORS AND WEALTH MANAGEMENT FIRMS

Registered investment advisors (RIAs), financial planners (FPs), and other wealth managers are responsible for investment and asset management of primarily the financial assets of an HNI or institutional investor. They are regulated both by the SEC at the US federal level, and by state authorities where they operate. Their typical fees are between 0.5 percent and 2 percent of assets managed. Each individual client portfolio is managed separately, with some characteristics of mass customization applied to the whole group or subgroups as classified by a set of factors, including risk tolerance, liquidity, and investment horizon. These portfolios can be a mix of equity, fixed income, mutual funds, ETFs, and alternatives. RIAs are best suited for investors who want to have an outsourced bespoke or semi-bespoke portfolio compared to an FoF/FoHF, but with the ability to discuss decisions with people managing the portfolio. This can be particularly important for HNIs who want to manage their tax burden, unlike investments in a commingled FoF pool.

Many HNIs and smaller investors who outsource their portfolio management to RIAs are also attracted to alternatives due to the higher returns they achieve compared to traditional investments. Demand from such investors has been a primary driver of RIAs allocating capital to alternatives in recent years. A third of the RIAs offered private equity investments to their clients,[8] and that number has been growing in line with client demand.[9] While only 10 percent of RIA client portfolios have private equity exposure,[10] more than two-thirds are interested in private equity, which points to a large gap between investor interest and allocations by RIAs. There is an opportunity for GPs to close this gap in coming years.

Alternative fund managers should approach RIAs not as a client but as a distribution channel with a strong influence on the client. Alternative funds get allocation from RIA clients in two ways. One is through the HNI for whom the RIA conducts manager due diligence and checks compatibility with portfolio objectives. The second is to be empaneled among the RIA product offerings. This approach includes signing agreements with broker-dealers to make investments available to the agents on the platform.

However, agents are restricted by what their home office allows them to sell. There is a lot of education and business development work, including some market cultivation, that will have to be undertaken by interested GPs. In recent years, unlisted real estate investment trusts (REITs) have taken this approach and have been richly rewarded: monthly aggregate RIA and wire house allocations topped billions of dollars.

The other big reason for advisor reluctance to invest client capital is the time commitment and labor-intensive nature of manager selection and the tedious subscription process. For RIAs who process electronic trades, the lack of "click and subscribe" is an impediment. One would expect, given the long duration of private equity and hedge fund commitments, that RIAs who facilitate these investments and offer them on their platform will also benefit from asset stickiness over the long run. These become differentiating factors for larger clients who will be the most suitable for an alternatives allocation, further increasing their attractiveness and contributing to their revenues. A tangential benefit is that all the allocation to alternatives is outsourced, which improves revenue efficiency for RIAs. By highlighting the benefits of offering the right alternative fund (yours), fund managers can find long-term partners with a growing pool of capital.

Obstacles to working with RIAs include the high minimum investment or commitment amounts of each individual fund, lack of a central repository to source funds, transparency, asset safety, and lack of familiarity with alternatives. Larger funds can afford to invest the resources to educate individual RIAs or groups, prepare educational material for client usage, and create bespoke investment vehicles, including feeder funds structured to accept lower individual minimums. They also can persuade RIAs to make their funds a gateway to other alternatives in the future and can negotiate long-term deals with RIAs in consideration of the substantial investment up front to forge the relationship.

For smaller GPs with limited resources available for marketing, there are other avenues. Some RIAs have created their own alternative investment platforms, and there are third-party platforms that serve RIAs, providing services such as custody (including no fee or low fee) and due diligence to assist them with their alternatives allocation. Technology is rapidly evolving to enable digitized subscription and confirmation.[11] Some RIAs have also established unlisted interval or tender offer funds that address issues with lower individual minimums, avoid capital call hassles, remove tax-filing complexity by using 1099s instead of K1s, and boost client confidence by complying with the 1940 Act.[12] One key reason GPs should join the RIA pipeline is that these agents become de-facto marketers for empaneled funds without an additional placement fee. This can be substantial savings for assets gathered through the channel.

One caveat: it takes a lot of sales effort to be accepted by RIAs. As such, smaller managers and GPs with less than 10 years in the business should explore other avenues before seeking distribution through RIAs. Real estate managers, however, will be better received, since RIA clients have a high affinity for real estate investments in their portfolio.[13]

4. FEEDER FUNDS

Feeder funds are special purpose investment funds whose primary goal is to "feed" capital to a master fund, which is ultimately responsible for investing and managing the portfolio. Feeder funds collect capital for investment into the master fund in a master-feeder structure or act as a sub-fund for the master fund.

The master fund can have multiple feeders for several reasons. One is to distinguish capital for tax or regulatory purposes (e.g., on-shore and off-shore structures, US and non-US investors, taxable and non-taxable investors, or for exclusion of certain investments that would otherwise be acceptable to the master fund). Another reason is to set up a structural tool to aggregate assets into a larger pool of capital, as in the case of commingled investments from smaller investors to make the fund large enough to entice a selective GP and simplify investor relations (IR) and operational management of the fund. Profits and losses are distributed in proportion to their investments in the master fund, except in cases where the feeder is meant to exclude certain types of investments. In this case, the feeder will receive allocation in other investments of the master fund (excluding prohibited investments), proportional to its investment in those alone.

Feeders can either be sponsored by a GP or an outside entity. In case of manager-sponsored feeders, there is no distinction between the master and the feeder as far as marketing is concerned, except for how the allocation is directed. We are more interested in the non-manager-sponsored feeders in this section, whose primary role is asset gathering for the master fund.

Here are key issues to consider while marketing feeder funds:

1. Feeder funds may be the only way for smaller investors to access a selective manager whose minimums for investment may be multiples of what they are able to prudently invest.
2. There is an additional layer of costs for setup and operating costs of the feeder.

3. In case of a wrap product, there are additional fees collected by the intermediary for creating the feeder and providing access to the investment.

4. GPs may prefer feeders to avoid dealing with too many investors directly, but this also creates distance between the manager and end investor. This would not be an issue for the larger managers with established brands; however, smaller managers dependent on small checks to collect a respectable AUM will find that the investor-manager distance can be detrimental to long-term growth unless an effective IR program is implemented. This could include open access to all investors in the fund. Whether or not they are directly investing in the fund or through a feeder, investors can be provided all investor communications, or are invited to special events such as webinars targeted at feeder fund investors.

5. LPs will not be able to conduct adequate due diligence but will be dependent on the manager of the feeder. This causes single investment feeders to be treated similar to FoFs, but lacks their diversification benefits. The manager of the feeder fund may, in some instances, procure access to the master fund's data room for its own investors.

6. Investors have been skeptical about somewhat opaque feeders, after seeing multiple feeders in the Bernie Madoff scandal. The largest feeder was the Fairfield Sentry Fund, sponsored by the Fairfield Greenwich Group, which raised $1.7 billion for its Madoff feeder. The allure to retail investors was access to an exclusive manager like Madoff, so they glossed over the lack of transparency, inadequate due diligence, and additional fees charged by the sponsor. There is less concern about the master fund in the case of well-established, blue-chip managers, but investors can and should always conduct diligence on the provider of the feeder.

Managers of feeders should create as much transparency as possible and shorten the distance between the fund and investor, while also providing value-added services to make the fees worthwhile. This includes thorough due diligence of the master fund, similar to what is expected from a FoF manager. Investors today need concrete evidence and not just claims of adequate safeguards, in light of issues that surfaced during the Madoff fraud. A thorough documentation of the processes, policies, and execution, in addition to evidence of compliance with such processes and policies, will be crucial. Face-to-face meetings between the master fund's manager and prospective LPs will go a long way toward winning over skeptical investors.

Feeder fund sponsors may be able to negotiate more favorable terms or qualify for better fee breaks in an aggregated feeder fund vehicle than investors would get on their own. LPs may also obtain the benefits of consolidated reporting across feeder funds in their portfolio by using the technology platform of a feeder fund sponsor. Feeder fund sponsors may be able to negotiate more favorable terms or qualify for better fee breaks in an aggregated feeder fund vehicle than investors would get on their own. Investors may also obtain benefits of consolidated reporting across feeder funds in their portfolio by using the technology platform of a feeder fund sponsor.

5. GATEKEEPERS

Gatekeepers are specialist advisors and consultants who assist investors with investment decisions and are a vital part of the alternatives investment process. They assist with creation of investment objectives and policies, portfolio construction and monitoring, and manager selection. As the name suggests, a manager's path to the LP goes through the "gatekeeper." Therefore, some fund managers and marketers wonder whether gatekeepers are obstacles or enablers during a fundraise—depending upon how well it is going. The better question for any GP is to ask, "How do you build a positive and constructive relationship with them, instead of a perfunctory, or inimical relationship?"

Gatekeepers play a large role in the asset allocation decisions of many different institutional investors and especially most pension funds—both public and, increasingly, private pensions. They are considered fiduciaries in the process. All gatekeepers conduct due diligence on GPs. Some offer services that goes beyond due diligence—essentially becoming an extension of the investor's staff and serving as an unbiased and objective "prudent person" and a "second set of eyes" for the investor. What they look for in a GP should parallel what a capable LP would consider for investment. After all, they represent LPs and seek to meet their clients' investment goals. Here are some of the primary metrics that gatekeepers evaluate a fund on:

1. **Performance.** Good track record, outperformance vis-à-vis risks, source of outperformance, consistency of returns, batting average, correlation with other asset classes, performance attribution to investments and team members (given their network, they can also parse out the source of performance and the attribution), deep and accurate understanding of the market.
2. **Brand and reputation.** Not just name recognition, but character and investment quality.
3. **Team**. Alignment of interests between the LP and GP, conflicts of interest, investment oversight and diligence, a stable and capable team.
4. **Fund mechanics**. Investment oversight and diligence, distribution of fund economics, disciplined investment process and execution, transparency, quality of IR and communication, alignment of pay and performance, robust bench strength of future leaders for the organization, adequate staffing, and other considerations.

Some gatekeepers act purely as advisors and others make investment decisions. Some institutions will not consider an investment without a recommendation by their consultant, while others seek confirmation after they have made decisions internally. Gatekeepers' services range from being pure advisors and providers of independent, third-party opinions on the suitability of an investment (prudent person opinions) to providing quasi-investment and quasi-CIO services that include asset allocation, policy development, co-investment decisions, risk management, portfolio construction, performance monitoring, and ongoing due diligence. In every case, they act as a first screen for the investor.

For marketers, there is no good answer as to whether they should solicit the LP or the gatekeeper for an allocation. It depends on circumstance. The authors typically approach both simultaneously, creating a push-and-pull marketing strategy.

Building relationships with consultants is a one-to-many approach and can be extremely productive. For the right product and team, consultants can broaden your reach to their entire investor base. Typically, consultants are open to accepting meetings—or at least to review fund marketing materials—as they have a larger staff compared to most individual clients and the meeting is another opportunity to benchmark and gather information about competing opportunities in the market. Most consultants also maintain a database of managers and update this information regularly, including performance information coupled with their observations.

In some instances, managers may fail to get a response from a consultant, and hence soliciting investors directly is also important. In one example, Hemali was setting up an Asia road show for one of her managers and contacted a number of LPs in the region. Within days, a consultant who represented many of the investors she had approached reached out to her requesting an update meeting. While an investor might decline a meeting, they may ask the consultant to review and monitor the fund if it is interesting to them.

Consultants and advisors, like placement agents and other service providers, have a vantage point that straddles the GP and the LP world. Given the flow of information they receive from either direction, they can serve as conduits of information and also provide a "sanity check" on the GP's market information and assumptions. Managers who develop a functional relationship and rapport with a group of consultants and engage them prior to fundraising can build relationships more easily, better understand their clients and their needs, and obtain valuable feedback on their strategy and competitive landscape.

CONCLUSION

While each group of investors (E&Fs, pensions, and others) has enough capital to incentivize a manager, we view it as an optimization problem. Managers who are building successful deal pipelines and executing are constrained by time and resource availability. Understanding investment objectives of different investor groups is a good starting point to assess if the product you are pitching would be an appropriate fit for an investor. Subsequently, you can construct a marketing strategy that is broad enough and not overly reliant on any one investor or investor group, and ultimately focus on obtaining allocations from a targeted list of investors with the highest probability of success. As with any marketing effort, the cardinal rule is to "first, know your customer," which provides the critical foundation for successful fundraising.

FUNDRAISING IN PRACTICE

CHAPTER 6

Premarketing and Marketing—an Overview

Marketing is critical to a fund's success. You may believe above-average returns are enough to attract investors, but this is a misperception. It is not uncommon to find a fund with superior performance failing to attract investors. This is often due to poor marketing.

The good news is that marketing alternatives is a craft that can be learned. As with any craft, you learn from those who are adept at it, but master it by practicing. No amount of independent study or listening to experts will teach you as much as doing it yourself. Before you go to battle, you need to arm yourself with the tools necessary, and in this book we will explore them with you. Once you are comfortable with the fundamentals of fund marketing, you will be able to adapt these methods to suit your personality, capability, and needs.

Fund managers (GPs and related persons) need to familiarize themselves with the expectations of investors, both institutional and high-net-worth individuals (HNI). A good starting point is the Institutional Limited Partners Association (ILPA) private equity principles, which seek to align the interests of funds and their institutional investors. These guideposts, which are equally applicable to other alternatives, were developed in response to the 2008 financial crisis. This crisis exposed the deficiencies of both funds and institutions in executing their fiduciary and functional responsibilities. Such scrutiny resulted in many improvements to investor relations (IR) functions that we see today—better transparency, governance, stewardship and adherence to fiduciary duties. (Note that marketing and IR are related but distinct functions, even if they are performed by the same individual or team. Chapter 11 will discuss IR's influence on marketing.)

Here are the ILPA principles anchoring IR practices in private equity:[1]

1. **Transparency.** Transparency not only means sharing information that is timely, accurate, and detailed to meet the needs of investors, it also requires the disclosure of fees, calculation methodologies, justification for expenses incurred, and timely reporting of nonroutine regulatory and policy violations.

2. **Alignment of interest.** Conflicts arise when the interests of funds and investors diverge. To minimize disagreements, resentment, or ill will, ensure terms are reasonable, underlying economics duly incentivize performance and equitably distribute profits, and partnership conditions are not onerous to or shortchange either party.

3. **Governance.** Given the level of autonomy and information asymmetry that favors GPs over LPs, put mechanisms in place to ensure there are clear boundaries around what is acceptable. Furthermore, there should be a mechanism for enabling proper monitoring and remedying a situation should there be a disagreement or potentially contentious situation that could arise between the two parties.

We highly encourage managers and investors to thoroughly familiarize themselves with the best practices outlined in the latest ILPA principles document.

PREMARKETING

Marketing is a continuous process in alternatives, it never really stops. For example, while some hedge funds may temporarily pause or close to new capital once they reach certain target AUM levels, most are in constant fundraising mode. In the case of private equity funds, the next fundraise often starts even before the current one is completed. Successful marketers are those who focus on the current fundraises and are always working toward the success of future fundraises. This process, premarketing, is a key ingredient of a successful marketing function in alternatives.

Reasons to premarket:

1. **Timing mismatch.** An LP may be unable to invest today while being genuinely interested in the fund. Some factors that may temporarily preclude an allocation include current liquidity levels, sufficient exposure to the asset class, and limited time to perform the requisite due diligence. These are excellent opportunities for a marketer to nurture their interest and lay the groundwork for future allocations.

2. **Informational interviewing.** Premarketing is a soft-sell strategy that could create benefits in the long term. LPs appreciate being able to learn about the fund without every meeting turning into a sales pitch. This two-way exchange is also an opportunity to learn about the GP before making a commitment, which is also known as "investment dating."

3. **Building relationships without fundraising pressure.** It is better to have initial conversations with LPs when they know you are not there to make a marketing pitch, rather than only reaching out to LPs during a fundraise. They will be less guarded and more receptive to a manager or marketer investing time and effort to educate them as part of relationship-building. Institutions appreciate the time spent to learn about the strategy, fund, and team well ahead of a fundraise, so they can have greater confidence about their investment decision and feel comfortable with the GP. To build credibility over time, be transparent at the outset and communicate in a manner that is consistent, reliable, and persistent (but not intrusive).

What Do You Need to Start Premarketing?

Premarketing by nature is unstructured; there is no specific requirement from LPs other than the willingness to learn about the manager. Most GPs start with existing pitchbooks and investor updates as the basis for a conversation. Updating information presented in older pitchbooks prior to meeting investors is a good practice; it shows commitment to the process and a genuine effort to bring them on board for the next fund.

GPs should approach fundraising as a resource challenge. Optimize the capital raise given the constraints of time and money. While you may be able to convert an LP that has never invested in your asset class or strategy, this effort may prevent you from targeting investors that are ideal for you and already looking to allocate to your strategy.

A common and potentially costly mistake while fundraising is not keeping LPs engaged. Fundraising is a hectic and time-consuming part of the asset management business. For most GPs, it is a distraction from their core competencies and responsibilities, but is essential to keep the wheels of the firm running. New managers often view a meeting with an LP as an accomplishment instead of identifying it for what it really is—moving the ball a little closer toward the goal post. The GP interview does not end after the meeting either; it has just begun.

Unless there is an outright rejection from an LP, keep the conversation going without being intrusive. After a meeting, send thank-you notes, and follow up with responses to questions raised or any additional information promised to an investor. In addition, obtain permission from the LP to provide regular updates and fund letters, so that the engagement continues as you provide a better understanding of your fund, strategy, and the firm. While adding LPs to the email distribution list keeps them updated and reminds them of your fund, active engagement is more fruitful, moving them toward an investment. Seasoned fund marketers regularly provide quick updates and call investors occasionally to re-engage with them, without rushing them to commit.

Investor communication best practices:

1. Reach out when there is something genuinely important to share, such as a new deal, an exit, a write-up of an existing

investment, an investment from a prominent LP, significant outperformance over the benchmark (hedge fund), an addition to or even departures from the team.

2. Do not request in-person meetings too frequently. You want to avoid meaningless meetings that do not add value to the LP.

3. Informal and unplanned engagements can be opportunities for candid conversations with LPs—these include coffee breaks, cocktail hours, meals, and other encounters at conferences.

It is good practice to have continuity in your interactions with LPs. Most large funds divide their investor list among IR and sales teams to help provide such continuity. By having a primary point of contact for each LP, it is easier to build stronger relationships and monitor changes to sensitivities and preferences over time.

TYPICAL MARKETING PROCESS

Essential questions for a fund manager to address as part of the marketing process include:

1. **Assessment:**
   - Who are your current LPs? What is the composition by investor segment? What is the investor concentration— top 5 and top 10? What is the geographical dispersion of current LPs?
   - What has been their investment experience? What was their alpha compared to a benchmark (hedge funds) or internal rates of return (IRR) compared to the public market and industry? For closed-end funds, what were their multiples of invested capital (MOIC), exit experience, and distributions? Where do you stand against your competition—what is your track record and is it an advantage?
   - For private equity, what percentage and number of LPs will re-up (existing investors committing capital to the

new fund), and at what amounts (higher or lower than their
current capital commitment)? For hedge funds, are they
likely to increase or decrease allocation in the coming years?

- Are LPs supportive of the new fund (private equity)? Is there
LP concern about fund size growing too large to impede
good returns?
- How many LPs who declined to allocate in the past could be
persuaded this time around? What were their concerns, and
have they been addressed adequately? If not, what should
be done?
- What will be the biggest obstacle to raising capital for the
new fund?
- Map out the team's strengths and compare them to the
competition.
- Address the most important question: what is your unique
selling proposition (USP)? What proof do you have to
substantiate your claims?
- Why should an LP allocate to you and your strategy?

2. Desired state:
- What is the ideal size of the fund?
- What is the desired LP composition by segment, geography,
and concentration?
- Create a target list of ideal and desired LPs.

3. Gap analysis:
- Has the anchor been identified?
- How many new LPs should the fund attract? What are
the desired characteristics? What is an ideal check size or
investor AUM range to target?
- Does the team have bandwidth to execute a strong fundraise?
What additional resources are needed?
- Is performance superior enough to attract on-the-fence LPs
from the prior fundraise and new targets?

- Are the relationships with target LPs sufficiently deep and broad? If not, is the solution to start building relationships now, to use a placement agent, or both?
- Do inadequacies in the documentation or communication exist? Can this be resolved before a fund launch?
- Is there a need for a strategy recalibration or modification? Will that be received well by current LPs? Will that make it attractive to new LPs?
- Can all members of the team tell your story spontaneously to LPs? Which members are excellent storytellers who can provide in-depth information to LPs to aid in their due diligence, and who needs significant coaching and practice?
- Are there additional institutional, organizational, or regulatory issues that should be remedied prior to the launch?

4. **Planning and budgeting:**
   - What is an ideal budget versus the actual budget? What are key priorities and compromises?
   - Which current LPs are likely to provide referrals and references? Who is on the fence about making an additional investment, and how can they be convinced? Who might redeem their investment (hedge fund) or not re-up for the next fund (private equity/venture capital)?
   - Where should roadshows be organized? Who will be the "host" LPs for the roadshow? Can an LP event be organized to connect with a larger group of LPs?
   - Are there conferences that will attract desired LPs? Are these ideal venues to make introductions? Do these conferences have speed dating sessions to meet new LPs?
   - What is the time commitment from the investment and operations teams? How can that be streamlined to be more impactful?
   - What is the expected timeline and what are key milestones?

- Where do you plan to market the fund? What are the regulations and how do you ensure compliance? (Ensure all documents are approved by counsel before launching or sharing.)
- Create all marketing documents and presentations, but secure their confidentiality through data rooms and access portals that are trackable. Make the content available to prospects, and monitor its use, revoking access once an investment decision is made. Follow up if LPs do not access the information in a timely fashion to confirm interest in the fund.

5. Execution:

- Is every LP you are reaching out to an eligible investor, and do they have a good reputation? Conduct a quick background search (e.g., Google, LinkedIn, common connections) on the LP and the individuals with whom you will engage.
- Do you understand the organizational structure of targeted LPs? Find out if they have the resources and experience to understand your fund's strategy and goals, conduct appropriate due diligence if interested, and invest.
- Have you identified the right people at the investor firm for you to direct the initial pitch? Seek referrals, if possible, to make the connections count.
- Do you have a good understanding of the LP's motivations and concerns? Figure out if the fund is a right fit for the LP's objective and portfolio.
- What is the goal of the interaction? The objective for each step is to move the ball forward toward the end zone. As long as there is progress at each interaction with the investor, consider it a success. Trying to rush the process will create additional risks and lead to an "interception" instead of a "touchdown."
- Do you have a process to maintain engagement after the initial contact? Interact with potential investors regularly,

and report both good and bad developments with consistency and transparency.

- Have you assessed how often you want to reach out to the prospect? Regular interaction does not mean reaching out incessantly. Do not pester the LP. While there is no hard and fast rule about how often to make contact, it is helpful to read the room and pick up on social cues. Simply asking the LP how often they would like an update solves this problem.
- Have you provided all information the investor would need to make a decision? Due diligence should be conducted to confirm facts; it is not an information-gathering process.
- How do you ensure there is knowledge sharing and responsibilities assigned for follow-ups with LPs? Document all interactions, questions, feedback, and recommendations from investors and other stakeholders (placement agent/consultant). Designate team members who will "own" the tasks and requests from LPs, along with specific deadlines. Do not drop the ball, especially during the marketing phase.

6. Process conclusion:
- Ensure all documentation is complete, and the fund administrator confirms the LP's investment.
- Keep engaging with the LP; do not move on after getting the check. How you conduct yourself after the LP's funds are received will be an important factor in allocating to your firm in the future.
- If there is a separate IR team, ensure there is a seamless handoff, but stay engaged to maintain the relationship with the LP. Referrals from LPs are a common occurrence.

While there are clear differences in marketing a hedge fund versus a private equity fund, the underlying principles are the same. The primary differences are contextual and not fundamental; they both strive to raise capital until they reach capacity. While hedge funds do not have a time frame to reach capacity—and can reassess and modify the capacity ceiling—that is not the case with private equity, which has a deadline to raise targeted capital. Private equity firms generally start another fund if they go past the capital target, whereas hedge funds can continue to add capital to an existing fund. However, both pause fundraising once they reach their fundraising goals and immediately pivot to premarketing.

One significant structural difference is that private equity funds will not seek replacement capital for redemptions until the investment period ends, whereas hedge funds will constantly raise replacement capital once the initial lockup ends. The economics of a private equity fund allow for a revenue floor (minimum guaranteed revenue for the firm) for the fund life, which allows a fund to manage its operations, including the marketing budget, better than a hedge fund that has no such guarantee. (This is also the reason why a larger percentage of hedge funds go out of business than private equity funds.) On the other hand, the fundamentals and structure of marketing hedge funds and private equity funds are similar. A good fundraiser can succeed in both, provided they have the relationships and adequate knowledge about the strategy they are selling.

For private equity funds subject to cyclical marketing, having a strong first close and developing fundraising momentum are critical to success. Before a marketing campaign begins, the fundraising team needs to establish the objectives of the fundraise and obtain internal buy-in. This includes agreeing on (1) the size of the fundraise, (2) whether the fundraise intends to actively change the investor composition—which may be an important issue to address as the fund matures from a primarily high-net-worth customer base to one that skews more institutional—and (3) entering into or expanding in a new geography.

The idea is to ensure that clear goals are shared by everyone working on the fundraise, and that adequate and appropriate resources (both staffing and budget) are dedicated to improve the probability of success in reaching the target. However, when it is a choice between turning down an LP who does not fit nicely into the target bucket or does not meet the fund's size goals, the GP will almost always default toward taking the investment.

As for a "shooting darts in the dark" versus a targeted approach, aiming to reach all potential LPs might seem like a good option and may be appropriate in some circumstances, but it is no different than telemarketing. The conversion rates will be very low, and a great deal of effort and resources need to be dedicated to make any meaningful impact toward reaching fundraising goals. This approach might turn counterproductive and send marketers on wild goose chases. Instead, it would be more productive to focus initial conversations on learning about the investor's goals, policies, allocation, decision process, experience with strategies similar to yours. Marketers should also identify relevant decision makers and influencers.

GPs should consider the size of an investment and other constraints that might be present. For example, an LP that typically writes $50 million to $100 million checks with a restriction that their investment cannot comprise more than 10 percent of a fund will not be a good candidate for a $250 million fund, even if the strategy is a perfect match for the LP's objectives. Gathering such information early on will help the GP decide if pursuing the LP will make sense.

GPs should also identify, as early as possible, an LP's specific conditions for investment, criteria for evaluating a manager, whether there are specific allocation buckets the investment or strategy must fit into—and if those are hard constraints or if there is flexibility. This information will dictate the level of effort spent on marketing to the LP.

For instance, the GP will find it hard to convince an LP to allocate capital to a strategy or geography where it has no experience or expertise (e.g., a Brazilian investment when the investor has not invested in emerging market funds). Even in cases where you are able to convince the LP to make an investment, the effort and time needed to educate the client about the strategy and risks will be substantial. On the other hand, if your fund strategy happens to be one in which the investor is actively seeking to gain exposure, it would be an easier fit.

LPs spend considerable time and resources researching a GP before they make an investment. Therefore, it will be helpful to know whether you are a new addition to a portfolio or replacing another manager. If it is the latter, you will have a higher bar to scale, as the prior manager already has a relationship with the investor and has undergone due diligence.

HOW TO EFFICIENTLY REACH NEW INVESTORS

1. Start by approaching the right LPs, instead of targeting them all.

2. Improve reach by seeking referrals from existing LPs. Referrals give credibility to a GP when they meet potential LPs. The prospective client will be more receptive to meeting with a manager recommended by another investor.

3. Host roadshows and events around existing geographies of LPs, which raises the probability of getting referrals.

4. Gather information through quick introductory calls, and ascertain the potential for investment before expending additional marketing effort. Maintain LP interest by sharing mass communication and occasional personalized contact.

5. Hire placement agents strategically: to augment resources, leverage agent's existing relationships, and expand into geographies or investor segments where the team has no significant relationships.

6. Be careful not to burn bridges; people do move around in the industry. Cultivating a quality relationship with a decision maker that later moves to another firm could mean a transfer of that professional bond. The only ones to walk away from immediately are those you should not have approached in the first place, such as ones with potential regulatory or reputational problems.

MARKETING TIMELINES

Private equity funds face time constraints, which means marketing efforts have set timelines. While there is no specific time limit until the first close, the partnership agreement will specify the length of time between the initial and final close. A common time frame for most private equity funds is 12 to 24 months. If there is a delay, the GP must obtain LPs' consent for fundraising extensions. Premarketing, on the other hand, should be a continuous process for an existing GP. For new managers, it should ideally be conducted at least 12 months prior.

SCREENING PROSPECTS

Should GPs or marketers spend an inordinate amount of time with LPs who have significant exposure to their competitors? If they agree to meet, this shows that the LP is interested, but know they may probably have enough exposure to your strategy and may not allocate more. The LP might be interested in meeting with you purely for benchmarking and market survey purposes. It may be imprudent to spend too much time with the LP in such cases, even if you want to be on the radar for a future allocation. In response, conduct the initial screening or LP qualification call, and then assess the situation.

Are they trying to replace a manager? How do you stack up against other managers (if that information is shared or knowable)? Most LPs are quite candid about their intentions if you ask them the right questions, although very few may volunteer information without a prompt. After discussing the LP's motivations, needs, concerns, and investing experience with your asset class and strategy, most GPs will be able to discern whether additional effort with that LP is warranted. Use the information you gathered to prepare your team for follow-up meetings with the LP, and ensure your marketing materials and presentations are effective in addressing any requirements and concerns.

Be prepared with additional information that may be necessary to take the engagement further. More important, if an LP has questions and concerns that only certain people outside the usual group of presenters can answer, make sure to include and prepare them for the meeting. For example, if an LP is concerned about company integration in a roll-up or platform strategy, include the operating partner when meeting the LP. Just the presence of the partner is a good signal to the LP that you are actively engaged and responsive to their needs and concerns, which will further deepen their trust in you and your fund.

REACHING OUT TO THE RIGHT PEOPLE

If you cannot connect with people who serve as a referral, reach out to those in your network—someone you met at a conference, share the same alma mater, or enjoy other common connections. If you resort to a cold call, it is best to reach out first to decision makers in your asset class. Just like in investing, there is a top-down and bottom-up style to managing investment offices. However, while the top-down approach is common among HNWI and SFOs, it is less obvious in institutions. While marketers can reach out to decision makers, they should expect, moving forward, daily interactions will occur with members of the investment team.

Typically it is the marketing team that reaches out to new contacts, unless they are referrals to a specific individual at the manager level who would then do the follow-up. If several people have relationships with the targeted LP, the person with a first- or second-degree connection might initiate the contact. Other ways to develop contacts would be connecting at conferences, conducting speaking engagements, and participating at other public events. The contact could be the person who represented the company; otherwise, find contacts from publicly available information.

We emphasize that it does not matter who initiated the contact or who was the first point of contact at the investor firm. Ideally, it should flow through the marketing and IR teams and some common repository such as a customer relationship management (CRM) system. Subsequently, it is entirely dependent on LP preference and GP availability.

While it is impractical for a small investor to seek regular engagement with the most senior partner or even the investment team on a regular basis, a sizable LP that writes the largest checks for the GP will likely receive favorable attention.

CONCLUSION

No matter who reaches out to whom, common tenets apply to any marketing effort: know your customer. Marketers will be severely handicapped in their efforts without understanding the LP's investment philosophy, policies, institutional sensitivities, decision criteria, assessment process, key players, investment exposure or liquidity, and experience—both positive and negative—investing in similar strategies.

In the next chapter, we discuss how marketers can set up a systematic process to maximize the team's impact, among other tasks and priorities.

CHAPTER 7

Premarketing and Marketing—Process, Tasks, and Priorities

n marketing, it is important to follow a systematic process. For experienced marketers, this process typically takes the form of a weekly task list.

The list includes tasks like:

1. Seek updates from investment team about fund and markets.
2. Respond to all requests from and promises made to LPs.
3. Reassess the fundraising pipeline.
4. Provide and receive subscriptions update from operations team.
5. Prepare for upcoming due diligence visits.
6. Share feedback, concerns, and pushback from LPs.
7. Update presentations and other data you plan on sharing with LPs.
8. Follow up with LPs who have not made progress toward a decision.
9. Review subscription agreements to avoid issues at closing.

Marketers must nurture and build their brands with care and diligence over time. How you deal with investors affects your reputation and that of your firm. The best approach is to focus on what will matter to your investors and whether you are prepared to address their needs.

There is no consensus on how much information should be shared with and what is relevant to LPs. Some frown upon what they deem to be too much or irrelevant information. Others might complain that the same information lacks breadth or depth. Even within the same investor firm, there may be different points of contact—such as the investment staff, operational or finance teams, their advisors or consultants—asking for different information or different formats.

Sometimes, the tax status of an investor—whether they are a tax-exempt entity subject to the unrelated business income tax (UBIT)—or the structure of its relationship with the fund manager (single-fund investor versus multiple-fund investor) may spark a data request from LPs. The task of the IR team is to parse out what is required, what is reasonable, and what would impose a significant burden on the investment, operations, or finance teams to fulfill the request.

Of course, you should apply sound judgment when information is being requested by a large LP or by LPs representing a significant percentage of the manager's AUM. Any pushback needs to be thoughtful, justified, and professionally communicated. You may point to widespread practice as a standard, but technically no standard exists. Private equity funds can use ILPA templates to make a case.

PITCHING THE PRODUCT

In contrast to responding to investors, there is proactive marketing communication that forms the bulk of investor interactions during a fundraise. Preparatory work for marketers involves creating marketing collateral and educating or prepping the team on expected outcomes from each customer interaction.

Before delivering your presentation to potential LPs, obtain an opinion about your pitch from trusted LPs, consultants, and placement agents. Do not test-drive your presentations with potential LPs; it will be a costly exercise leading to missed opportunities, and potentially tarnish your reputation and adversely impact your fundraising momentum.

Seek feedback without making it onerous, appearing disingenuous, or impacting your relationship with LPs.

Everyone in the company should be able to deliver a short marketing pitch effectively. Differentiate between the best investment managers and presenters. One LP described a founder and portfolio manager as a "dead duck." The best presenters can engage an audience with a communication style that resonates with LPs and gains their trust.

Always identify objectives and constraints for the team that will be present at a meeting. The minimum information you will need is about the investor's organizational goals, its prior experience, and the background of the LPs representatives likely to join the meeting. The marketing team should be able to highlight key messages to be delivered—framed to relate to LPs and address potential concerns.

The same pitch delivered multiple times can create an air of monotony and kill the presenter's energy. How do you keep it fresh and engaging? Tag teams will work. Change the list of team members at follow-up meetings, so the LP will not think that it is a rerun of an old pitch. Ensure you present new information to the LP or their advisor to avoid repetition.

Leave no stone unturned. To seasoned marketers, every person present at an investor meeting or with whom they interact elsewhere is important to the investment decision, no matter how junior or senior they may be. Prejudging the value or importance of people is detrimental to the marketing effort. A marketer may not know the internal organizational dynamics or who has the ear of the decision makers.

Your job is to convince the LP of the value your fund will add to their portfolio. The better everyone understands the strategy and develops a liking for the fund team, the higher the likelihood there will be a positive outcome. This is also an opportunity to build relationships for the future. There are many instances in which relationships that were built when an LP representative was new to the firm or served in noninvestment roles later yielded great results in fundraising when they moved to another firm or took on an investment role.

OTHER CONSIDERATIONS

One important issue for GPs to consider is to properly structure the entities and mechanisms. The objective is to improve the tax efficiency of carried interest earned through entities that are structured to minimize tax liability. If you anticipate capital allocation from US pension funds, add ERISA compliance expertise to the list of qualifications needed when hiring a law firm, as these have legal disclosure and due diligence requirements.

If there is excess interest from one type of LP, how should a GP turn down a potential opportunity? If the fundraising strategy is executed well, this is unlikely, since LPs being actively courted are those that are coveted by the GP. However, if there is immense interest from one segment of LPs and tepid response from other investor types, the GP may want to accept the investments until the maximum desirable threshold is met and then slow down the marketing to that segment. Buying time without creating a negative disposition is important. No LP wants to feel that they are less desirable than other LPs, especially after being solicited by the manager. They will argue that "my money is as green as anyone else's." Any ill feelings will sour the relationship now and cannot easily be redeemed in the future.

NEGOTIATIONS DURING MARKETING

Negotiate with an eye toward prioritizing the importance of LPs, depending on how much capital they have in the fund. If a larger percentage of LPs with soft-circled capital want to change certain terms, it can potentially be an indication that the terms are not in the right ballpark and need to be revised. Whether the requested changes come from a few larger investors or a group of smaller investors does not matter—they still affect the GP's bottom line. Good side letters should be investor specific. If covenants in the side letter are overly broad, or impact other LPs in the fund, it should be a part of the fund documents instead of a side letter.

LEGAL ISSUES

There may be a need for local legal advice if the fund is being marketed globally, especially regarding registrations prior to marketing funds in these jurisdictions. This could include national private placement regime (NPPR). Regulations differ by type of vehicle as well (e.g., private equity, hedge fund). In some regimes, premarketing without naming the vehicle, or reverse solicitation if you have not done premarketing, is allowed. Reverse solicitation is easier when a PA is engaged. Pick a law firm that understands marketing regulations globally and can provide a marketing regulations matrix for each region or country.

In the last two decades, the alternatives industry has been subject to various regulatory requirements and investor information needs brought on by a changing investment environment. Some scrutiny is due to industry expansion. The diversity of experience among LPs will require a new regulatory paradigm and investor protection measures. Another reason for scrutiny from investors is risk management due to the shortcomings of many GPs during the financial crisis of 2008.

Increased regulatory oversight also came about as the industry matured. Examples include the tax treatment of carried interest, privacy regulations in several states, and data disclosure requirements from GPs and from LPs to beneficiaries in the case of Freedom of Information Act (FOIA) requests to public pensions and other regulated entities. Other catalysts for heavier industry regulation are self-inflicted, such as pay-to-play scandals and insider trading. Understanding LP sensitivity to the issues and their awareness of regulatory changes are key while marketing to and interacting with them.

MARKETING A FUND FOR THE FIRST TIME

New GPs should hold startup costs to a minimum and avoid incurring costs that can be delayed. Some large-cost items are setup and marketing, especially if a placement agent is involved. Final agreements and documents can be postponed until there is support from LPs to generate a minimum viable AUM. Placement agent fees are paid after the LP has been admitted to the fund and can be negotiated to allow flexibility without up-front costs. Understanding how investors view advantages and disadvantages of investing with a first-time manager would assist with crafting a message and increase the efficiency of the marketing spend. These include:

> **Advantages:** Outperformance,[1] more co-invest opportunities, flexible terms for preferred investors, limited partner advisory committee (LPAC) seats, entry to new geographies, and deployment of new strategies.[2]

> **Disadvantages:** Short or unverifiable track record, new team, uncertainty about their ability to deliver on promises, lack of established processes, and execution uncertainty.

A new GP must meet *all* the following criteria to be considered by LPs:

- ✓ Good track record of the principals and partners
- ✓ Sound investment philosophy and sustainable strategy
- ✓ Offers standard industry terms or better
- ✓ Alignment of interests
- ✓ Strong team and well-known service providers
- ✓ Good investor communication and excellent investor relations
- ✓ Robust operational capability

Partners of first-time funds and emerging managers should head the fundraising effort, even if there is a marketing lead, as familiarity with the manager removes another LP concern. Make sure you have a compelling personal story, explain why you wanted to start a fund, discuss clear attribution on past deals and ability to source future deals, and demonstrate the benefit to the LP.

How good is your network in terms of vouching for you, your capability, and your narrative? How are you different from existing funds, and how will you convince the LP of your ability to deliver results?

Given there is no prior history of working with the LP, they will question your team's ability to work cohesively and effectively. Investors will examine each interaction with the team for signs of confirmation or invalidation of their initial impressions about them.

One of the best examples of how some LPs look at first-time managers comes from a CIO of a family office. They believe emerging and undiscovered GPs are like the "hotshot gun slingers" who can find that elusive treasure and have the "fire in the belly" rarely seen with established managers. First-time GPs will do well to show this fire and to back it up with the skills and discipline to prove themselves. Without this passion, it will be difficult to convince an LP to back first-time managers who are critical about their strategy and investment process. Just be careful not to appear desperate or that you are "trying too hard."

First-time GPs should also be willing to sweeten the terms to make the fund attractive enough to LPs and offset some of their concerns. Emerging PE managers can increase the size of their check and the total capital deployed by encouraging co-investments. This will help raise a larger fund next time. However, there is a fine line between offering a more attractive deal and being desperate to a point that concessions will negatively impact the fund's prospects, economics, or strategy execution.

If you have an anchor LP, placement agent, or gatekeeper willing to work with you, it is acceptable to be transparent about wishing to revise the terms. Seek their input before making a decision. Involving them in the process not only demonstrates you are fair, transparent, and open to feedback, it also creates a sense of "we're all in this together" attitude and ensures there is alignment of interests among all parties. Some LPs are open to paying the GP more when the results are superior (back-ended economics or higher carry share) and support a management fee structure that makes your fund viable.

Concerns arise when management fees far outweigh the cost of running a fund. Since a fund's costs vary, many early backers of first-time funds will ask for a budget to ensure the manager will be viable at the expected minimum fund size. They will also seek to cap the size of the fund to ensure it can survive, but not thrive, on fees alone.

In addition, a pro-forma budget allows the LP to see the team will be well-compensated for their value-add, instead of economics being concentrated toward the founders or owners.

Undoubtedly, LPs who back first-time GPs are underwriting a higher risk compared to more established managers and also have an expectation of higher returns. Early backers may see a component of venture investment with first-time GPs. They seek, and receive, a higher return for the risk they take through lower fees and preferential terms.

First-time managers do carry startup risk because they lead smaller teams, and even if they have good ideas, their execution is far from certain. One way to gain access to expertise is to outsource some of the team's functions to well-known service providers. For example, auditors should be larger, well-known accounting firms. One caveat: you may want to hire them, but they may not be receptive, since they do not need your business. The GP should convince them of the growth potential of the fund. (Some have active emerging manager programs that incubate promising teams.) You may find the same with the fund counsel and fund administrator. Do not cut corners when hiring service providers; find other places to cut costs.

First-time GPs would do well to go after a handful of recognizable LPs—institutional or otherwise—to receive recognition by association. A mentor once gave this advice: "You won't lose your job investing in a manager backed by Yale, Harvard, or MIT." Association with blue-chip names gives the investment staff more confidence to invest with a first-time manager and that the staff will not appear imprudent to have assumed that risk.

INVESTOR RELATIONS

Most LP representatives are fiduciaries and are answerable to others. Similarly, they expect GPs to be answerable to their investors and fulfill their obligations to the beneficial owners and stakeholders. LPs need accurate and timely information that will help them monitor their GPs and make decisions at the right time. Even outside of the fiduciary relationship, it is the LP's money that GPs are investing, and it is the LP's right to know how their capital is being managed. A properly functioning investor relations program is a necessary and essential part of alternative investments. This includes timely reporting, transparency, proactive information sharing outside of regular reporting, and prompt responses to other investor queries and requests.

If LPs are not receiving the level of service they rightfully expect, there will be several repercussions for the GP. For one, a dissatisfied LP may withdraw some or all of the investment from the fund, or they simply will not re-up when the manager raises funds in the future. In addition, poor service can lead to investor complaints and calls to partners and senior executives, distracting them from their primary functions of investing and operations. Finally, less-than-cordial relationships with LPs can damage the reputation of the firm, create an adversarial relationship and lead to negative interactions. As such, a highly effective investor relations effort is invaluable to the GP.

DEALING WITH REJECTION

An emerging-market-focused hedge fund with a sub-$50 million AUM but consistent performance was unable to generate any institutional LP interest, despite repeated solicitation. The fund manager persevered with the outreach and received the first institutional allocation after six years of regular and thoughtful communication with an endowment. Shortly thereafter, AUM grew to $300 million.

A fund may be rejected for many reasons, but marketers need to understand the underlying cause and find creative ways to address them. Seldom is the rejection outright. Some common soft rejections:

- "Does not fit our portfolio"
- "Not allocating to any new relationship" or "only re-ups right now"
- "Too busy with existing portfolio" to spend time on new relationships or allocation

- "Client's not interested"
- "Sorry, that time does not work for us." (repeated multiple times after requesting in-person meetings)
- "Over-allocated to the strategy"
- "Why don't you send us the info and we will get back to you later?" (usually in response to a request for a follow-up meeting, after the initial meeting with the investor/advisor)
- "Let us know after you have raised $XX million."
- Asking only about the progress of the fundraise, not the fund or strategy
- Generic, ambiguous, vague, or nonspecific responses to your queries about their interest

Whether getting a soft or hard decline, it is important for marketers to maintain a professional relationship and to learn the reasons for the rejection. Sometimes, the LP may be reluctant to share the information or unwilling to be forthright. While this is outside of the marketer's control, LPs are more likely to provide feedback to someone who worked hard to build the relationship and has proved to be credible and transparent.

For closed-end funds, the two common options of closing on an LP commitment include rolling closes (as soon as an LP commits) and a series of prescheduled closes (first close, second close, . . . and final close). The general advice is to "close on the money as soon as you can." However, a series of closings with preset dates is more efficient and economical than closing on every single LP whenever they are ready. Announcing the date for the next close will have the effect of calling interested investors to action, but it can also backfire if there is insufficient demand and allows for investors to withdraw from commitments before the next close.

However, rolling closings can be more costly overall. A GP in a weaker position could opt for rolling closes after every commitment and demonstrate momentum, while a GP in a stronger position can meter out closings more regularly. The most in-demand GPs can dictate a single date or two and know the LPs will not push back. Others discount first closes and reach the quorum necessary to be noticed by others.

Fundraising is a function of how much the LP wants to invest in you and how much available capital the LP has to invest overall (liquidity). Providing an LP with flexibility around closing dates, especially from one year to the next, can be marginally helpful in dealing with liquidity issues.

During closings, LPs also expect a closing opinion from counsel to cover limited liability, and tax and regulatory issues, including private placement.

CONCLUSION

Headline numbers touting large and successful fundraises grab stakeholder attention in the industry. However, marketing campaigns are similar to farming. Much of the effort happens behind the scenes and is process dependent. For a successful harvest, you need time, the right nutrients, effort, and a bit of luck (weather). In marketing alternatives, premarketing is the foundational effort (like tilling, deweeding, and prepping in farming) that secures required resources and prepares the soil for a good crop season. Yet, no amount of premarketing in itself will guarantee a good fundraise. Marketers need the essential elements—market mapping, targeted solicitation, right resources and budget, process-oriented campaign management, consistent effort, and a little bit of luck (like good weather in farming) to ensure a successful fundraise. Despite being arduous and time-consuming, a successful fundraise is distinctly achievable by focusing on processes and adapting best practices from successful marketers and marketing campaigns.

CHAPTER 8

Documentation for Funds

Today, no business transaction can be finalized unless it is written in a contract and signed. Investing in alternatives is a business deal, and it is in the interest of both the fund manager and investor to document the transaction.

As it stands, there are no industry-standard documents used for fundraising. This is understandable, given the plethora of strategies, structures, and jurisdictions that cover the alternative investments space. Therefore, it is essential to ensure contractual agreements satisfy legal and jurisdictional needs and delineate boundaries that safeguard the interests of investors and other stakeholders.

There are other documents already commonly used in the industry—the private placement memorandum (PPM) or offering memorandum (OM), limited partnership agreement (LPA), and subscription document (sub docs). One of the most common investor complaints is the growing complexity and length of these documents.

If you have not formed a fund or have not been through the entire fundraising process, it might be beneficial to familiarize yourself with a sample set of documents. You do not want to be surprised or caught unprepared when discussing the documents with an investor. You can get these from your lawyer, from the SEC, or online from institutions that are subject to public disclosure. Although your fund counsel is the expert on what should be in the documents, your familiarity with them will be an asset when raising funds—and during the flurry of side-pocket agreements, each with its own nuance, that are needed in negotiations to close the investment.

As negotiations over terms and fees progress, that complexity only adds to the already unwieldy documentation requirements. Investors would prefer a streamlined and standardized process across the industry. However, many sponsors want to ensure their "unique" strategy and approach are reflected in their documents. They fear a standard template might leave them with risk and constrain them by removing flexibility to execute their strategy effectively. There is a necessary struggle between the two, and at this time there is no standardization of fund documents in sight.

In October 2019, the Institutional Limited Partners Association (ILPA) released a model limited partnership agreement that aims to reduce complexity and costs for fund managers and investors. That might change, as there is a clamor from private individuals to invest in high-performing alternative investments as they hunt for yield, and from fund sponsors wanting to tap into that demand. Unlike sophisticated investors with substantial resources to justify the cost of reviewing and negotiating nonstandard documents, the ordinary investor is more comfortable with the standard template, even at the cost of some flexibility.

The following are some commonly used documents in fundraising for alternatives.

1. PRIVATE PLACEMENT MEMORANDUM (PPM)

For now, alternative investments are private transaction investments; there is no public market for transacting in hedge funds or private equity funds. As a private transaction, information describing the objective of the fund, fundraise, transaction, risks involved, and agreed-upon terms that will govern the transaction would be shared with prospective investors for investment consideration. The PPM acts as the primary source of disclosure for the fund offering in the alternatives space. It should cover both the structure as well as the operations of the fund.

A PPM typically includes the following:

- Description of the fund and the sponsor

- Summary of the offering, limited partnership agreement (LPA), and other documents
- Investment strategy
- Fund domicile and jurisdiction
- Investor qualification and suitability
- Management information
- Service provider information
- Risk factors
- Valuation policy and methodology
- Fees description (including all fees ultimately paid by the investors, such as performance fees, management fees, operating or advisory fees, and transaction fees)
- Financial statements of the fund (if applicable)
- Taxation and tax liability disclosures
- Restrictions such as nontransferability (without manager approval) and lock-ups.
- Legal and regulatory disclosures
- Notices about securities laws
- Current or past litigation involving the sponsor, related entities, or personnel
- Conflicts of interest disclosures
- ERISA notices, if the fund is accepting ERISA investments

The PPM should help mitigate risks and liabilities associated with transacting unregistered securities faced by a seller, including claims of inadequate disclosure, omissions, misstatements, or misrepresentations. It provides adequate information to the buyer, both positive and negative, to help in making a prudent investment decision.

2. LIMITED PARTNERSHIP AGREEMENT (LPA)

The agreement between different stakeholders in the fund is governed by the LPA. This is the actual governing document of the partnership. Due to the complexity and variety of strategies and structures, standardization of the LPA is far from a reality. The goal of the LPA is to assign and specify the rights, liabilities, and obligations of the parties to the agreement (fund managers and investors) and to regulate the relationship between them.

Since investors are only liable to the extent of their investment amount (hedge fund structures) or commitment amount (private equity structures) while the fund managers have unlimited liability, the LPA is a key document in delineating the risks and liabilities between them.

Here are some of the key topics covered in the LPA:

- Details of the fund: the formation, structure, and entities
- Rights and responsibilities of the manager or sponsor, such as the annual reports, regulatory compliance filings, audits, and record keeping
- Rights and responsibilities of the investors
- Limitations, liabilities, and indemnifications for the manager, investor, and other stakeholders
- Fund duration and life cycle (for private equity funds)

Profit and Loss Allocation Process

As discussed earlier, an investor's liability is limited to the amount of committed capital, but the liability of the fund manager is unlimited because investors are essentially "silent" partners in the venture.

Furthermore, given the complexity of profit allocation based on hurdles, catch-up, clawback, and other contingencies, it is crucial to clearly articulate the process to ensure the fund manager and investor both agree to the profit and loss allocation. The following are the components of the process:

- Tax allocation methodology
- Fund dissolution and wrap-up
- Distributions and reinvestments
- Assignment of rights and power of attorney to the fund manager to act on behalf of the fund for all required functions—such as buying and selling securities, voting the fund securities,

complying with or amending documents—to ensure fund
continuity until its dissolution

- Amendment process
- Legal domicile and jurisdiction

3. THE SUBSCRIPTION DOCUMENTS (SUB DOCS)

A subscription agreement provides information about an investor's
willingness to join the limited partnership. It also substantiates the
qualifications of the investor for the fund through assurances and warranties. While there is no standard industry document, subscription
documents generally adhere to SEC Rule 506(b) and 506(c) of Regulation D that governs exemptions of private placements from registration.

It is important to note that the completion of the subscription documents by the investor does not automatically imply the investor has
become a subscriber to the fund. The manager has discretion over
accepting the subscription for an investor to join the fund. Some of the
standard requirements are sacrosanct (qualified investors only); others
can be at the discretion of the manager (e.g., waiving minimum investment thresholds).

While the pertinent information in the subscription agreement
for joining a limited partnership varies depending on the law firm
preparing the documents, it typically covers important investment
qualifications such as net worth, investment experience, and other factors for the investor to join. It is not unusual to see separate documents
or separate sections within the document for individual investors versus
institutional investors.

The document could cover a range of issues:

1. Suitability of the investor, based on whether they have to be
   an accredited investor, qualified purchaser, or any legally
   mandated status that may vary by jurisdiction.

2. A subscription agreement portion that covers the representations, warranties, acknowledgment, and acceptance of various aspects of the investment. This could include investment risks, potential for loss, communication, privacy, and legal jurisdiction.
3. Confirmation of receipt for other documents (PPM/OM, LPA and others).
4. Indemnification of the manager, if not covered by the LPA.
5. In case of nonaccredited investors, supplemental information to ensure that they meet the criteria of sophisticated investors, and they understand the fund strategy and investment risks they are undertaking.

Subscription agreements, as with most other documents, require that a minimum percentage of investors approve future amendments.

4. SIDE LETTERS

Side letters are agreements between a particular investor and the fund, agreeing to terms that differ from the terms offered to other fund investors. A side letter usually arises from the investor wanting terms that are more favorable to them, vis-à-vis the general terms of the fund. The reasons for a side letter vary, from the simple issue of the investor seeking better terms for its investment, to more complex issues due to either regulatory or legal requirements.

Without side letters, some of the investors will not be able to or willing to invest in the fund per the existing terms. A fund of funds may want a shorter lock-up or preferential liquidity in line with what it offers to its own investors; another investor may have a requirement for specific documentation, reports, or investment to satisfy a regulatory need or a fiduciary requirement. Ultimately, it falls on the manager to accept the terms requested by an investor, acknowledging that these might place other clients at somewhat of a disadvantage. An investor willing to write a larger check or a strategically important investor will have a better chance at receiving the terms they seek.

Common types of side letters:

1. Favorable economics, including fee waivers or a share of the fund revenue
2. Preferential liquidity, including a lock-up waiver or gate priority
3. Most-favored-nation (MFN) clauses that grant the investor automatic matching of any favorable terms or rights granted to any other investor in the fund
4. Preferential transparency, including the ability to get information at a more frequent time, or access to information generally not made available to other investors
5. Co-investment rights, or a right of first refusal for co-investments

Despite side letters becoming a more common occurrence, funds entering into side letters must still do so carefully, for both business and legal reasons. Agreeing to terms that put other investors at an actual disadvantage might anger and alienate those other investors, expose the fund to litigation, or be considered egregious enough to warrant the regulator's attention.

Since side letters have a higher priority versus the LPA, their provisions govern the relationship, instead of the corresponding provision in the LPA. Where these conflicts do not adversely affect other investors, it is fair game—as in the case of performance fee reductions or waivers but still may be subject to disparate impact or disparate treatment claims. In these cases, the loss of fee revenue impacts only the manager and not the fund or other fund investors. While no one's the wiser during good times, a preferential liquidity does create legal problems when other investors were gated and not allowed an exit (HFs) and would be considered a violation of the fund manager's fiduciary obligations to impacted investors. Sponsors should carefully consider ramifications of any side letter and seek legal counsel to help determine compliance with the law in fulfilling obligations under the side letter agreement.

In case of retroactive rights, or rights activated at a later date, such as the MFN status, the fund needs to have a process to both activate the provisions and communicate terms with those investors. Since side letters almost always create conflict with the LPA, it is essential for funds to fully understand legal concerns such as the impact on fiduciary responsibilities and regulatory compliance. Additionally, they should attempt to mitigate issues by communicating to other investors about the existence of side letters and seeking investor consent when appropriate.

5. INVESTMENT MANAGEMENT AGREEMENT

The agreement between the fund and the investment manager (IM) defines the services the IM will provide in consideration of the compensation it will receive. It delegates and assigns the discretionary decision-making authority to the fund manager, to manage the fund in accordance with the investment strategy of the fund. It also gives the fund manager the power of attorney to manage investor contributions and the duty to advise the fund accordingly.

Sharing of Documents

Since marketing the fund starts even before fund formation, one key document needed is the initial pitchbook or current fund update, which is used to soft-sell the fund to prospective investors. It is followed by formation documents, which include the incorporation and fund registration documents. A good practice is to upload and organize the documents in a data room—a restricted-access, secure data storage where investors can review proprietary or confidential information and documents that are made available by the fund manager to help the investor ascertain suitability of the fund for an allocation. These data rooms can be as simple as a password-protected online or virtual drive to as sophisticated as custom-built platforms that facilitate secure information sharing. Typical data room documents include the PPM, LPA, fund presentation, track record, investment memos, all policy documents of the fund and firm, track records, and past investor communication. This could also include the sub-docs.

ADDITIONAL DOCUMENTS

In addition to documents normally shared with investors, the fund might also require an operating agreement between the fund manager and the management company, specifying how ownership and responsibilities or rights are assigned among the principals. Depending on the asset class or fund type, there may be requirements for SEC and state filings and an obligation to register with the SEC, CFTC, or as an RIA.

Other documents often requested by investors:

1. Due diligence questionnaire (DDQ): this should contain most of the information listed in this section, as it forms the primary due diligence document
2. Organizational structure
3. Audited financials for previous funds or previous years, if the fund is still in the marketing stage
4. Investor communication, such as annual letters and annual general meeting (AGM) materials, quarterly letters, and investment notes to investors
5. Operations documents and policies, such as the compliance manual, valuation policy and methodology, employment and HR manuals, code of ethics, conflict of interest policy, operations overview, IT process and information security, disaster recovery plan, and ESG policy
6. Formation, constitutional, and regulatory documents, such as the certificate of registration, Form ADV, and articles of incorporation
7. Service providers list and backgrounds
8. Investment pipeline
9. Deal analysis, including source, due diligence results, and investment decisions of all deals considered—whether passed on or invested
10. Investment memos and case studies
11. Tax and legal opinions from outside legal and tax counsel

12. Attribution analysis and value-added analysis by investment and by partner/analyst
13. Value creation by GP, sponsor, or IM
14. Fund presentation, pitchbook
15. Team bios, track record, and partner/team attribution
16. Investment review, investment due diligence
17. Portfolio analysis
18. Market studies and white papers
19. Risk—gross exposures and net exposures

In addition to these documents, investors often request information in specific formats, or ask for copies of internal documents—like the management/partnership agreement or compensation summary for the partners and team members—for their review.

A marketer needs to be familiar with these documents and their content. As the face of the firm, marketers create the first impression of the firm with investors. Familiarity with these documents enables the marketer to anticipate and address investor concerns regarding the strategy, firm, or fund, and also provides solutions that can convince a potential investor to commit to the fund.

Additionally, it is critical for both parties to follow complete documentation on time. We know a placement agent who lost a $40 million commitment from an LP due to documentation delays. The agent represented a fund manager who had not closed on the investor's capital, even though the LP had turned in signed agreements six months earlier. The lesson: you do not want to go through several months of soliciting, due diligence, and partially onboarding an LP, only to lose that client due to a small but avoidable lapse in documentation.

Managers and fundraisers should ensure there is a set process for tracking information and document sharing, for both operational efficiency and regulatory compliance. All investor documents need to be stored properly for future retrieval, with strict privacy policies that exceed regulatory requirements.

CONCLUSION

Since there is no standard document in the industry, the fundraising process is more complex than necessary. Understanding what is expected by investors and organizing documents to make information clear and comprehensible will ensure a less burdensome task, especially when repeated numerous times during fundraising.

It is prudent to have an initial conversation with investors to figure out how they want you to support them with their documentation needs—and follow their advice. However, be cognizant of investors with limited experience investing in alternatives and provide proactive assistance without being intrusive. Fundraisers need to have discernment to differentiate and cater to individual investor needs.

Since the job of a fundraiser is to close the deal, they should ensure investors complete the necessary documentation to the satisfaction of your fund administrator, legal counsel, and their own teams.

CHAPTER 9

Pitchbooks and Presentations

Pitchbooks or introductory presentations usually mark the first step in the marketing process and serve as an introduction to the team, strategy, and fund. The pitch needs to tell a story that exemplifies why the manager is exceptional and creates a succinct, memorable, persuasive, and compelling case for the fund's inclusion in the investor's portfolio.

While the overall goal of the marketing process is to get an allocation from a prospect, what should be apparent to any thoughtful marketer is that marketing alternatives is a long-term journey with multiple stages. Each step must advance the conversation or investment process to the next level. Think about American football, where the overall objective of the quarterback is to score a touchdown; one common strategy is to advance the ball 10 yards at a time until it reaches the end zone.

Similarly, the immediate objective of a pitchbook is to persuade the investor to consider an investment, even if there are many steps to complete before there is an actual allocation. The pitchbook should get the investor interested in and comfortable with the strategy, fund, and team. While there are exceptions to the rule, we will focus on what is effective for most situations.

One common mistake is to see the pitchbook as an end, rather than a means to an end. This results in novice and even experienced managers encapsulating the entirety of the marketing process within the pitchbook. Showing up to a 30-minute meeting with a 100-page pitchbook does not serve anyone's interest. Investors are better served by a focused presentation that hits the main points effectively, even if there is much more to convey. It is imprudent to assume any investor will spend a considerable amount of time learning about the fund even before any assurance of profitability in the investment.

This is not to suggest a pitchbook should be short on content or lack transparency. Strike a balance between displaying too much information in the presentation and not adequately explaining why your strategy deserves an allocation. Finding an optimal balance requires a careful analysis of key messages you wish to convey and how those messages should be delivered. One solution is to solicit feedback after mock presentations to a select group—such as those who have seen similar presentations, like placement agents—that will help you find that balance.

ELEMENTS OF AN EFFECTIVE PRESENTATION

Effective presentations start with framing the pitch from the investor's perspective. Anticipate questions that could be top of mind for investors, and answer them as comprehensively as you can without being overbearing. The following are some examples of questions you should ask yourself about potential investors:

- What kind of investors will find the strategy appealing?
- Why will they be interested, and what elements of the strategy will interest them?
- What will be their level of familiarity with the strategy?
- What would be their concerns, and what messages will resonate with them and alleviate their concerns?
- What are the attributes these kinds of investors look for, even before they have the initial conversation with a manager (e.g., pedigree, performance track record, reputation, uniqueness of strategy, and other traits)?
- What is your value proposition, and why would it appeal to prospective investors?

The pitchbook should address these questions in a clear, consistent, and concise manner. Successful storytelling means finding the best way to communicate this information in a short period of time, effectively and efficiently. Investors care less about what you know than what you have done. They care about what you can do now, what you will do during the expected term of their investment (or fund), and how those activities will help investment performance. They absolutely care about why investing with you will help them reach their investment goals and management of their portfolio.

However, the investors' level of familiarity and understanding of the subject may differ depending on their investment experience. It is important to ensure a minimum level of clarification is provided to cover the basics, but do not be overbearing such that experienced investors would find the presentation tedious.

ESSENTIAL CONTENT OF A PITCHBOOK

Most managers start creating a pitchbook with an inkling of a storyline, instead of having all the twists and turns addressed before putting together the presentation. Effective presentations ensure that key messages of "why we are different" and "how that differentiation adds value to the strategy" are called out and highlighted. Some managers adhere to the dogma that any information that does not serve to differentiate you from your competition does not belong in the first few slides of the presentation.

THE MVP

One way to address what issues need to be covered in an introductory presentation or pitch is to borrow from the land of venture capital investing: seek to come up with an MVP (minimum viable product that covers the basics but is enough to get the client's attention). In the case of pitchbooks for alternative investments, the MVP should cover a number of topics.

Executive summary. The first few seconds of a presentation or meeting are crucial in setting expectations for what follows. The audience is making its own judgment about the quality of what is coming and deciding on their engagement levels. Many managers include a crisp executive summary as a good way to capture investor interest and ensure they are positively dispositioned toward the presentation.

Team. Investors back both the manager and the strategy. They would be interested in learning about the background of the team members in addition to their position, responsibilities, credentials, and experience. This information helps them conduct due diligence by finding common connections who can validate certain claims made by the manager. Not everyone who is essential to the functioning of the fund is or needs to be employed internally or full time. However, investors would like to know if the team has experience working together, and if their strengths and weaknesses complement each other.

While it may not be possible to list everyone in the team, the presentation should include members of both the investment and operations teams. For larger teams, most managers focus on members who are directly involved with the fund. Smaller funds may be able to accommodate listing the entire team. In addition, it is important to disclose staffing by office locations, as physical presence may create tax and regulatory nexus issues for investors and it also demonstrates geographically diverse coverage.

Investment strategy. Articulate clearly how investment decisions are made by explaining the parameters, rules, processes, risk tolerance, and other criteria that guide the team. Strategy is one way to implement an investment philosophy; it should illuminate investment and exit conditions and choice of securities. A strategy that does not neatly fit into the allocation buckets of an investor (e.g., by asset class, quantitative versus fundamental) will have to overcome this hurdle.

The strategy description must include the relevant components: the investment universe, investment horizon (long-term versus short-term), security (stocks, bonds, derivatives), exposure (long-only, long-short), liquidity (private, illiquid), size (large-cap, mid-market), geography (United States, global, emerging markets), leverage (unlevered, two to three times), industry (technology, healthcare, broad, diversified), stage (venture capital, seed, early, growth, late-stage), and management (activist, active, passive). The fund manager should also articulate the objective of the fund precisely and clearly, including the investments' correlation with benchmarks, volatility, and risk/return expectations.

Investment philosophy. Philosophy is a set of deeply held beliefs, assumptions, and perceptions. An example in the hedge fund space would be whether you believe in active, activist, or passive investing. The use of leverage and short selling are also philosophical choices.

Edge. The most important factor to highlight is your edge, or market advantage. Prepare to substantiate your edge and its sustainability. Having an edge is the "secret sauce" that drives superior returns for your strategy. For example, what inefficiencies in the market are you tapping into and capitalizing on that other managers have missed or have not fully exploited? This is truly the unique selling proposition for an alternative investment.

Track record. While past performance does not guarantee future results, a track record provides some confidence the outcome will be favorable. A hedge fund that has never been able to generate alpha (or returns higher than that for an appropriate benchmark) is unlikely to have the skills needed to generate outperformance, compared to someone who has consistently delivered alpha in diverse market conditions. A track record must be measured against an appropriate benchmark, otherwise the data would not be of practical use.[1] It is important for managers to select a benchmark and clarify its relevance in comparing the risk and reward characteristics of performance. A private equity manager who has an established track record of generating consistent deal flow and adding value to companies in different market cycles has a better possibility of delivering consistent performance.

Results of simulation/back tests (Quant HF). When real-life returns cannot be demonstrated due to the discovery of an "arbitrage" opportunity or other such situations, investors may rely on back-testing their hypothesis to demonstrate viability and validity. Most quant strategies fall into this category until they can show real-world results later in their life cycle. Investors are open to accepting back-tested results as an alternate metric, but with some allowance for value loss as these shift from back-testing to actual execution.

Deal sourcing and selection (PE). One of the drivers of returns in private markets is access to proprietary deals unavailable to others. These deals are not subject to price discovery through competitive bids, which allows for a favorable entry price into the company. Investors want to understand if the manager has proprietary deal flow data and also wants to understand the depth of such flows.

Value addition (PE). Regardless of market conditions, managers can create value for companies they have invested in by activities like improving operations; opening up new avenues for their products; improving managerial strength, quality, and focus; accessing their network for advisory services and expertise to improve the operating performance of a company; their ability to tap into capital markets for financing or to lower the cost of debt; and their ability to attract other investors by restructuring and strengthening the company. While there are numerous ways to create value, successful managers have both the ability and manpower to deliver added value.

Case studies. Case studies showcase your performance to the investor. Be wary of cherry-picking examples, as most astute investors will look into your track record and find the ones that have not done so well, and the SEC will not look favorably on this practice. Be prepared to address what went right, what did not work as expected, and lessons learned. However, it is important to highlight your successes and explain how you consistently add value.

Risks. Some managers may present risks in the investment presentation; others will include them in more detailed investment documents such as the DDQ or PPM. An investment thesis that ignores investment risks is half-baked and shows the manager is either unaware of the risks or is reluctant to share them for fear of scaring away investors. This is a red flag to LPs. Most managers list expected risks underlying a strategy and enumerate ways in which they are mitigating these risks.

Investment terms. A listing of the fees and terms for the fund is a requirement. They must be consistent with what the market offers, but exceptions are fine if investors are convinced higher fees or less favorable terms are warranted by fund performance. Favorable terms are always welcomed, and at times demanded, by investors, but only with some further scrutiny of product quality. The fund structure is another topic to address in the pitch.

Disclaimers. It is important to protect your intellectual property and also adhere to legal and regulatory requirements in marketing alternatives through adequate disclaimers. Failure to do so will invite unnecessary and costly regulatory and legal risks. While a boilerplate disclaimer might work for most funds, to ensure compliance it would be best to have a lawyer draft a bespoke version or at least review the standard version.

Economic interests. There are some situations when fund economics (e.g., investment officer compensation) are of interest to investors, especially in cases where these are shared with entities beyond the fund management team (which includes the operations team). If investors have reason to believe key players are not properly compensated for the value they bring, they may worry these high-performing individuals can potentially leave the fund, which would impact returns. This can happen in cases where founders have a diminished role, and there is a transition to a new group of individuals.

Contact information. It may be strange to see presentations without contact information for the fund, but they do exist. While there may be other ways for the investor to find this information, including email signatures and business cards, inserting this in the presentation makes it easier for the prospect to contact the fund for any questions or concerns.

The content of effective pitchbooks will vary based on the type of fund, its structure, and its strategy. It is critical to ensure each fund addresses important issues, even if they are tangential to the strategy, that might pose lingering questions. Clarifying them will help the investor focus on your pitch instead of being distracted by unresolved issues.

All information shared in the presentation should be your original work product or otherwise properly cited. This also applies to artwork, images, and other noncore trivialities. Consider purchasing the rights to use content for further dissemination.

DRAFTING A PRESENTATION OR PITCHBOOK

Since most LPs use a pitchbook as the basis for screening managers, it is important to ensure they are effective in communicating the message and encourage them to invest time and resources in evaluating the fund. Therefore, managers need to consider a few essential elements while drafting their pitchbook:

1. **Be mindful of the investor's time.** Managers and marketers need to optimize time with investors and make a winning case for allocation.
2. **Present clear and accurate content.** Information presented should be easily understood, accurate, and comply with laws and regulations that govern alternative investments in the jurisdiction where it is being marketed.

    Take a page from Apple founder Steve Jobs. He made sure every piece of content he presented had a purpose and believed any additional information is a distraction that weakens a pitch.

Each section of his presentations had a key point, which he would drive home using simple words, data, and visuals.

3. **Storyline.** Make sure the order in which you present the information follows a rational path, tying in with what comes before and after. An engaging storyline is a critical element in ensuring you will have a receptive audience.

4. **Format, style, and design.** A visually appealing presentation not only keeps the audience's attention, but is effective in conveying the message.

Remember to keep it simple. A simple narrative conveys messages effectively. Condense complex issues, and re-emphasize and reinforce messages using the "say, say it, said" technique: (1) say what you are going to say, (2) say it, and (3) conclude with a recap of what you have said. We often forget details but tend to remember interesting stories we hear. Case studies will illustrate your argument emphatically, not from a theoretical perspective, but in real-world execution.

If there are topics, processes, or technical terms that might not be familiar to some prospective investors, provide context to ensure they are educated about the subject. You do not want the lack of familiarity with the terminology or process to become a stumbling block, preventing them from investing with you. Find ways to make the unfamiliar familiar—compare and contrast it with well-known concepts, highlight key elements, and address the "So what if I invest with them?" question. Don't overpack information into every slide. Too much text, innumerable data points, or a visual overload imply you have not synthesized information into relevant messages for your audience. The risk of overexplaining is that the presentation becomes too long, explanations become rudimentary, some information is irrelevant, and it will sound condescending to experienced investors who are familiar with the subject. The end result could be investors dismissing the pitch as lacking in depth.

PLAN, PROCESS, AND PRODUCE A GOOD PITCH

The pitchbook is a tool to convince investors to allocate to your fund. Use it effectively by stating what your clear value-add will be to a portfolio. When making a case as to why a manager is exceptional, explain how this translates to their own portfolio; connect the dots for them and highlight the result for maximum impact.

One common mistake is to title the slide with the topic being presented, instead of the message it wants to convey. One effective technique from the world of management consulting is to create a storyboard or storyline by writing out the messages on each slide before filling in the data (bullet points, charts, etc.). The slide's content should support the point made in its title. The idea is to ensure the storyline is consistent, compelling, and clear by flipping through the slide titles. By starting with the narrative, it is easier to maintain the flow and continue the linear storytelling. A linear narrative is much easier to follow than one that creates suspense; suspense works better in entertainment, not investment.

The time spent in the ideation and preparation stage—discussing, planning, and analyzing the information before you start putting together the presentation—is a great investment in ensuring the pitch is effective and branding consistent.

1. **Decide on key messages you want to deliver.** For the best impact, each message needs to be self-contained and add to your investment strategy or objective.
2. **Select data points that prove the key messages.** Substantiate your claims with concrete evidence, or the presenter will see a skeptical audience instead of a convinced and eager investor.
3. **Order the messages into a storyline that flows naturally and linearly.**
4. **Segment the pitch into manageable parts.** These will provide opportunities to reinforce the messages within the sections. This is an effective way of using the "say, say it, said" technique discussed earlier. Consider additional techniques and tools you may wish to use.

5. **Pick a presentation design, color scheme, and style that represents your identity and brand.** Extend that branding across all communication and marketing materials—including fonts, icons, and color scheme. Building a brand takes time and effort, is best worked on during ideation, and should be applied consistently across messaging.

6. **Number the pages.** This ensures you can reference the information and direct your audience to the right point, helps you pace the presentation appropriately, and lets you pick and choose topics you want to elaborate on and others to quickly glance over. When investors raise an issue you have already addressed, instead of fumbling through the pitch, redirect everyone to the relevant page. You will come across as efficient and organized.

IMPORTANCE OF CONSISTENCY

Be consistent throughout the presentation. Use the same terminology, even if interchangeable words are acceptable. If showcasing multiple case studies or data points for the same topic, use the same format, structure, metrics, and schematics or graphs. Human beings are pattern recognition machines; the brain is hardwired to look for patterns, and once the pattern emerges, it is easier for them to focus on issues you want to highlight.

If the presentation is inconsistent, it reflects poorly on the fund and raises questions about the quality of information provided. Trust is gained, not offered, and the time it takes to work through inconsistencies will make it difficult to communicate your messages and will raise doubts about the quality of the team. The allocator should not be hearing different messages from different people or in different presentations and letters.

While it is important for a presentation to look visually appealing and professional, it matters more that you know the information and are able to address any questions raised. The most effective presentations are not ones that distract from the main message through an overload of information on one page. They are not a complex story conveyed like a mystery book that needs the investor to play detective, or simply fails to present what the investor wants to know. Visuals should only be used sparingly to help explain or convey a message, and then if needed, to add to appeal to what otherwise might be a dull and drab presentation. We are not advocating for sloppy presentations but cautioning against turning it into a slick product brochure. It helps to remember that the effectiveness of your presentation is measured by whether your listeners understand what you are conveying and if they are convinced about the value you are offering.

One of the cardinal sins in novice presentations is a multiplicity of fonts and formats throughout the presentation, caused by working on each slide separately instead of focusing on the presentation as a whole. A simple tactical remedy is to make changes to fonts, formats, and styles on only the "slide master." Most professional organizations create a template to be used for all their presentations, reinforcing your brand's visuals.

Investors should not be getting information that is inaccurate or outdated—both of which are easy to spot and correct before they are sent out or shared. There needs to be an internal review before any sharing. Outdated information would raise concerns about cherry-picking information and hiding negative performance or recent operational issues. It portrays an image of a firm that is not functioning at peak performance levels. A regular and timely update process will help prevent this and is easy to implement.

CONCLUSION

In their presentations, most managers focus on the decision-making process—the strategy over the philosophy—what drives the decisions or the thought process underlying them. A seasoned investor wants to understand the underlying principles that drive these decisions. If a manager is unable to articulate this thinking, it would reflect poorly on the firm, or is an indication the firm is not self-aware of these drivers.

Be sure to articulate precisely how returns were generated, what were the contributing factors, and what really set the fund apart through the value-add leading to these healthy results. For example, a private equity fund may have taken over a company's operations and turned it around, an activist hedge fund may have pushed for changes, or a fund is a short seller signaling to the market about hidden problems in a company. It is important to call out the actions that monetized value-add and drove performance for the fund.

If you can leave the investor interested and engaged, the pitchbook has achieved its goal. As the saying goes, "A good start is halfway to success."

CHAPTER 10

Placement Agents

The role of placement agents has developed very significantly over the last 20 years from a relatively low value introductory agency role to that of a true full-service advisory role. As the fund-raising market becomes ever more competitive, the importance of strategy and planning has never been higher.

—Andrew Sealey, CEO, Campbell Lutyens

L aunching and completing a global fundraise, especially one that becomes a protracted endeavor, is time-intensive and needs skillful positioning to distinguish your fund from others. At times, such fundraises can be fraught with unexpected challenges. First-time funds, funds launching in challenging market environments, and managers with unconventional pasts can be at even a greater disadvantage during the fundraising cycle.

Additionally, GPs face restrictions on advertising their products and must find other ways to reach potential LPs, articulate a well-crafted story, and convince them to invest. The number of investors that GPs can reach using internal resources can be limited, since this is a difficult process to scale. LPs have constraints as well; their time is limited, and their investment and market knowledge have information asymmetry. No matter how unique the strategy is, a fund cannot be successful unless it attracts capital. Enter placement agents (PAs), a group of intermediaries whose primary role is to bridge the LP-GP gap.

A PA can be one of a broad range of intermediaries whose role is to help funds raise capital. They are often referred to as third-party marketing (TPM) firms. PAs have existing relationships with qualified investors and are licensed by an appropriate securities regulatory agency where they operate. The PA's job is to raise capital, quickly and efficiently. However, the value of many PAs extends well beyond their assistance with raising capital. Since PAs engage with multiple firms and investors, they possess a vantage point from which they can advise fund managers on issues ranging from a fund's optimal size and prevailing market terms, to how a fund should be structured to appeal to the largest number of investors based upon the fund's strategy. PAs provide fund managers with access to investors. "There are three things a placement agent needs to have for me to consider working with them—access, access, access," said an experienced fund marketer. They can enable connections to investors who otherwise would be hard to reach. The importance of PAs in marketing alternatives cannot be overstated.

STRUCTURE OF PLACEMENT AGENTS

PAs focus on two main areas: origination and placement. Origination, also called deal origination or deal management, is the function of obtaining high-quality investment mandates from GPs for raising money and managing related information flow. Project management, which addresses the organization and execution of the fundraising process (e.g., status updates, roadshows, logistics) is typically considered a part of deal management. Placement, or sales, is the function of raising money from qualified LPs for GP mandates. In a larger PA firm, the roles may be defined; for smaller firms, these may be overlapping functions.

Full-Service Placement Agents

Full-service PAs have a global network, often with local agents that have access to local relationships, and they can be a complete extension of the marketing team. Functions and tasks handled by full-service agents could include defining the marketing scope, preparing marketing materials in coordination with the fund team, creating project plans, developing strategy (e.g., identifying prospects, crafting the message), and executing a plan (conducting roadshows, following up with LPs, and obtaining commitments).

Full-service agents have extensive relationships with LPs, possess a broad view of LP activity, and hear market feedback regularly—all of which are helpful to a GP in crafting a compelling marketing strategy. They are also able to tap their prior experience as intermediaries for those LPs and other GPs to provide detailed information on investors' concerns and interests. They can create solutions that may appeal to a particular LP and help convert others who need additional incentives to make an investment. Many full-service agents are typically compensated on a percentage of funds raised. The definition of funds raised varies from "funds raised by the agent" to "total funds raised, including those where the agent did not have a role to play." When the compensation is based on "total funds raised," the fee as a percentage of the funds raised is much lower compared to the "funds raised by the agent" model.

Finders or Functional Agents

As the name suggests, the focus of finders or functional agents is on finding potential LPs. These agents are typically from smaller firms that focus exclusively on cultivating strong relationships with LPs and introducing them to funds. They may even be affiliated or duly licensed individuals who function similarly to independent contractors. Functional agents, by design, are single-purpose entities and many times will rely upon the support of your internal teams to make sales, complete documentation, and ensure regulatory compliance. GPs must ensure they are adequately staffed to maximize the introductions provided by functional agents. Finders' compensation many times is based on the number of introductions made or a monthly fee and not on the size of an investment. Some lawyers question as to whether this is a dead or dying option, given regulatory posture.

Boutique Firms

Boutique firms are usually smaller firms focusing on a single investor category or a particular geographic segment. Services and expertise offered will vary by firm.

BENEFITS OF USING A PLACEMENT AGENT

Broad Reach

PAs can become extensions of an internal marketing team or a completely outsourced function. Funds have a small window of time to raise money, especially in the case of private equity funds where there is a transactional time period between fund closes. PAs broaden marketing reach to qualified LPs, including endowments, foundations, pension funds, insurance companies, and other interested parties.

Trusted Relationships

LPs need to trust a GP to make an investment, especially if they have not had the opportunity to observe a manager over time. PAs have spent time with LPs already and enjoy established credibility. They have the ability to solicit investors on behalf of your fund, providing the trust the LP is seeking that your fund may not be able to provide. An unknown or emerging GP will have a hard time even securing a meeting with the LP. The PA is that bridge.

This is particularly important in regions such as the Middle East and Asia where personal interactions and relationships are highly valued, and in locations where regulations can significantly impact a fund's marketing strategy. Where there is an expectation of a high-touch interaction, having boots on the ground is necessary for success. Since it may not be practical for funds to have a presence in every region of targeted prospects, PAs that represent multiple funds can make the economics of "local presence" viable.

Manager Quality Certification

Regulators, and potential investors, expect PAs to have conducted extensive due diligence on the GP to market the fund to potential LPs. This is similar to the IPO underwriting process. A PA that interacts with several investors and solicits their feedback on the fund can help both the fund and LPs bridge information asymmetry.

Track Record of Efficient Fundraising

Both emerging and established GPs are more successful in fundraising when they use PAs (see Figure 10.1). A successful fundraise not only builds stature with investors, but also helps with deal flow.

FIGURE 10.1 Fundraising success of private equity funds closed in 2018 YTD by placement agent use and manager experience (June 2018)

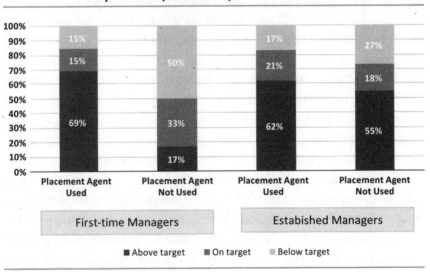

Source: https://www.preqin.com/insights/research/blogs/placement-agent-success-in-2018

Geographical Expansion

When teams do not have the relevant experience, relationships, or licenses to raise money in targeted geographies, it constrains GPs from raising funds globally. Having a licensed professional who speaks the local language, understands the culture, and has deep local relationships is essential. An additional benefit is that someone in the same time zone can better address questions and assistance requests than an internal team half a world away. A GP showing up sporadically in a region can hardly compare with a local PA who has spent time building trust with investors through regular interactions.

Strategic Advice

PAs with plenty of experience fundraising for various GPs and who have built strong relationships with LPs have their pulse on the market, investor appetite, and funding status. They can guide GPs in making strategic choices, such as the timing of the fund launch, fund size, amount of the initial and subsequent closes, information on other competing fundraises during the marketing period, fund structure, and trade-offs. Some can also help GPs with issues such as team structure and staffing levels, finding the ideal investor base that aligns with the fund's long-term prospects, and providing managers with insight on obtaining information about individual teammates' track records from previous employers.

Tactical Advice on Terms and Assistance with Negotiations

Given their breadth of experience with LPs and fund sponsors, PAs are an excellent source of information on terms the market can bear. Terms that fall outside the "market standard" are viewed with skepticism and can become a hurdle. These go beyond familiar conditions such as fee structure, fund term, and transaction fees. Some terms that can be obstacles for investors include preferential exits, preferential returns, Most Favored Nation (MFN) rights, Limited Partner Advisory Committee (LPAC) seats, co-investment rights, excusal rights not to participate in certain investments of a pooled investment, in specie (in-kind) redemptions, enhanced reporting or portfolio transparency, information confidentiality or Freedom of Information Act (FOIA) reporting, and other conditions that are more likely to be negotiated and agreed to in a side-letter agreement.

A GP is not necessarily expected to keep abreast of market terms. Managers are expected to focus on the portfolio between fundraises. However, a PA who is engaging with LPs and GPs will understand trends and be able to assist clients with terms the current conditions warrant. They are familiar with creative solutions employed by other emerging and established GPs that can be applied to problems a fund manager might encounter.

Communication Strategy

Highlight your fund's unique value proposition and leverage what the PA knows to tailor the message around what makes it a suitable fit for LPs. Excellent PAs can help identify likely concerns and objections from LPs, collate criticism and feedback from potential clients, and process them into actionable or rectifiable tasks for the GP. This is not only about alleviating concerns, but also about crafting the right message that makes both the manager and fund a compelling fit for LPs. Experienced agents are a great asset for managers in achieving that goal.

Market Continuity

A typical GP conducts a fundraising cycle followed by an investment cycle during which managing relationships with existing investors is a priority vis-à-vis building new relationships. If the GP is a small firm whose limited resources precludes it from doing both, there are limited new relationships it can develop. Such managers could benefit from aggregated market information they would otherwise find difficult to obtain. PAs actively engage with LPs at all times and have a read on market conditions and investor disposition, valuable information around which to plan and execute a successful fundraise.

Investor Screening

Given their wealth of relationships, PAs are equipped to assess a prospective LP's interest in the fund, current allocation to similar strategies or geographies, target allocation, liquidity, and other constraints. They can also identify an LP's key decision makers, internal processes—and more importantly, concerns and motivations. They will be able to leverage their relationships to ensure you are speaking with the right decision makers for more efficient and effective fundraising. It makes better use of a GP's time to secure an allocation and increases the probability of success, especially if in-person meetings are necessary. They also save on what could be significant costs of pursuing unsuitable or unqualified investors for the fund.

Assessment of Potential Success

PAs are compensated through commissions on funds raised. LPs assume that funds the PA represents have been screened to ensure they would be a good fit. After all, it is in the PA's economic interest to only pursue deals that have a realistic probability of closing.

Speaking with PAs is a great way to check a strategy's probability of success. Since placement agents are primarily paid success-based fees on fundraising, it is unlikely a GP would find an agent interested in taking up your assignment unless there is a reasonable probability of success; PAs will critically evaluate your fund before they take up the assignment. If you see reluctance from multiple agents, then it is time for the GP to question its strategy or check for issues that may be an impediment to raising a viable fund.

Tracking the Performance of New Funds

While existing funds can rely on their audited track record to gain trust with investors, the first-time GP is unlikely to have such a report. They must rely on information collated from reliable data sources and personal experiences to build out a reasonable representation of their own performance. This difficult task is made even more arduous when they are barred from using performance history from previous employers or partners who might view the new fund launch as competition.

Experienced fund attorneys and PAs who have dealt with many first-time fund launches can help the GP find a way to satisfy investor demand for a reliable track record while complying with the agreements and restrictions around the use of proprietary data from their past experiences.

Post-fundraise Engagement with Potential Future Investors

GPs of illiquid funds are not in the business of helping LPs find buyers for investments they wish to divest. While timing a liquidity sale is possible with hedge funds after the expiration of a lock-up period, fund flows into and out of PE are at the discretion of the manager. As such, there is a growing marketplace for the sale of investor interests in a fund, also called secondaries.

Some PAs use secondaries as an opportunity to benefit from an immediate transaction and create future relationships. They will find LPs to buy the secondary interest, while getting them to simultaneously invest in the GP's next fund. Alternatively, if the GP is already fundraising, PAs may find LPs to invest in the current fundraise with the condition that they be allowed to buy a secondary stake from an existing investor. This can be a winning proposition for all parties, the existing LP, new LP, GP, and PA.

ASSESSING THE NEED FOR A PLACEMENT AGENT

PAs are service providers that are rightly compensated for the value they bring to the table. Therefore, GPs need to do a build versus buy analysis before deciding on the need for a PA. Beyond the numbers and money, the implicit value of the agent in helping a GP achieve its strategic goal—be it a successful fundraise, diversified investor base, or another objective—may be critical to the firm and would be better accomplished by using a PA instead of doing it in-house. Some GPs hire a PA even for premarketing, especially if they anticipate some challenges in a future fundraise. In these instances, the PA is paid a monthly retainer, which may be a draw against future fees collected during the actual fundraise.

Should the GP decide to hire a PA, then it needs to choose which kind of firm to use and what type of relationship structure will be needed to meet objectives. Typically, PAs prefer an exclusive mandate where they would be the only ones raising money on behalf of the fund, other than the GP's own marketing team. However, there are nonexclusive mandates or specific purpose engagements such as split mandates and top-offs that are seen in the industry.

A split mandate implies there is more than one agent raising capital for the fund. Most often, a smaller agent is sought for its targeted reach that ideally would complement that of the primary placement agent. Top-offs are typically mandates from large and established GPs seeking assistance in a specific geography or LP type (pensions, sovereign wealth funds, and others). They will carve out a specific amount of the fundraise for that external agent.

WHAT TO CONSIDER BEFORE CHOOSING A PLACEMENT AGENT

The contractual agreements and nature of the PA business makes it difficult to change course in the middle of a fundraise. Even if a manager is able to do so, it comes at a cost of valuable time during fundraising. Therefore, managers need to avoid such mistakes by considering the PA's:

- Experience with the asset class and geography that aligns with your needs.
- Breadth and depth of relationships with the clients you want to target.
- Track record of successful fundraises: firms that have worked with funds in the same range as yours will be most appropriate.
- Average time for first close and final close.
- Number of simultaneous fundraises and maximum number of mandates they will agree to at any time; ensure staffing levels on your mandate as is appropriate.
- Any competing strategies they are representing or hoping to represent.
- Service level agreements should align with your needs and must be explicitly agreed upon prior to accepting the mandate. In situations where the firm is providing value-added services other than capital raised, there should be an explicit agreement on what those services are and how they will be evaluated even if they meet those conditions.

- Percentage of incomplete or stalled mandates.
- Whether there are any conflicts of interest, client complaints, or regulatory action. The Financial Industry Regulatory Authority (FINRA) has a database for investors to check a placement agent's history and to find out if any broker/dealer or their agents have any regulatory actions against them (https://brokercheck.finra.org/).
- Compensation terms and structure; structure it with incentives and clauses to best align with your realistic goals.

Other issues:

- **Expense allocation guidelines as to what out-of-pocket expenses can be reimbursed.** Given an agent can represent multiple GPs simultaneously, there should be an allocation methodology that incentivizes the agent to discuss your fund but also be explicit in the conditions for such allocations. These costs typically relate to travel, creation of marketing and due-diligence materials and, sometimes, additional work done on behalf of the client. While these are all "market standard," they need to be specific and agreed to at the onset.
- **Payment timing.** Typically, PAs are paid at fund closing. However, the fees come from the GP's share of revenue and are usually not assessed to the fund. Therefore, the GP needs to have sufficient resources to cover costs of using an agent prior to earning enough revenue to pay for ongoing expenses and agent commissions.
- **Turnover at PAs.** The industry is tackling this issue, as it is important to ensure there is continuity in the fundraising process. Identify if there is a turnover problem—especially at the senior levels—by asking for turnover numbers in the past few years. While the reasons for turnover are many, one common theme is around whether the team is compensated well. Agents need to be incentivized appropriately to raise capital for the manager.

THE KIND OF MANAGER DESIRED BY PLACEMENT AGENTS

PAs have two primary constraints in operating their business— relationships (quality and quantity) and time. They want to partner with GPs who can optimize both.

Relationships are nurtured over time, and the PA's reputation is a huge factor in building and maintaining investor relationships. If a fund that the agent markets is unable to raise the targeted capital or if performance is subpar, it creates a reputational issue with LPs and impairs long-term prospects. Marketing a fund that outperforms the market enhances the agent's reputation with LPs. This agent will have better prospects of raising capital for future funds they represent.

GPs with an excellent chance at raising capital are those who tell their story well, possess a strong pedigree and history of collaboration, have an exceptional track record, and have at least one key LP backing them. Make the first impression count; you will not get a second chance. Agents want to ensure the funds they present to LPs stand up to scrutiny and make a good impression. The better GPs are at this, the easier it is for agents to market funds and increase the probability of a fundraise's success. It may seem obvious, but agents cite the primary cause of bad fundraising experience is the lack of a collaborative partnership with the GP, despite it being in their best interest to be more synergistic. Since time is a constraint, agents will want to ensure GPs they take on are easily coachable.

RISKS OF USING A PLACEMENT AGENT

Most PAs market multiple funds, often 10 to 20, at the same time. This enables an agent to quickly shortlist fund options based on initial screening criteria before engaging in a more serious conversation with LPs. However, when a fund is crowded with other funds and presented to an investor, there arises a concern that the PA would focus on an easier sale, rather than an appropriate one in which the strategy and investor portfolio are the best fit. Some GPs also worry that their fund may not get the requisite attention if the strategy is more complex or takes a bit more time to pitch to the LP. Other GPs are concerned by PAs representing strategies similar to theirs, which creates an inherent conflict of interest.

Do these risks outweigh the benefits of using PAs? Experience can be mixed. First-time funds represented by agents perform significantly better than ones that do not. Similarly, funds represented by top-tier PAs, based on the number of funds they place and amounts raised, also generate statistically significant higher returns. Another consideration is the restrictions placed on some public funds engaging with PAs, as a result of the pay-to-play schemes during the early 2000s. Some notable players (private equity funds) agreed with regulators not to enlist PAs when soliciting public pensions. Some states such as Illinois, and cities like New York City, have banned PAs outright from soliciting public pensions. Other states will require PAs to register as lobbyists to market to certain investors.

FINDING THE RIGHT PLACEMENT AGENT

- Beware of the Rolodex versus relationships. PAs who have a contact name at investor firms exhibit mere Rolodex access and nothing more. Good agents have strong existing relationships with key decision makers and are knowledgeable about the LPs' internal processes, decision criteria, organizational structure, sensitivities, and concerns.
- PAs should play the role of an advisor or a coach, depending on the GP team's experience. An agent with a wealth of knowledge from previous engagements should be able to steer your team toward successful strategies and avoid pitfalls, with gameplans customized to the targeted LP. It is crucial that PAs help refine your pitch to create a convincing rationale for investor allocation. Some GPs are already adept at communicating with LPs and may need only an occasional boost. Others also provide project management support.

- GPs with existing funds should ask the agent to do a prospect analysis and check if there is an overlap of clients between those they represent and those you already serve. Ideally, you would like to see some common clients and that other prospects are similar to your investors. Reach out to LPs on both the PA's list and yours to verify the agent would be a good match for your firm.
- Ensure PAs have a successful track record of working with funds that are similar to yours or that they have a desirable client list. Make sure they are not also representing or have recently represented a competing fund. Dig deeper into the fundraises that did not meet the target; more can be learned by understanding failures than dwelling on successful fundraises alone.
- A GP and agent must have a close working relationship to achieve a successful partnership; good cultural fit is often ignored.
- The PA is a professional, not a miracle worker. Despite the agent's best efforts, the responsibility of convincing an LP ultimately rests on the GP. The agent can act as an advisor, offer access to investor relationships, and provide feedback. They cannot, and should not, guarantee an investment. The PA's commission-based fee structure highlights this point; GPs understand an allocation is not guaranteed and pay only for a positive outcome. It is increasingly customary to put a PA on retainer. This helps address the economic risk to an agent working on difficult fundraises. Without such retainers, PAs may not be willing to bear fundraising costs for emerging managers or funds using complex strategies aimed at a limited investor audience.
- Match your PA's expertise to your needs. If you have a marketing team, the best PA would be the one whose client list is complementary to yours and aligned with your fundraising goal. If your fund already has strong backing from existing

investors and only seeks to diversify its investor base in a new geography, then base your choice of a PA on that goal. However, if interest from existing investors is less than exciting and fundraising appears difficult, engage with a PA that has a wider network and experience to help your team overcome these obstacles.

- How important are you to the PA? If you are too small or unknown and do not have someone at the agent's firm championing you or your fund, the two of you may not be a good match. However, if you have existing or potential relationships with a PA's other partners (such as boutique investment banks), these factors may swing you toward the agent.

- An important criterion in a PA is the level of engagement its senior partners and experienced members will have in fundraises. Without involvement of senior partners, a fundraise may not be seen as a priority by staff and could suffer from a lack of focus and effort.

- PAs should work with a GP's internal team to ensure efficiency in the marketing process. If all are working in parallel, ensure the efficient use of the team's time and resources, including time spent traveling to and from investor locations. Coordinate schedules to meet with several investors in one trip, instead of traveling back and forth.

REGULATORY COMPLIANCE OF PLACEMENT AGENTS

In the United States, broker/dealers are registered with the SEC and must also be a member of FINRA, which enforces the rules of the SEC. Agents who work for a US broker/dealer must be licensed to do so by FINRA. In other countries, PAs must adhere to rules of their country. It is common to find jurisdictional regulators for PAs, such as the Financial Conduct Authority in the United Kingdom.

Finders, even if they are only introducing potential clients and are not part of any discussions, may need to be registered as well. Finders may be subject to state and federal registration and licensing rules.

It is extremely important to make sure PAs are duly licensed, because violations can have severe consequences. In a 2013 case against Ranieri Partners LLC, the SEC brought enforcement action against the firm and one of its senior managing partners relating to the investor solicitation activities conducted by a consultant on its behalf. This consultant was not registered as a broker-dealer with the SEC. Ranieri was charged with "causing" the violation of the registration provisions of the Securities Exchange Act of 1934, and the managing partner was charged with aiding and abetting the violations.

It resulted in a fine of $375,000 for Ranieri and $75,000 for the managing partner. It also restricted the partner from supervisory functions at any investment advisor, broker/dealer, or other SEC-registered market participant. As for the consultant, in addition to a disgorgement of more than $2.4 million in improper compensation and paying prejudgment interest, he was barred from association with any broker/dealer, investment advisor, or other SEC-registered market participant.

PLACEMENT AGENT FEE STRUCTURE

There is no standard PA fee structure due to the variety of services offered and varying levels of fundraise difficulty. That said, a typical fee would be around 2 to 2.5 percent of the funds raised, spread over a couple of years. Some agents are open to investing a portion of fees into funds for which they are raising capital, to show alignment of interests with investors and to keep an ongoing relationship with fund managers. There may also be a global fee arrangement in which the agent is paid a smaller percentage (significantly lower than 2 percent) of the total fund raised, including from current investors. In this case, the agent acts as an extension of the internal marketing team and is expected to play a much broader role.

Some agents will insist on a retainer to cover expenses while they are soliciting investors for the fund. These retainers are offset, fully or partly, against commissions earned later by the agent. Expenses incurred by the agent, such as for travel, are reimbursed by the fund manager.

Fees also vary based on fundraise size and perceived difficulty in raising capital for the particular strategy or fund. Established funds pay a much lower fee than emerging funds based on the effort required to fundraise.

PAs tend to favor tail provisions in their agreements. These let agents earn a commission on the funds raised for a period of time after an agreement ends. Since most of the work happens up front and the time it will take to close varies greatly by investor, a tail provision protects agents from losing revenue due to variables beyond their control. To incentivize agents to keep up their performance throughout the fundraise, managers might offer a tiered-scale commission where compensation rates increase after meeting certain thresholds.

CONCLUSION

PAs are a vital part of the alternative investments landscape. The most successful ones are trusted intermediaries who help managers succeed in their fundraising efforts. However, they do add a layer of cost that may not be affordable or justifiable to some managers. By co-opting them to be a part of the team, they are complementary resources with access to LPs that the manager may find difficult to access. The crucial job of the GP is to find the right PA that meets its needs.

CHAPTER 11

Effective Investor Relations

I nvestor relations (IR) serves a vital role in a fund. The IR team is not just a conduit for information flow between LPs and the fund; they also are the face of the organization to most LPs invested in the fund and the broader marketplace. How they handle their roles influences investor attitudes toward the fund itself.

In many alternative funds, the role of marketing and investor relations is carried out by the same person or group of people. Except at very large funds with expansive resources, an IR title is typically given to anyone responsible for fundraising, marketing, and sometimes also business development. (Note in some PE organizations, business development can refer to a deal sourcing role and not a capital raising function.)

There are several reasons why funds have overlapping IR and marketing functions. First, both deal with investors, and having one point of contact at the fund streamlines the relationship with investors. Second, most small and midsized alternative funds do not have a large staff, and it is common for one person to be responsible for, or play a key role in, multiple functional areas. The third reason is for the sake of relationship continuity in closed-end funds (structured private equity).

In a fund life cycle where a period for fundraising is followed by investment, the marketer loses contact with the investor until the next fundraise. Such intermittent relationship-building efforts are not optimal for building a long-term bond with investors. Investor relations, on the other hand, goes on continually even after the life of a fundraise.

If the IR and marketing functions are handled separately, there must be defined processes to ensure smooth handling of the same investor between the two departments. Some of the larger firms further separate the IR and marketing functions by geography or client type (e.g., pensions, E&Fs) to ensure continuity in relationships with investors.

It might be helpful to view IR as similar to account management in a business; both are essential to building lasting client relationships. Unlike sales, which is short-term, volatile, and transactional, good account management is patient, consistent, and a relationship-builder. As a *Harvard Business Review* article put it, "acquiring a new customer is anywhere from five to 25 times more expensive than retaining an existing one."[1]

When the IR and marketing roles reside in the same person, how can one excel at both? The key is to find a way to extend expertise in one area to another. For example, a successful business development executive at an alternatives firm had both responsibilities. While she loved and excelled at marketing, she did not care as much for IR and so she found a way to extend her passion for marketing to IR.

When she sends out newsletters as part of her IR duties, she would also call investors to talk about it, since this gave her an opportunity to lay the groundwork for a future fundraise. Every interaction was not just a part of the IR process; it was an opportunity to connect with investors in anticipation of future sales. That change in perspective led to unsolicited glowing reviews from investors about her handling of IR.

GOAL OF INVESTOR RELATIONS

The singular focus of the IR person is to serve the investors' needs. The IR leader must be an excellent communicator who can tell a good story and must also have the humility and good temperament to listen intently to investor wants and expectations. They should be sensitive to the investors' disposition and concerns, and act swiftly to resolve issues before they become a recurring problem.

One common IR mistake is not clearly informing investors about the frequency and medium of communication, the availability of statements and documents, and the fund's performance expectations under different market conditions. Investors do not want to be surprised by a manager's decision or action, or the fund's performance. Irregularity of communication leads to many of these issues. If a GP does not know the investors' disposition toward the fund at any given time, it may be time to reassess the quality of their IR program. The remedy may be as simple as a phone call to each investor to provide an update and listen to their feedback and concerns.

Effective IR must seek to convert a sale into a strategic partnership with the investor, earn the investors' trust as one who knows their needs and portfolio objectives, strive to proactively understand and provide solutions to their problems, and liaise between the fund and investor to ensure the client's satisfaction. A thoughtful and well-executed IR program not only provides excellent service to investors, but the fund also gets access to the LPs' network for information, advocacy, references, deal flow, market insights, competitive benchmarking, competing fundraises, among other hard-to-get data and factors critical to fund survival and growth.

INVESTOR ADVOCATE

IR managers are advocates for investors within the fund, representing the voice and viewpoints of investors to others within the firm. If a fund truly seeks to meet investor needs, how can it neglect the LP's point of view? IR gives investors a "seat at the table" when the fund is discussing a course of action that affects LPs.

As an IR manager inevitably becomes the face of the fund to the investor, what happens if he or she leaves the firm? While it is advisable to streamline communication with an investor by having a single contact, other people at the firm could also reach out systematically. There should be an effort to build a much broader relationship base that supplements the efforts of the IR manager.

Funds can take a leaf from a consulting firm's playbook. There is a relationship manager for each client, but there is also a team that nurtures and extracts value from this connection through cross- and up-selling to the client. Further, this team approach brings more strength to the client relationship—varying personalities of different team members may be a good match for the client's own team.

Primary IR functions include:

1. Build relationships with investors, both decision makers and influencers.
2. Seek client satisfaction to retain them within the firm.
3. Ensure robust two-way communication between the investor and the fund.
4. Increase the client's value to the firm and vice versa.
5. Gather market intelligence.

The bottom line is to treat investors as clients of the fund, and therefore they should be served in the same way as any company serves its clients.

IR AS AN ESSENTIAL DAY-TO-DAY ACTIVITY

Effective day-to-day investor relations is both a science and an art. It is partly a trade, a skill that can be learned and cultivated, and also a process that can be broken down into repeatable steps. This sounds simple but it takes finesse, dedication, and diligence to do it well. While each firm has different IR responsibilities and expectations, a common requirement for an IR professional is to stay abreast of current regulations governing your activities.

The IR lead must ensure activities adhere to the law and be aware of any update to regulations. For example, when it comes to marketing, alternatives are generally restricted from soliciting to the public. That means private issuers are allowed to solicit and advertise a private placement—but only to verified accredited investors.

Be Responsive to Investor Questions and Ad-hoc Requests

Investors expect accurate, complete, and timely responses to their questions and concerns. While IR strives to be responsive, a lapse could occur during periods of active fundraising. It is crucial for the IR lead to be an organized multitasker with a formal process for follow-ups.

Know the Interests of Your Investors

Primary investor concerns are typically centered around a fund's portfolio, performance, and structure. In addition, it helps an IR professional to be knowledgeable about the market in general. Reading excerpts from an investment memo might give an IR person some background, but does not provide a deeper understanding that the investor might seek. Keenly observe the fund's investment discussions to elevate your level of understanding of the process and its decision frameworks. The level of knowledge an IR person displays will inspire more confidence in investors and pave the way for continued commitment to future funds. Do not "fake it till you make it," because this approach often sours investor relationships, as LPs lose confidence not just in the IR person but also the firm.

Prepare and Disseminate Investor Communication

Typically, IR is responsible for writing fund updates that summarize fund and market performance, as well as providing commentary on events and situations that can impact the portfolio. Collating information from internal and external sources may seem easy, but this is rarely the case given the number and diverging priorities of people involved. Be aware that any of the materials to be used for marketing must comply with applicable rules.

A note of caution about overcommunicating: do not bombard your investor with information such that finding relevant data becomes a search for the proverbial needle in a haystack. We have received booklets from managers that were the length of a novel or a textbook. Investors have to keep tabs on multiple managers, and if the report length discourages them from reading it, the communication is as good as useless. Be intimately familiar with the fund's investment philosophy and strategy.

A fund investor's primary concern is monitoring performance. That performance must stem from being true to the strategy and investment philosophy executed by the manager during the fundraise. Any deviation presents a risk to the investor.

So long as the fund is performing in line with expectations, the primary condition for investing with you is met. However, if performance diverges from the market, even your most "long-term" investors will start questioning the fund's investment prowess. It is in these times that your understanding of the fund's strategy and investment philosophy will be critical in communicating how conditions have impacted your strategy's performance. Strategy drift is a poison pill for most funds.

Build Strong Relationships with Investors

There is a reason why LPs and fund managers are called partners. The principle behind this relationship is to ensure you have aligned interests. The most successful IR professionals are ones who care about their investors and seek to work with them for a mutually beneficial partnership. This engenders trust, which becomes a feedback loop. The more you trust, the stronger the relationship, and the stronger the relationship, the easier it will be to trust each other.

Distribute Investor Reports and Statements on Time

IR assists with, and in some cases even oversees, the production and distribution of regular investor reports and statements. One cannot overstate the importance of the timely dissemination of statements and reports to investors. These are their regular reminders of whether the decision to invest with the GP is a good one. Any delay in distribution will be noticed and flagged and will also be held against the fund by the investor. Given the frequency, the set timelines, and involvement of external service providers, distribution of these reports is a routine task that should not be delayed without a force majeure. Any delays, errors, or omissions will trigger calls to the IR representative and constitute a professional lapse that would tarnish a carefully built reputation for the fund.

Schedule and Conduct Periodic Investor Events and Annual Meetings

While periodic communication can be a good way to keep in touch on matters relating to the fund, investors do not need extended interaction with the fund manager. It is not practical, or even a good idea, to take the manager's time and focus away from the portfolio. However, there are times when it is necessary for managers to be available for investor questions, such as during quarterly updates and annual meetings. IR usually coordinates these events and tries to get as many investors as possible to attend.

Track Investor Questions and Sentiment; Inform the Rest of the Team

Investors ask questions or share their concerns because something is not meeting their expectations. Funds must take feedback seriously, act quickly to resolve an issue, and prevent it from recurring. Once the problem is resolved, document the issue and resolution. Ensure others in the team are aware that this issue has come up with an investor, so they can proactively take steps with other investors that might be similarly affected. Some firms create a frequently asked questions (FAQ) report to document responses to investors' questions and concerns, and align the team on these responses.

IR reps should ensure each investor complaint, concern, question, or request is addressed fully, accurately, and within a reasonable time frame. A good practice is to acknowledge receipt of the query, set expectations as to when there will be a resolution, and follow up afterward to ensure the solution met investor expectations.

Create and Manage the Firm's Social Media Presence

Social media presence is a highly divisive subject. Some firms completely shun any kind of publicity, while others embrace it wholeheartedly while staying within regulations. Alternative funds are increasingly embracing social media as Gen Z and millennials explore alternative investments, especially in venture capital where GPs could connect with both investors and startup entrepreneurs. Social media represents a brand-building exercise worth embracing, as it can be used as an IR tool to build engagement with existing and potential investors.

Seek Investor Feedback and Establish Benchmarks for the Fund

Successful IR professionals not only communicate with investors, they also actively seek feedback from them. This includes investor reactions to fund performance, transparency, strategy, frequency and quality of communication, market news, newsletter length, and so on. Find out how your firm compares to competing funds and your LP's top performers. If a firm truly wants to be best-in-class, it needs to take the risk of conducting such comparisons and strive to do better in areas needing improvement.

IR BEFORE AND DURING THE FUNDRAISE

The role of investor relations during a fundraise is very much like that of a marketer. While Chapters 6 and 7 on premarketing and marketing covers the subject more comprehensively, we will discuss some critical marketing elements briefly here as it relates to IR in the context of a fundraise.

Getting Ready

Work with the management team to decide on fund parameters and terms. Prepare the investor presentations, maintain and update due diligence documents/data room. Ensure data is up-to-date, complete, and accurate.

Create a list of investors to target by tapping existing leads, databases, personal and professional networks, references and introductions from existing investors, and so on. In the case of a successor fund, confirm reinvestment interest from existing investors. Identify the most likely LPs, and create a customized target strategy for each one, depending on what investors look for in a GP. Gather market intelligence to identify new product demand and market size.

Build relationships with investors and intermediaries, since most IR teams are short staffed and cannot reach all the prospects they targeted for a fundraise. Educate yourself about portfolio construction and be knowledgeable enough to discuss the fund's fit and value addition to a prospective investor's portfolio. By educating yourself, you can shield the investment and operations activities of the firm from excessive distractions due to fundraising demands. Ensure the team is available, well prepared, and ready to handle a due diligence visit. Learn as much as possible about the investor's due diligence process, and share it with the team to set the right expectations internally.

Interacting with service providers and intermediaries is essential for business development and cultivating references. Marketers need to ensure appropriate focus on consultants and gatekeepers, given that adverse investment decisions are made even prior to reaching the end investor.

Once the investor confirms intent to invest, ensure all necessary documents are received and duly accepted to be legally binding on both parties. We have found instances where LPs have withdrawn their commitment if there is an inexplicable delay in receipt of the subscription and a fund close.

IR DURING TIMES OF CRISIS

How a firm handles its IR during a crisis reflects the strength of this process. Regardless of circumstances, firms with a very active and effective IR program succeed in retaining a large percentage of LPs during difficult times or getting many LPs to re-up compared to competition that did not follow some basic principles.

Share Important News Immediately

During the life of a fund, problems arise that need to be shared with investors. Whether it is internal (such as an operational failure or departure) or external (such as a regulatory change that might impact your strategy), these challenges need to be disclosed without delay. It is not good for investors to hear about it elsewhere, have time to form their own opinions, and perhaps misinterpret the issue. They will lose faith in the manager and question the fund's transparency when it runs into trouble. If you develop a reputation as a manager who shares only good news, this can significantly damage your relationship with the investor. By being up front and transparent, mutual trust will endure.

Do Not Spin Difficult Messages

There is a price to pay for bad decisions by the manager or failures that the investor thinks should have been mitigated. Whether the investor is right or not, the manager's tendency is to sugarcoat bad news. But investors can see through a spin, because they will try to find more information from multiple sources. The result is a skeptical view of the manager who did not convey a truthful analysis of the situation and offer remedial action. If the issue will continue to have an impact in the future, it is important to try and set the right expectations. If at all possible, resolve the problem right away to avoid any lingering effect on investors.

Thoughtfully handling the dissemination of unsavory information, including key departures from a firm, will gain the trust of your investors. Remember, stopping a crisis from escalating through competent IR is as important as launching a successful fund for the long-term prospects of the firm.

Raise the Level of Investor Communication

Human beings are conflict averse. Some have the ostrich mentality: a tendency to bury one's head in the sand in hopes that problems will disappear. As we saw during the 2008 financial crisis, several managers did not know how to address the market downturn that was massively impacting their portfolio, and they had no way of mitigating a broad-based decline. Without having a solution to present to investors, many managers fell short on communication. Others, who only chirped about good news, were glaringly lacking transparency to investors. Disheartened investors voted with their capital allocation and moved money away from managers whose IR program failed to perform during a crisis.

On the other hand, some managers shared with investors what they knew and set clear expectations about when they expected to have better answers. Others went one step further and increased the frequency of investor communication. Managers who were transparent and listed concrete steps they were taking to mitigate the impact of the crisis found favor with investors during and after the crisis. A good rule of thumb is, "If you know information, share. If you don't, set an expectation as to when you would be able to share." However, setting expectations too far out in the future will not absolve managers from investor concerns and queries. Most investors report on their managers quarterly to their internal stakeholders and boards. Ensure that timelines reasonably align with that cycle.

Sending Periodic Letters Alone Is Not Enough During a Crisis

Letters do not give investors an opportunity to ask questions or convey concerns. During times of crisis, investors need a forum for interactive discussion. To be efficient, a GP should connect with investors through conference calls, online meetings, or other mediums, for example, with the LPAC, to provide an update followed by a question-and-answer session. During these group sessions, do not let a single investor dominate the conversation. First, it takes away the opportunity for others to directly question the manager. Second, if the dominant speaker is negative, an atmosphere of pessimism will permeate the discussion—a situation no manager desires. Some managers screen questions from investors. We are not big proponents of this practice, unless it is a genuine effort to identify thoughtful questions and ensure that there is a broad range of topics addressed during the meeting.

Do Not Change the Content or Format of Periodic Communication

Picking and choosing what information to present to investors is not a good idea. It signals to the investor that the manager is not being transparent and may be hiding something detrimental. Even when information is disclosed as usual, but the write-up focuses on a different time frame (such as emphasizing annual instead of quarterly returns), it might raise investor suspicion, even if the GP believes it is inconsequential.

Educate the Team about How to Communicate Effectively during a Crisis

IR reps may be the investor's main contacts for the fund, but they are not the only ones that interact with the LP. Therefore, the IR team should educate the firm on what to communicate to ensure message consistency and distribute updated FAQs as necessary. This policy should hold consistently, but it is especially critical during a crisis, since information will be constantly changing and volatile. Ensure there is a firm-wide communication policy and information sharing process to make sure everyone is aligned and only authorized personnel are disseminating information.

Hire a Good PR Firm

Sometimes, it is better to hire a PR firm to craft your communication strategy during a crisis. This approach is generally appropriate for internal crises (such as performance, a team split, operational or regulatory deficiency). PR professionals likely have dealt with similar issues with other clients. Even if they have not, these are professionals whose expertise is to manage crisis communication which the team may desperately need.

Seek Assistance from Fund Counsel

In the hectic pace of activities during crisis management, the last thing a manager wants is to commit a regulatory or legal faux pas that creates a challenging situation. Ideally, it is good practice to run your messaging by fund counsel and seek approval before sharing it with investors. Be mindful about the cost of such counsel.

LICENSING AND REGULATORY REQUIREMENTS FOR IR

IR in and of itself does not have a specific licensing requirement. However, to the extent that there are role overlaps, one should consider them under the umbrella of fund and fund marketing regulations. While the registration requirements vary from state to state, here are some regulatory requirements managers must know. As usual, it is important for managers to seek the opinion of competent counsel. Furthermore, the focus on US regulations makes it less applicable for global managers, other than to offer a template.

For those who wish to work in IR, desirable accreditations include chartered financial analyst (CFA) and chartered alternative investment analyst (CAIA). Licensing requirements vary by jurisdiction. Some IR professionals do possess licenses such as FINRA Series 7, Series 65, and Series 3, or commodity trading advisor (CTA).

We cannot reiterate enough the need to hire a competent attorney who can help navigate the maze of requirements by jurisdictions and geography. In the United Kingdom, the FCA regulates the business and might require implementation of Senior Managers and Certification Regime (SMCR), and European Securities and Markets Authority (ESMA) for the rest of Europe.

CONCLUSION

IR is a key element that determines the long-term success of an alternatives firm. It is also one of the easiest functions to differentiate yourself, provided it has the right people, resources, and organizational attitude that fosters customer-centric processes.

Given its overlap between investing and marketing, IR professionals should have the intellectual curiosity to know enough about investments and investing strategies to speak with authority to investors. Successful IR professionals are not only good communicators but also excellent organizers who are able to manage multiple priorities and juggle several conversations and projects simultaneously. Even though a small fraction of investor interactions will be adversarial, they need the poise and confidence not only to handle them without confrontation but also to find common ground and mutually beneficial agreements. They should be adept at building relationships and not be shy about taking the initiative to find the right targets and start a dialogue.

Effective IR is not an exact science. There is no algorithmic method that would address all situations an IR team encounters. Neither is it an art where the creative genius of savvy practitioners will spontaneously conjure up brilliant solutions. It is a trade that can be learned with a disciplined adherence to meticulously detailed processes and an understanding of the simple reality—the entire fund works for the investors and protecting investors' interest is the primary objective. Investors are willing to forgive a poor investment decision, but a deficient IR experience is never forgiven or forgotten. The secret of successful fund managers is an immaculate execution of one aspect that is entirely under their control—a good IR experience.

CHAPTER 12

Due Diligence

llocating capital to a fund manager is a complex decision for an investor. The cost of a wrong decision is quite high. Unlike a physical product, which comes with an actual product to test and review with performance guarantees, professional services affords no such assurance and LPs rely on due diligence prior to making an investment decision.

Allocating capital holds risks for the LP. While the GP must abide by certain expectations and boundaries, they manage investor capital without any real supervision from LPs. Alternative assets show the highest dispersion of returns compared to other asset classes, and obviously returns cannot be ascertained a priori. A GP is not required to hold a certification or license to ensure adeptness in managing LPs' money. While the pedigree of a GP can be a substitute for skill certification, there is no measure for integrity.

This makes it difficult for an LP to determine which GPs can generate the best returns in the future, so in-depth due diligence provides some assurance that the GP's performance is likely to meet expectations and that risks are well understood. It is the modern-day equivalent of looking a horse in the mouth; LPs will rightly follow the maxim "trust, but verify." GPs should not only understand the reasons for investor due diligence, they should invite the scrutiny to build a strong relationship based on mutual trust.

The 2008 global financial crisis put the spotlight on issues of governance and performance volatility in alternatives. Additionally, instances of fraud perpetrated by principals and employees of alternative investment funds—Bernie Madoff, Sam Israel, Daniel Kamensky, to name a few—have led LPs to demand adequate risk controls prior to investing.

DUE DILIGENCE PROCESS

Every LP follows its own process for due diligence, measuring GPs on a set of criteria that can change based on how appropriate an investment is for their portfolio. However, there are some common checks that most investors will do.

Desktop Due Diligence (DDD)

The usual first step in the due diligence process is desktop due diligence (DDD). Past the initial screening of a GP and after ascertaining interest, LPs want to further understand the fund's strategy, process, terms, regulations, and risks. They also want to conduct a quick initial vetting of the investment management team. This is done from the comfort of an LP's desk with access to multiple data sources, supplemented by a few quick phone calls. DDD could be further separated into three broad and overlapping buckets: document review (a review of documents and/or data room access for confidential information); confirmation of claims by analyzing fund performance and its fit with the investor's portfolio, and by cross-referencing public and private databases for information verification; and preliminary investigation into the track record, team, and background, and by using online searches about the team and its investments to verify claims.

Many LPs will first ask prospective GPs to fill out a due diligence questionnaire (DDQ) asking a broad set of questions to help them make a decision. Most LPs rely on popular DDQ formats, such as ILPA,[1] AIMA,[2] or MFA[3] questionnaires. To address common LP concerns, funds typically create a standard DDQ to share with prospective clients. The practice of using standardized DDQ templates has opponents, who believe GPs use DDQs as a marketing tool. A standardized document from a respectable entity such as ILPA or AIMA could potentially lull LPs into accepting ill-suited answers to legitimate questions. While that could be true, sophisticated LPs will use a DDQ as a starting point that covers relevant topics, and a review of the DDQ can actually prompt more important questions to explore with the GP.

Access to a data room[4, 5] that houses important LP documents and confidential information is usually provided right after confirming investor interest. Sometimes, this would entail the LP signing a nondisclosure agreement (NDA) to review documents. Most data rooms have built-in NDA requirements during an initial log-in.

Almost all data room providers feature access tracking and reporting—information that would be valuable in marketing to nudge LPs if they have not accessed the information or follow up with investors who have spent a lot of time reviewing materials. GPs should also keep data access current and revoke access for LPs who no longer need it. It is good practice to connect with the LP before any access is revoked; this also provides an additional opportunity to confirm or rekindle investor interest.

After reviewing documents, LPs may send follow-up questions to GPs. Some LPs prefer a surprise call to confirm information on sensitive topics or to hear impromptu responses that they may deem more credible. GPs and their representatives must handle such impromptu calls with an appropriate level of diligence. If junior staffers are asked questions they cannot answer well or are requested to comment on sensitive topics, they should be encouraged to include senior partners in the conversation, as investors appreciate hearing directly from the partners.

Many LPs will also conduct online searches for publicly available information on the GP, the fund, past and current investments, the team, prior employers, and other public records relevant to their investment decision. This preliminary search serves to confirm claims presented by the GP and uncover any intentional omissions. Only after a positive outcome from DDD will LPs allocate further resources for the task.

Investment Due Diligence (IDD)

After conducting DDD, what follows is a series of calls, emails, and in-person meetings, including a visit to the GP's office, and perhaps even the portfolio companies. Investment and operational due diligence (IDD, ODD) can be simultaneous or separate streams depending on the LP and the topics could also be overlapping. Information that LPs seek in this phase may include general fund and firm information, investment strategy and philosophy, investment process review and analysis (research, selection, due diligence, portfolio addition, performance monitoring, eventual exit), fund terms, fund oversight (IC, LPAC, board of directors including independent directors), and so on.

Due diligence on a new GP necessitates an additional level of scrutiny and assessment of risks specific to that particular firm. These include determining whether the GP's experience and track record are appropriate for the fund strategy. Seasoned LPs are aware that the conditions responsible for their track record may not be replicable due to shifting investment environments and other "environmental" factors such as access to a specific data set, infrastructure, supervision, and proprietary networks that helped generate those returns. Some factors that are considered in making that determination include market conditions during the same time period, actual portfolio risk relative to benchmarks and comparatives/competition, use of leverage, and consistency of returns. GPs will be better served to critically examine these conditions and be confident in their ability to bridge any gap ahead of a due diligence meeting. Furthermore, if the LP worked with a prior GP that had shortcomings, strive to present how your firm can add value without speaking badly of the predecessor. A "lessons learned" section is usually well received by LPs.

While a fund's track record and performance are important, what is even more relevant are qualitative assessments of the GP. For example:

- Was the performance achieved while staying true to the investment strategy and philosophy?
- Does the GP have a well-defined, documented process for the team? How does the GP address deviations from that process?

- Does the GP track and adequately correct missteps, mistakes, and inadequacies? Is there a concerted effort to learn from mistakes and prevent them from recurring?
- While the portfolio manager is ultimately responsible for the investment decisions and performance of the fund, is there a process where decisions are scrutinized and challenged to ensure that complacency and overconfidence do not cloud investment judgment?
- Is there a reasonable basis to expect the GP to continue performing in a similar fashion during different market conditions (or perform directionally in a specific market condition for a cyclical strategy)?
- Is the performance due to chance, or a result of the strategy and the GP's skill?
- Are outliers contributing disproportionately to the performance of the GP, and is there an expectation such outliers would exist in the foreseeable future?
- Is the GP actively engaged with the investee company, and do they address underperformance appropriately? Does the track record show they are able to exercise control and prevent investment losses at underperforming companies?
- Is there an abundance of investment opportunities to choose from? In PE funds, has the GP developed an active and broad deal pipeline (including an emphasis on proprietary deal flow) that is sustainable and of high quality? Is the GP entering into an investment with thoughtful and specific plans to create or unlock value, and is that plan fully executed through an eventual exit?

One common question LPs focus on is scalability of the strategy. How much capital can the strategy easily deploy without impacting performance, and does total AUM currently deployed under this strategy (including by competing firms) remain under the upper limit? Not only do GPs need to have a clear and compelling response to LPs, they should also ensure the rest of the investment team buys into the AUM limits strategy.

For first-time funds, LPs are typically interested in the growth of the firm and future fund sizes. GPs should be thoughtful with their answers—for example, future fund sizes can be determined by investment staffing levels and expected exit timelines will depend on their strategy and process. A response that includes a plan, process, and commitment to stay devoted to the strategy and philosophy for the foreseeable future is seen as more convincing as it takes away one more portfolio uncertainty for the LP.

While it is impractical for a portfolio manager to meet with every prospect, you should ensure LPs who have progressed in the due diligence process are able to secure a meeting before deciding. LPs will also interview members of the team to ascertain their roles and experience and judge their service quality. LPs might view any reluctance as a sign that "something is off."

If a personnel change means the team would lack depth to pursue the fund strategy, LPs need to account for such risks. Another issue LPs focus on is the "culture" of the team. They want to see a positive work environment, an ethos that focuses on investment results, and "doing the right thing." LPs have walked away when they felt the firm's employees were not treated well, working conditions were poor, or simply no one other than the founder had a voice. Small gestures, subtle nuances, and the tenor or cadence of interactions within the team can convey a lot to an experienced investor. GPs should understand that culture cannot be faked, and experienced LPs are quite good at identifying incongruities between words and action. A positive culture is not just a due diligence checklist item, it is often the reason for a firm's continued success.

Additionally, LPs will seek terms that are offered to other investors who have made similar capital allocations to a fund. GPs should expect such questions and be prepared to answer them candidly. This would include any side-letter agreements, most-favored-nation (MFN) agreements (meaning if some other investor is offered terms that are better than their current terms, the better terms will be offered to the investor as well), or preferential terms entered with any other LP; when check sizes are in the same range, the LP will often ask for a similar agreement. If offering such terms to a new investor is an impediment, GPs should be prepared to explain the situation carefully to new LPs or risk losing a potential investment.

One consistent investor due diligence request is for full disclosure of conflicts of interest. GPs are expected to invest alongside LPs at levels that are meaningful to them, and at liquidity terms that favor LPs. Related persons[6] serving in key positions in the firm or with authority over client funds is seen as a conflict. Such responsibilities are best assigned to outsiders, including a preference for regulated third parties (such as custodians, administrators, etc.) to be solely in-charge of actual client assets. Sometimes the conflict may be unavoidable, especially at a small or new firm with limited assets, but GPs should be prepared to defend it during due diligence and potentially still be at a loss due to the conflict.

Operational Due Diligence (ODD)

Alternative managers enjoy an extremely high level of autonomy in their investment process, and LPs want to ensure their capital is safe and performance is on par or better than expected. Due diligence of alternative managers tends to be broad, detailed and robust. In addition to investment issues, good LPs will look into noninvestment-related points of failure during this stage. Operational due diligence (ODD) is necessary not only to prevent a collapse due to fraud or poor risk management, but also to ascertain proper functioning of a fund and an ability to fully execute a proposed strategy.

Even as early as 2003, operational issues were the cause for failures of half of the hedge funds analyzed by consulting firm Capco.[7] Problems included improper representation or valuation of investments, lack of proper controls around cash movement, improper trading or trade processing, and other operational issues. As a result of past fund failures, there is a growing emphasis on operational excellence by GPs and LPs, especially in a technology-dependent world that grapples with technical glitches and nonavailability of critical infrastructure such as power, telecommunications, and internet connectivity (see Table 12.1). Due diligence will focus on middle- and back-office functions of the firm and occasionally on the service providers that perform the function on behalf of the fund.

TABLE 12.1 **Major Operational Topics for Assessment and Confirmation During Due Diligence**

Overall fund structure and operations
Trading, authorization, reconciliation, restrictions, and trade compliance
Fund governance, legal, administration, and compliance
Risk monitoring, risk management, and risk mitigation of individual positions and overall portfolio
Reporting and valuation
Finance and accounting—expenses charged to the fund versus manager, shadow accounting
Access control and tracking of banking, securities, cash accounts
Technology and strict access control to information and systems to relevant individuals
Business continuity
Alignment and conflicts of interests
Social and political impacts—ESG, diversity, fairness in dealings

Most often, ODD is conducted on-site, with some amount of preparatory work done up front so that shortcomings can be identified and remedies may be recommended by the due diligence team. Rarely is an investment turned down immediately unless the GP is unwilling to accommodate changes and remedies sought by the LP.

Most LPs will want independent verification of financials and performance information provided in a marketing pitch (such as audited financial statements or a direct message from the fund administrator providing the fund's NAV, performance, and explanations for any restatements). By making a directory of independent service providers available to LPs and setting up service level agreements with them, verification can become less of a hassle during fundraising. In addition, valuation of assets and procedures for valuing illiquid or infrequently traded assets must be established and documented for LP and auditor verification.

Adequate staffing is necessary for the proper functioning of a fund. High turnover is a red flag for most LPs. LPs will seek information on the size of the staff, their experience, capability, and any redundancies and contingencies. Many investors seek compensation history and variable compensation related to investment performance. Funds where the economics, especially carry or performance incentive, is concentrated on certain individuals instead of being adequately shared with the broader investment team, should not expect to gain favor from LPs.

In addition, some LPs will demand a staffing history and information on any outsourced support. They may request to speak with past employees and ask about compliance with stated employment policies (including clear segregation between investment and operations functions, related party employment, background files, and internal actions against any employee). While staffing adequacy poses a challenge for smaller and newer funds, it is an essential element for investment protection, and many GPs find hiring qualified outside consultants offers assurance to potential LPs.

On-site ODD will involve multiple interviews with those in the middle- and back-offices, a review of policies and policy compliance, demonstration of critical systems (trading, reconciliation, order management, portfolio management/DSS, and others), access management, and key person dependencies or deficiencies of proprietary systems. GPs who have invested in conducting an internal review of their operations are well positioned to meet this scrutiny, and these reviews also prepare the operations team to respond to LP queries during due diligence.

Access to assets (cash, securities, brokerage, lines of credit, etc.) is an important part of ODD, especially after past instances of fraud and self-dealing have left LPs without adequate recourse. Prime brokerages, administrators, auditors, and banks are familiar with these confirmation requests, but the GP should document the entire cash movement process and make it available to LPs when requested. Establishing adequate access and authorization controls and providing a robust process on who is able to establish or change access for banks, prime brokers, and custodians is a must for all GPs.

Astute LPs look at the size of the investments to see if they match up with what is in the investment documents and analyze whether the size of investment is warranted by the nature and promise of the opportunity. GPs will do well to proactively analyze their investments and be intimately familiar with the data, process, history, investment thesis, and outcome. Familiarity with the portfolio and past investments provides investors with confidence at a time when they look to identify problems.

Most LPs view strategy drift as a real concern. A drift makes it very difficult for LPs to manage their own portfolio allocation and control risk exposure. The reason for investing in a GP is to tap their experience and expertise in a certain realm and with confidence in the strategies they are implementing. This may not be possible when the GP drifts away from the tried-and-true process, opening up the portfolio to risks of underperformance. GPs should be prepared to present their rationale if that drift was due to changing circumstances—and highlight skills they were able to leverage to mitigate transition risks and dispose the fund to a favorable performance.

Reference and Background Checks

Given the fund's autonomy, limited regulatory oversight, and potential for severe loss or fraud, the quality and character of the team are of paramount importance. Positive background and reference checks are necessary for any investment. GPs should add to this process by conducting background checks on all senior personnel prior to each fundraise for private equity funds, and on a regular basis for hedge funds. Any issues should be flagged and addressed immediately; these could include unforeseen or long forgotten problems that crop up in due diligence. It is better to address any reference issues proactively, with your side of the story.

Common checks and references conducted by investors during due diligence include:

- Background check for partners/CEO/COO/CCO/IR personnel (including lawsuits, criminal or civil actions, personal finances, education or professional credentials and experience verification)
- References from previous and current LPs
- References from senior leadership of portfolio companies (past and present)

- Discussions with interested investors who did not commit capital
- References from service providers and professional acquaintances
- Background checks for unknown service providers such as auditors and fund administrators
- Interviews with past employees

After reference checks and office visits are completed, there may be additional meetings, calls, or email communication necessary prior to deciding whether to invest with a manager. A courtesy call from an LP, even if the decision is unfavorable to the GP, is customary to continue an ongoing relationship after completing a comprehensive due diligence process. If there is no follow-up from an LP within a reasonable time, GPs may benefit from proactively seeking a response without rushing them or appearing too eager.

INVESTORS: PREPARING FOR DUE DILIGENCE

During due diligence, an investor's primary goal is to seek evidence and corroborate positive assessments of the team and strategy that initially got them interested in allocating to the fund. At the same time, they seek to uncover any red flags to help prevent embarrassment, loss of capital, fraud, or professional harm. LP representatives would want to gather enough information and evidence for their investment committee or senior managers and supervisors.

Investors want to ensure the strategy they were interested in is actually the strategy that is being executed; there are no discrepancies between what is expected and what is being delivered. They seek to uncover any deficiencies in strategy, implementation, or execution, not just with the investment process but also in the fund and firm operations and management.

They also want to ensure compliance with all regulations, norms, and policies as laid out in the fund documents. This is the right time to identify risks investors are not getting paid to undertake, including succession issues, inadequate operational infrastructure, lax regulatory compliance, and inadequate fraud prevention.

The process will be more efficient, productive, and meet the goals of the LP and fund manager only if both spend adequate time preparing for it. Even when due diligence is exploratory, it is an opportunity for the GP to re-emphasize messages, provide evidence to back up claims in the pitch, and convert an LP's interest to an investment. Some GPs do not put in the requisite effort when they know an LP is conducting exploratory due diligence, but this is a serious mistake and a lost opportunity to forge a long-term partnership with LPs. Exploratory due diligence is a confirmation of LP interest in the fund. One critical issue LPs should pay more attention to is the long list of exceptions that the GP has made in agreements—such as restricting redemptions, in-kind redemptions, fees, and placing other obstacles to investor liquidity in hedge funds or setting a low bar for extensions and changes to the LPA while adding a high bar for manager removal in private equity funds.

Sometimes, an LP might deem it necessary to seek written responses from GPs to critical questions instead of raising them during a meeting. By allowing GPs adequate time to respond, LPs can ensure their answer is complete, accurate, and documented as compared to impromptu responses during a meeting. GPs might also want to avoid responding immediately to questions for which they do not have a complete or accurate answer.

Most successful LPs do not rely solely on the data shared by the GP, but also on their judgment and intuition honed over time through experience and picking up clues. This may involve reference checks and cross-references that go beyond the list provided by prospective GPs. In one instance, Hemali had provided an LP 10 references for a GP; the LP went on to conduct more than 60 reference checks through its own network. Whenever possible, LPs seek feedback from other investors who walked away after due diligence. Most larger institutions engage outside investigators and conduct background checks on key individuals. Even smaller LPs can find a lot about the GP and key personnel by conducting an online and social media search.

MANAGERS: PREPARING FOR DUE DILIGENCE

The most important things a GP can do is to ensure consistency in messaging, provide evidence, and demonstrate actual implementation. There should not be incongruity or inconsistency, even if it is tangential, for a smooth due diligence. GPs need to check through their documents thoroughly to ensure data is consistent and accurate before they are presented to investors. Even if a GP is willing to correct inconsistencies, it reflects poorly on the quality of output from the manager and will raise questions about attention to detail. LPs will rightly doubt the GP's ability to focus on complex investment details when they are unable to do so in an easily reviewable document.

GPs should set up internal DDQ review processes before any information is shared with LPs. This means there should be a dedicated group of individuals, or a team, within the organization with adequate seniority, experience, knowledge, and responsibility to thoroughly review all information and data within DDQ documents and other marketing and fund documents for consistency and accuracy. It is equally important to have documents vetted by the fund's counsel for regulatory and legal compliance before external dissemination.

A good practice is to ensure the DDQ is factual, without being overly stylistic or verbose, and is focused on answering relevant questions succinctly. The language should be acceptable in a professional communication. The intent of the document is to be transparent and should seek to gain the trust of the investor and strengthen the relationship. A coherent and transparent DDQ goes a long way in building investor confidence and establishes that the manager is willing to and capable of answering difficult questions candidly. It will also portray the team as a competent entity who can be trusted with investor capital.

Some LPs have their own DDQs and would seek to have that completed instead of accepting the GP's standard DDQ, to ensure all questions and topics they care about are addressed and to ensure consistency in the way they consider multiple GPs. While the bespoke DDQ does help the LP, it adds work and complexity to the due diligence process and marketing workload. It would be helpful to have your responses to LPs' questions, including those in a DDQ, cataloged and stored for future reference and dissemination. This creates a modular approach where you are picking and choosing from existing answers, instead of redoing work.

A comprehensive FAQ based on LPs' questions should be maintained and updated. The FAQ is useful in onboarding new team members and effective for internal education and knowledge sharing. It is also a valuable tool in ensuring sensitive or difficult questions are consistently addressed by any team member. Many fund managers find the exercise of educating the entire investment team and relevant operating team members, and conducting mock interviews for team members, to be of tremendous value.

A scout's motto applies here: be prepared. A junior staff member may be called on for an impromptu due diligence interview or might find themselves engaged in a conversation with an LP during an annual general meeting or investor conference. For marketing purposes, the staffer becomes the face of the firm at that moment and could affect the LP's decision to invest or continue investing. Hemali has seen many LPs ask junior team members the same question, "What are the partners' strengths and weaknesses?"

Most LPs provide an agenda for an on-site due diligence visit to improve productivity and efficiency of the process. If there is not an agenda, marketing teams may create one and submit it to the LP for prior approval. LPs usually drive the due diligence process; GPs will be better served by making it collaborative, stepping in if the process is not moving forward or in a direction unfavorable to an investment.

SECRETS OF EFFECTIVE DUE DILIGENCE

GPs with a robust strategy, dependable process, reliable infrastructure, strong team, and superior track record should view due diligence as an opportunity to uncover any inefficiencies or deficiencies that are not apparent, so they can strengthen themselves for the future. It is similar to receiving free consultation from their LPs on how to improve the strategy, process, people, and the fund in general. LPs who are conducting due diligence have already shown their willingness to put in time and resources in pursuit of an allocation to a GP's fund. By being transparent and open to suggestions and recommendations from investors, the GP is showing a desire to listen and learn, which helps LPs overcome minor objections or concerns that may impede an investment.

Effective due diligence involves collecting information from multiple sources and cross-referencing them to ensure they fit together, not signaling inconsistencies or foreseeable red flags. LPs will not, and should not, take the DDQ as complete and accurate. In fact, nothing in the due diligence process is sacrosanct. They will approach it with skepticism that to some GPs might appear excessive. While it is important to have mutual respect and trust between the LP and GP, it is the LP's responsibility to ensure suitability of the investment, a GP's trustworthiness, and the likelihood that this strategy would succeed and fit their investment objectives. GPs should expect skepticism and react appropriately to questions that seem to cast aspersions on the information or the intent. A GP is unlikely to face the same treatment once the initial "kicking the tires" phase is completed and the LP makes a commitment to the fund.

"ONCE AND DONE" VERSUS COMPREHENSIVE PERIODIC DUE DILIGENCE

Some LPs understand the value of periodic due diligence to ensure material changes are discovered promptly, before it is too late to prevent a loss. This process does not need to be as involved as the original visit; it just needs to reverify assumptions and stress test factors critical to the success of the fund. Periodic due diligence confirms compliance with regulations and with stated processes for investment research, execution, and risk management. While it is additional work for a GP who believes heightened scrutiny is unnecessary since processes and philosophy remain unchanged, this exercise builds LP confidence and promotes a stronger relationship. Both can work out a schedule that will have a minimal impact on the team's investment activities and operations—while providing value to both parties in the long run.

Experienced LPs typically ask for all communication from a GP, including investor letters and news announcements from the past few years. GPs should have due diligence packets ready to share with investors, including relevant investor presentations, memos, and newsletters. This packet will help set baseline expectations of what kind of communication transparency LPs should expect, and chronicle the evolution of the GP's thoughts and reactions to market conditions over time. Following up an LP's query must be timely; there is simply no excuse for delays.

When it comes to information sharing, LPs in any fund do not like disparate treatment, despite larger LPs pushing for more transparency and involvement. While LPs understand there will be preferential treatment of larger clients and seed investors, they will only accept it if that preferential treatment does not infringe on the rights or performance of their own investment. Most LPs will not object to the GP cutting fees or charging a lower carry that does not impact other LPs in the fund, to attract desirable LPs. However, even the appearance of impropriety in sharing of information with the fund's LPs would be viewed with disdain and can harm the GP's ability to market the fund.

GPs with teams in multiple locations should expect to be quizzed about their functioning and value addition. While in theory, localized teams should provide an investment edge, LPs could be concerned about loss of efficiency and performance if the GP and team are unable to function effectively due to distance and dearth of effective supervision. LPs like to understand the levels of autonomy and process controls, to avoid situations like rogue trader Nick Leeson, who engaged in fraudulent derivative trades due to insufficient supervision and brought down Barings Bank in 1995. Recently, the pandemic has alleviated some of these LP concerns around remote and virtual work.

One creative solution to the problem of dealing with each LP doing their IDD/ODD at their own times—which results in duplication of work for the GP and drains on essential investment and operational resources needed for the functioning of the firm—is to conduct group due diligence. Potential LPs are invited to conduct due diligence on the GP at the same time, thereby crunching timelines and streamlining the process. One GP was able to complete a multibillion-dollar raise in excess of $5 billion within a short fundraising timeline of a few months by using group due diligence. LPs will also benefit from listening to and learning from the questions, concerns, and insights of other investors. At this time only in-demand GPs are able to exercise this approach.

AVOIDING COMMON MISSTEPS IN DUE DILIGENCE

It can be disheartening to see LPs rely on a boilerplate template for a process as critical as due diligence. Trying to force fit a predetermined process and questionnaire on a complex investment decision reduces the value of discovering uncommon but foreseeable issues that could determine the outcome of the investment during the investment horizon. In addition, overreliance on a fund's track record during due diligence, or at any time during the investment decision, can be highly misleading. As every investment disclosure rightly states, "past performance is not an indicator of future results." LPs should take that disclosure at face value—it is possible that parameters underlying such performance, including AUM, market conditions, and competition for similar deals, may have changed.

Analyzing a track record will inform an LP's judgment about the likelihood and magnitude of replicating results in the future. LPs are also likely to develop a better understanding of the strategy and decide for themselves if a GP and fund is suitable for the investor's portfolio. GPs need to make it easy for LPs to analyze their results. This will help avoid accumulating LPs who will face buyer's remorse and depart at the most inopportune time, or who will impact re-up rates as your fund and strategy is no longer appropriate for them. As a bonus, the sooner LPs decide on unsuitability, the better it is for the GP. They avoid spending time on prospects who are unlikely to commit capital, so they can use their time and resources for those who are more likely to do so.

Many LPs and alternative investment professionals fail to fully comprehend business continuity risks, including key person risk, succession risk, fund termination, and capital return issues. Additionally, for new fund managers, they need to have financial backing to continue operations until they can raise capital and achieve breakeven. That should be part of every due diligence; though it is a rare occurrence, this low probability event has a high impact.

LPs will not allocate capital after a due diligence exercise unless the GP exhibits a comprehensive understanding of the strategy, the team is found to be capable and trustworthy, the infrastructure is robust, and risks are appropriate for the expected returns. It is incumbent on both the GP and the LP to make a sincere effort to understand each other and be completely transparent with information, views, and observations.

GPs should seek feedback from LPs who decide not to commit capital to the fund. By showing sincerity without engaging in egotistic debates, GPs can benefit from learning about the concerns of the LP and attempt to mitigate them wherever possible. The willingness to engage even after the investment fails to materialize enables a GP to build an ongoing and positive engagement with an LP for future allocation and cultivate a positive reference.

CONCLUSION

One effective risk mitigation tool an investor has at their disposal in alternatives is conducting adequate investment and ODD. While some investors adhere to a purely checklist-driven due diligence that fails to uncover hidden issues, astute investors understand due diligence can mitigate investment risks and help foster greater learning about the firm and team. Many managers should change their perception on due diligence as a necessary evil to a productive and constructive examination that can assist them in identifying potential uncompensated risks in operations, strategy, and implementation. In addition, thoughtful management of the due diligence process can limit impact on investment resources. Creative solutions, such as group due diligence, are gaining acceptance from LPs. Despite what form due diligence takes, the process must always be viewed as transparent and thorough.

CHAPTER 13

Marketing Funds Globally and Marketing Global Funds

C apital is fungible, and it flows to the place of greatest return wherever in the world it might be. Risks, regulations, and diversification considerations act as barriers for the free flow of capital. For those accepting capital, the source is secondary to the need for capital. LPs allocate capital to maximize their returns within the constraints of their risk appetite, liquidity needs, and regulatory constraints. Empirical evidence bears testimony to the risk reduction benefit of global diversification. Even for the United States, which enjoys the lowest volatility of returns for any single country (see Figure 13.1), there is value in global diversification as it lowers overall portfolio volatility, irrespective of the higher returns sought by such portfolios (see Figure 13.2).

Yet most LPs are likely to exhibit a preference for their home country (see Figure 13.3). They, like most people, show signs of familiarity bias.[1, 2] LPs are more familiar with the investment options and risks at home. Investing in another country, on the other hand, necessitates learning about a region that might be quite different from their own, with its own peculiar opportunities, risks, regulatory regimes, and systemic issues. Most GPs also could be deterred by the cost of opening a local office abroad. At the minimum, these factors serve as a barrier to optimal exposure, if not a barrier to entry, to foreign investments.

FIGURE 13.1 **Volatility of returns by market**

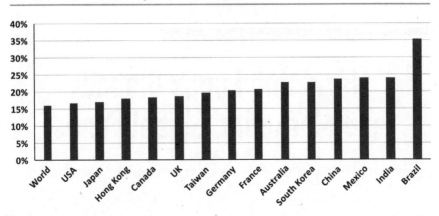

Source: Authors' analysis using InvestSpy Calculator using Performance for country ETFs by iShares

FIGURE 13.2 **Correlation Matrix for Stock Market Returns by Country (February 3, 2012–December 27, 2019)**

	Germany	UK	France	USA	World	Japan	Hong Kong	India	Mexico	Emerging Markets
Germany	1	0.79	0.92	0.56	0.63	0.25	0.37	0.42	0.39	0.52
UK	0.79	1	0.83	0.54	0.61	0.28	0.41	0.41	0.39	0.53
France	0.92	0.83	1	0.58	0.66	0.26	0.37	0.44	0.42	0.55
USA	0.56	0.54	0.58	1	0.96	0.14	0.23	0.55	0.6	0.76
World	0.63	0.61	0.66	0.96	1	0.2	0.31	0.62	0.67	0.86
Japan	0.25	0.28	0.26	0.14	0.2	1	0.47	0.11	0.12	0.17
Hong Kong	0.37	0.41	0.37	0.23	0.31	0.47	1	0.25	0.19	0.43
India	0.42	0.41	0.44	0.55	0.62	0.11	0.25	1	0.52	0.71
Mexico	0.39	0.39	0.42	0.6	0.67	0.12	0.19	0.52	1	0.74
Emerging Markets	0.52	0.53	0.55	0.76	0.86	0.17	0.43	0.71	0.74	1

Source: Authors' analysis using InvestSpy Calculator

Data: Performance for iShares benchmark ETFs by country/market

FIGURE 13.3 **Share of investors' portfolios in issuers' currencies**

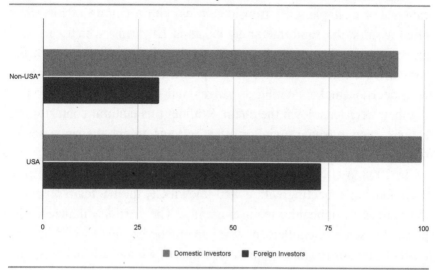

Source: https://www.nber.org/reporter/2021number1/global-capital-allocation-project

The United States is an outlier in that it attracts global investors despite the home-country bias of foreign LPs. America is seen as a safe haven for capital, with its adherence to the rule of law and democratic government with checks and balances, stable financial and banking system, the world's most popular reserve currency, a largely free market economy, and a plethora of investment opportunities. Such a unique confluence of beneficial factors for investors is rarely seen elsewhere in the world.

Other countries, especially developing economies, install high barriers to entry with constraining regulations for foreign investors and capital controls. In this context, how are GPs to seek capital from foreign LPs? It is a burning issue for many, especially emerging GPs who cannot afford to invest their limited marketing budget chasing after low probability targets.

CULTURE MEETS STRATEGY

Understanding culture is a key aspect of global marketing, and marketing alternatives is no exception. When US LPs meet with foreign

GPs, cultural dynamics can be the deciding factor in who gets an allocation. For example, GPs from countries with a culture of hierarchy often assume the same hierarchy exists at LP firms, which can be a grave mistake. They fail to understand that in organizations with flat structures, the decisions are rarely top-down and are often bottom-up, with decision makers acting as judges and enablers instead of pushing their decisions down the chain. Without this cultural context, their actions, even in trivial social or office settings, might alienate a potential investor.

In 2008, a US institutional investor was on a due-diligence trip to Asia. During a meeting with a well-known GP, the US team observed the manager's unhealthy team dynamics. The portfolio manager displayed his sense of entitlement when he grabbed a cup of water that the head of investor relations poured for himself, without any acknowledgment or thank you. Such entitled behavior was the last nail in the coffin, and the US team walked away.

American GPs could fall into the same trap. You will be well served to understand the cultural context of the foreign LP's due-diligence meetings. In the United States, it is a good practice to address the presentation to everyone at the meeting, even if the decision maker is the focus of the pitch. Ensure everyone in the room feels important, because people you might least expect could be pivotal to the decision.

On the other hand, the egalitarian approach might not work in regions where hierarchy is part of the culture. The GP could offend foreign LPs who feel they were not treated with enough respect. In addition to honing their pitch, GPs and marketers also should learn to read the room to see how the rest of the foreign team treats the decision maker. If they are deferential, focus your pitch on that person.

Take another example: punctuality. Some cultures have a more casual attitude toward punctuality, while others see it as a mark of professionalism. Find out what the cultural norm is and adapt. Employing a "buffer time" when investors expect meetings to start and end on time, or vice versa, could end up in disaster. GPs with buffer-time expectations will learn a costly lesson where punctuality is obligatory.

While one can find LPs worldwide, there are regions where investors in global funds tend to congregate. The United States is an obvious one, as it is the largest market for alternatives and has a fairly large number of LPs with holdings abroad, who understand the value and risk of investing in assets overseen by foreign GPs. Canada is another such region, with its huge concentration of large pension and sovereign wealth funds; Europe is a region of LP concentration with its wealth management, and SFOs and MFOs. The Middle East has the world's largest concentration of sovereign wealth funds; Asia is also home to sovereign wealth funds and large family offices. Australia–New Zealand are known for their superannuation funds.

With such opportunities around the globe, where should a GP focus? Since time and resources are practical constraints, prioritize the home market for your marketing efforts, and then regions where there is a high probability of complementary strategy and check size. Only after excelling at these markets—handling operations well and backed by the right resources—should GPs look at other regions. Remember to prioritize the list of LPs you could solicit, provide the right resources to ensure your efforts can succeed, and persist with the effort. It is bound to take more time, effort, and resources than you expected to get a check from even an interested LP—and not every interested prospect turns out to be an investor in the fund.

UPCOMING REGIONS

Some regions are developing their own concentration of LPs in alternatives. Latin America has a large number of pension funds that can take long-term investment risks, since they are catering to a rapidly growing younger demographic. Many developing countries are witnessing a huge explosion of high net worth and ultra-high net worth individuals. Countries where financial system regulations ban foreign investments or make their compliance requirements onerous are also changing their rules due to demand for diversification.

This large market will open up opportunities for global asset managers. However, they tend to favor well-known and larger funds because they are more familiar. For US GPs not in that camp, solutions include partnering with a well-known local name for a cobranded feeder fund, procuring a publicly disclosed investment from a large local investor, establishing a local office (an expensive option that may pay off if it can generate investments and fundraises), or hiring a well-connected and respected placement agent.

MARKETING ACROSS COUNTRIES

Marketing in multiple countries comes with a set of unique challenges, compared to a purely local marketing effort. One primary issue is the plethora of regulations in each region. The lack of common regulations or even a common construct for GPs to follow makes it very difficult to navigate. There is a concerted effort to align some regulations, including a push toward allowing retail investors entry into alternatives, mandating enhanced disclosures, and standardizing reporting requirements by asset class.

While the intention is noble, even the act of sharing information with interested investors in a different region may be subject to local regulations. That means GPs should pay special attention to the legal and regulatory disclosures required by each country. Failure to include obligatory information in the marketing materials can have serious consequences for the manager due to noncompliance.

In addition, GPs must keep on top of the changes in regulations where the fund is being marketed. It is crucial for GPs to ensure necessary filings are made prior to marketing the fund and to seek the advice of counsel to abide by the regulations of each country. The marketing should only start when you can ensure there are processes and procedures to comply with applicable regulations, maintain filings, and fulfill reporting requirements as required in each of the countries where the fund intends to market.

Hiring legal counsel in each geographical area is an impractical task if there will be no real marketing impact from a country. It is better for the fund to prioritize its marketing efforts, as without prioritization the chances of success are limited. Remember that in many countries, even if the investor is interested in committing to the fund, they need permission to invest from their local regulator. This can consume a lot of time, budget, and resources during the fundraise for both private equity and hedge funds.

Importantly, fund performance in a new locale will differ from past experiences. Currency fluctuations can significantly impact an investor with a foreign stake. If there is reporting or tax payment required based on the fund's performance in the local currency, this may have significant unintended consequences as well. For example, in the late 2000s, wealthy Indian-Americans invested in rupee-denominated fixed-income products in India. The currency depreciated significantly during the time and investors experienced a loss, yet investors were forced to pay taxes on their interest income. They had to wait until the investment matured and they were able to repatriate the principal back to the United States to realize the losses, even as they paid phantom taxes in the prior years.

It is not necessarily a GP's responsibility to educate LPs about a region and its associated macroeconomic or investment issues, but the GP could make efforts to do so. Educating an LP about a foreign market might not be a good use of limited time in an introductory meeting.

Does this advice hold true for emerging market GPs? One common mistake they make when pitching to US investors is to spend significant time talking about macro issues. This is painfully evident when GPs from most developing economies start their fund pitch with a country primer (even for large nations like China, India, and Brazil). Managers should send the fund materials in advance, including a section on macroeconomic, regulatory, and other investment-related topics prior to the meeting for LPs to read.

There are exceptions to the rule. For example, it is the LP's first foray into the foreign market, and there is a need to make them feel comfortable with that country's macroeconomic, political, or investment risks. If the LP is sophisticated and interested in speaking with the GP, it is reasonable to assume there is a familiarity with the investment landscape—or they would spend time learning about it before meeting. It is easier to do a quick recap if it becomes evident during talks that the LP could benefit from learning about this market, rather than wasting time up front.

Creating a pipeline of foreign prospects and marketing to them will be more expensive and time-consuming than targeting domestic investors. Different time zones alone make it difficult for timely communication. In addition to cultural barriers, lack of on-the-ground resources and the necessity of travel add to the cost, inefficiency, and time consumed. However, there are some solutions to mitigate some of these issues: hiring a good placement agent may not only be an effective and efficient way to get access to these investors, it might also be a government requirement to use local registered advisors or brokers. Another solution is to aggregate meetings, such as holding country-specific conferences. These events are a great way to meet specific investor types or investors from a specific region.

CONCLUSION

Raising funds in a country other than the country of domicile of the fund is time intensive and represents additional operational and fundraising challenges. These challenges require a thoughtful consideration that leverages internal resources and identifies key service providers who can facilitate the process and ensure a fund is not undertaking undue risks. Given the plethora of investors across the globe, it would be beneficial to prioritize the effort to focus on investors with limited investment friction. Diversifying the investor base will be beneficial to both fund investors and the fund manager in the long run.

CHAPTER 14

Toolkit for Emerging Managers and Difficult Fundraises

S ome fundraises are inherently more difficult than others. Despite your best efforts in planning, execution, and resource allocation, sometimes fundraises require more work than expected or are beleaguered by headwinds that make success difficult. Others become difficult due to missteps in fundraising. Difficult fundraises may include those from emerging managers, first-time funds, country-specific funds from developing nations, a niche strategy with limited investor appeal, and a strategy that does not neatly fit into the asset class buckets as defined by institutional investors, among other issues. In this chapter, we present solutions that would raise the likelihood of success while reducing the fundraising burden.

EMERGING MANAGERS

Fundraising for emerging managers has always been more difficult than for established managers (see Figure 14.1). In 2020,[1] emerging managers received only 21 percent of total capital commitments to private equity managers, even if they made up 52 percent of funds. Moreover, 42 percent of the funds raised less than $100 million but the slice for emerging managers was only 2.4 percent of the total capital raised.

FIGURE 14.1 **Private capital raised ($B) by manager experience**

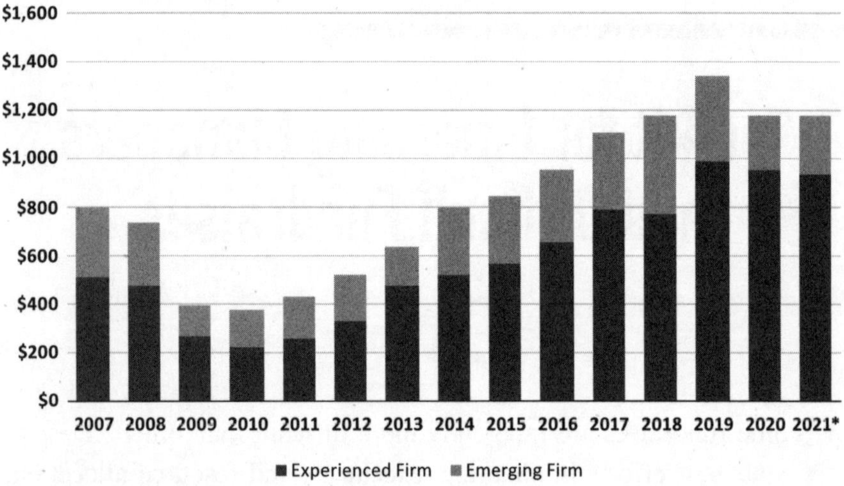

Source: PitchBook Data, Inc.

Emerging managers find it difficult to raise funds for several reasons. It takes time for an investor to get comfortable with a manager—to understand the strategy, get familiar with the investment philosophy, conduct due diligence—and align on such mundane issues as finding time to meet. This should be no different than what an investor is expected to do for established managers but who come with some credibility and brand recognition, which a new manager lacks.

Emerging managers also do not have the track record, established team, or processes that investors can rely on to more quickly earn their confidence. There is investor reluctance, due to possible continuity issues of first-time funds—an inability to maintain a team or raise enough capital to fund operations—even when performance is not an issue. Reliable data on the percent of first-time funds that never come back to market with a successor fund has been elusive, but anecdotally there are sufficient numbers to warrant attention. An investor who has invested the time to conduct research, do due diligence, and build a relationship with a manager will be averse to reinvesting the same amount of effort with a new manager. Emerging managers also can be naïve about high investor expectations when it comes to operations and investor relations. This could be another source of friction for investors that managers should take steps to avoid.

Investor apprehension with emerging managers reflects doubts about their ability to attract enough capital to make the fund viable. No early investor wants to jump into a fund only for the manager to decide to close shop due to capital-raising issues.

So why should investors bother with emerging managers? Empirical evidence shows that first-time funds outperform established funds by a margin of plus 6 percent annually.[2] This is due to multiple beneficial characteristics of emerging or first-time managers—including better investment choices given limited capital to deploy, concentration in less-efficient market segments or securities, not having to manage underperforming assets from previous investments, a management team heavily reliant on superior performance for their compensation, and rationing risk allocation appropriately. Emerging managers and smaller funds tend to outperform larger funds, and that makes them attractive to investors, despite having other challenges. Those very issues do impose a higher fundraising toll on smaller, emerging funds.

In some cases, there are mitigating factors that make the fundraise easier, relatively speaking. This includes a well-established track record, such as in the case of spin-offs from established funds, first-time managers who had been managing portfolios (HFs), or senior investment professionals who can find reasonable attribution of their involvement and value addition to a portfolio. In any case, it is dependent on the previous employer or firm to allow a first-time manager to use track record to attract capital. Should such an arrangement exist, it would also imply explicit or tacit support of the manager by the larger established fund manager, which provides shadow branding and credibility to an emerging manager. While it is impractical to expect such arrangements to be common—after all, the new manager might emerge as a challenger to the established manager—it is possible to construct a track record that finds acceptability among prospective investors.

To do so, collate information from public sources to avoid confidentiality and proprietary information issues. Another option is to get corroboration from "those in the know," including company management, service providers, and others involved in the deal. A third possibility, more acceptable to investors, is to have a dispassionate third party, such as an accounting firm, confirm the claims made in the track record. The industry relies on the norm, "Trust, but verify." Such verification requires considerable investment of time, resources, and goodwill; third-party verification eases the effort and shares the information to all interested parties, moving the ball closer to the goal post.

Last, there is the question of whether the track record is replicable. Success achieved under vastly different conditions at an established firm may not necessarily be possible with a different team. In addition, a lack of supervision, absence of prior relationships, new back-office support, fundraising demands, the need to manage cash flow and other entrepreneurial demands can now crop up as an independent firm. Some solutions include outsourcing infrastructure, partnering with a fund platform that takes care of operations and creates a link to established relationships with providers, finding a seed investor who invests capital to fund the operations for a period of time in return for a stake in the fund or firm, and providing referrals from credible sources regarding the ability of the first-time or emerging manager to deliver results.

Recommended Solutions

Emerging managers should start with the right expectations for a fundraise. It will take longer and be more resource-intensive than you expected. Without properly planning for these two factors, you will be tempted to fight, micromanage, and be disappointed—all of which lead to bad outcomes. No matter how stellar you think a manager's past experience is, it is up to the investor to buy into that claim. Going into a battle without the necessary tools (your track record and evidence of your investment acumen) will lead to undesirable outcomes. While investors understand that track records will be difficult to obtain for first-time managers, you must still find a solution. Do not hide behind the excuse, "My track record is the proprietary information of my previous employer" and expect investors to accept it. Provide as much concrete evidence as possible, even if that means triangulating and recreating the track record from public information and verifiable sources. The exactness matters less than directional—but believable—evidence.

Build strong relationships with the people you work with, so they will champion your efforts even after they leave the firm. At the least, ensure you have not burned bridges with any of them. You can be sure that prospective investors will call them to confirm your claims and track record. Their endorsement can be potentially valuable.

Do not overhype a short track record. This causes potential investors to view everything you present with skepticism and discount your genuine claims. Instead, emphasize processes, consistency of results and repeatability, or reasons for sustainable advantages.

Build your brand. There are many ways to do so—write articles for reputable publications, get speaking engagements, cultivate a social media presence, and develop whitepapers that show thought leadership. Carefully recruit a board of advisors and directors who can help not only open some doors for you but also give your image more credibility from the brands they have already built.

You should invest in a world-class team and a robust infrastructure for operations. If necessary, raise capital to fund the operations of the fund management company before raising capital for your fund. The goal is to remove the points of concern for potential investors. Some can be easily addressed—such as the need to build necessary infrastructure to fully execute and deliver the intended strategy. Investor relations experience—before, during, and after the fundraise—will create a brand for you as much as your performance does. Good investor relations will let your investors give you a chance to prove yourself in tough times.

One common mistake emerging managers make is looking at required documentation as a burden, rather than an opportunity to provide a compelling reason for the investor to invest. Private placement memorandums (PPMs) handled in a perfunctory, "let's get this over with" attitude are less impactful than ones that tell the complete story and does justice to the main characters and plotline—the manager, investment philosophy, strategy, operations, governance, and risk management. PPMs should not just be a list of what needs to be disclosed, but also answer the who, why, how, and what-ifs. It should make a compelling case as to why the investor should consider you for an allocation.

Invest the time and resources to find an anchor investor or seed investor. First-time managers are understandably reluctant to part with a share of the economics, and they are hesitant to invest time, scarce resources, and efforts into a difficult task. However, the ability to secure the backing of a large investor with the necessary economic muscle to back you for the long term, assuming performance meets expectations, will alleviate concerns of other managers about fund viability and reinvestment risk. They can provide you the brand behind the brand.

You can seek emerging manager programs at institutions. Investors tend to follow a leader, such as a respected institutional investor, when the risk is significant. Capital commitment from a recognizable name is a catalyst that can change the direction of the fundraise, but the probability of landing an institution is fairly small for most first-time and emerging managers. That probability increases by targeting programs geared toward accepting emerging managers. Capital from such institutions as well as the learnings from the ensuing due diligence process will be valuable for courting other institutions.

Last, do not forget to focus on the deal pipeline. Investors are going to question you on upcoming deals and your ability to source value-added opportunities for the fund. On the other hand, closing on deals during the fundraise will create strong momentum for the fund. Some LPs have pools of capital dedicated just for the "pregnant primary", i.e., GPs who are typically over 25% invested during the fundraise.

FUND SIZE ISSUES

Emerging managers need patience and good judgment when deciding on the size of successor funds (for private-equity-structured vehicles) or when seeking additional capital for existing funds (for hedge fund vehicles). This is true for all fund managers, but especially so for managers from emerging markets who have multiple thresholds to cross to secure an allocation. Most managers are eager to grow fast and want to rapidly increase the size of their AUM without adequate consideration of market demands and expectations. They may not be able to increase the fund's return if the AUM gets too big, too fast.

This could go against expectations from investors that private equity managers can handle larger investment checks required for bigger funds and have capability to add value to larger portfolio companies at different stages of maturity. Similarly, hedge fund managers also worry about the market impact of large investments and increased illiquidity of a security as their holding size increases in relation to the float available. Investors are, for well-established reasons, reluctant to support larger funds that on average generate a lower investment return compared to smaller funds, ceteris paribus.

Humans are prone to a higher self-assessment of their own performance. Managers are no different when assessing the performance of their funds versus similar funds and other fund managers. In addition, they have an inflated estimate of the need for their strategy in an investor's portfolio allocation. All these can lead to emerging managers being aggressive in shooting for a larger fund or a larger successor fund than what the market would reasonably support. Further, they err by being in the market too early—before there is enough evidence to convince prospective and current investors that the manager is ready to jump to the next level. Of course, there is the lure of larger management fees the manager can collect with a bigger fund.

In some cases, the focus on larger funds does stem from a personal goal of, say, wanting to manage more than $1 billion AUM, having a competitive streak, or searching for validation of their achievement ("my fund is in the same league as the globally recognized funds"). However, these managers must be measured and purposeful in deciding fund size and capacity for long-term success.

There are legitimate reasons for pursuing a larger fund size. In public markets, if there is higher liquidity due to a systemic change (such as regulatory changes in emerging markets that increases the free float), raising individual check sizes can be justified. Another reason could be to avoid co-investments or syndication that sustained previous funds and increased stakes in portfolio companies. There could be a case where larger investments of the manager substantially outperformed smaller investments, and there are identifiable reasons why the larger investment worked relative to the smaller ones. One cannot presume to know all the reasons why a fund size or strategy capacity could be markedly larger; it is important to ensure that reasons presented would be convincing to prospective and current investors. It is not uncommon for some investors to start paring down allocation as the strategy AUM increases, while others wait for the fund to grow larger before they make an allocation.

In addition, as the size increases, the resources available need to be in line with investor expectations. As an example, a larger fund that is allocating to more companies or taking larger stakes that entail more board positions than previously should have the necessary resources to fulfil those obligations faithfully. A hedge fund investing larger checks would have to ensure there are adequate trading resources to ensure minimal market impact.

Investors will invariably ask a first-time GP about future growth expectations and the size of future funds. The GP must be prepared with a thoughtful response. Some managers answer this question by focusing on mapping fund size to check size and the size of teams that can support a deal. For example, on a $1 billion fund, you could have $100 million checks and 10 deals per fund, plus four investment team professionals per deal (a partner, two vice presidents, and another executive).

Should the fundraise fall short of expectations or take too long to complete, one risk is investor skepticism as to why others were not committing to the fund. Managers who have been thoughtful about rightsizing their fund, where there is capital large enough to faithfully execute the strategy, but small enough to maintain a supply gap creates a fear of missing out (FOMO) effect for future funds. It is a great strategy. So it is with hedge funds that have been closed to new capital for a long time only to see the flood gates open when market conditions prompt an increase in capital that can be put to work effectively. Such was the case with some of the largest hedge funds during 2008, which had previously been closed to new capital and encountered overwhelming demand when they reopened during the 2008 financial crisis, as the market fell precipitously.

Unfortunately, this is not the case for many emerging market PE funds, which typically take a longer time to gain traction and fall short of fundraising goals due to their aggressive and unrealistic AUM target. This in turn results in difficulty raising future funds.

One reason for failing to meet fundraising targets is that a strategy or region is too narrowly defined, so investment opportunities are very limited. A manager may be tempted to look for opportunities elsewhere, but there will be consequences for such strategy or geographical drift. If there is a strategy drift, managers should be prepared to explain to and convince investors that the shift was warranted. For example, a regulatory change that restricted the ownership stake in a company could justify the strategy change, because it pushed the fund to increase the number of investments.

Some Recommended Solutions

Rightsizing the fund is a matter of skill, market awareness, judgment, and discipline. Eagerness to grow rapidly might prove detrimental to the manager if not handled well. For hedge funds, there is not a set limit and timeline to meet fundraising goals, unlike private equity. Such private equity time constraints may force the manager to make suboptimal decisions if the pace of the fundraise is in danger of missing the AUM target.

Survey the market. Ask advisors, consultants, LPACs, and potential investors for input about the intended size of the fund. Be willing to push for a higher AUM, but only after understanding the costs and impact on this and future fundraises.

Hedge funds are not immune to size issues. If they become too large for their strategy, investors would see it as an asset grab and redeem at the earliest viable opportunity. The manager may be able to stave that off through superior performance, but it is not uncommon for sophisticated investors to pare down exposure to the manager as AUM increases, even if performance aligns with expectations.

Go to market with a new fund only after the previous fund is nearly fully invested—and the manager has bandwidth to handle it and there is an investor need to diversify across vintages. However, if there is a perceived rush to invest in anticipation of a successor fund, current investors will be disaffected, and prospects will need reassurance. Managers should be transparent about the pace of investing and earn the confidence of current investors, which can be demonstrated by returning capital. The fundraise for a future fund will get off to a flying start only when current investors support it and the re-up rate is strong. Otherwise, it becomes a needless exercise that hampers future fundraises.

It is unwise for emerging managers to rush the launch of another fund without adequate exits, unless there is overwhelming evidence that the portfolio is bound to deliver blockbuster results at the exit, or there is tremendous investor support to launch a new fund for a multitude of other reasons. These include market conditions opening up an opportunity that might disappear if the fund launch is delayed.

INHERENT CONFLICTS: MULTIPRODUCT MANAGERS OR SPONSORED FUNDS

Multiproduct managers are those that handle competing or complementary funds with the same investment ideas, internal and external resources, and oversight. (Successor funds and private equity funds at different stages of their life cycle are excluded in this discussion.) Prospective investors are suspicious of managers that invest simultaneously through multiple funds, believing they are more interested in asset gathering than generating the best performance.

There are also questions about inherent conflicts of interest in allocation of time and investment opportunities among the multiple funds they manage. One concern is that when a fund is falling behind, the manager would focus on the better-performing funds instead of fixing the laggard. Some institutions have unwritten policies against using multifund managers or insist on applying additional scrutiny.

Sponsored funds are those backed by a broader organization such as a bank, asset manager, government, corporation, or other entity that join the investment management process as an investor, service provider, regulator, or market participant. These funds can be perceived as self-dealing, with issues of governance and loyalty that can deter investors. In some cases, the perceived conflict is real, as in the case of bank-sponsored funds that may be obligated to use their backers' advisory, brokerage, corporate banking, and investment banking services. These funds might have gotten a better deal, with a higher level of service, elsewhere.

The fund might also be barred from investing in opportunities involving the sponsor's competitors. With such hurdles, why would the sponsor and investment team even start the fund? The fund team wants to benefit from the broader resources of the sponsor. In turn, the sponsor wants to buy the skills and expertise of the fund team, or they want to partner with the fund team to take advantage of market opportunities that they otherwise could not, due to regulatory or operational constraints. Sponsors also see the value of cross-selling the fund to existing clients, which diversifies revenues and risks while growing the overall size of the business.

ADDRESSING THE CONCERN OF INVESTORS

Multiproduct Managers

Multiproduct managers need to convince investors that each product is adequately staffed and has sufficient resources to succeed with the necessary operational and supervisory oversight. In addition, they should also delineate the guardrails under which they will operate and ensure investor interests are protected. Multiproduct firms are more stable, as they can rely on the diversification of revenues and risk to tide over challenging times, have deeper pockets to attract and retain talent, promote cross-product learnings, benefit from scale economics, strengthen relationships with outside service providers and counterparties, and leverage a common operating platform that reduces costs.

This needs to be demonstrated and substantiated. Yet, there is a corner of the market that simply does not play in this sandbox. It is for the manager to figure out who does not want to participate and to fish in a different part of the ocean to remain efficient and productive during fundraising. It is not in the best interest of the manager to try to change minds; it is more productive to find investors who share your thinking, see value in what you offer, and are willing to back your strategy.

For those who are interested but have concerns about product focus, one course of action is to lead investors through periods of difficulty in one or more funds when others were performing well and show how there was corrective action taken and additional resources allocated to the fund to ensure performance improvement. Show evidence of your actions, not just your intentions.

When dealing with multiple products, some funds will be significantly larger than others; they could even be orders of magnitude bigger. Managers need to enforce mechanisms to ensure each product gets equal priority. This could come through incentive structures for the team, priority terms, or other structural constructs. Consciously avoid structuring funds and fund terms in a manner that pits one strategy against others. Ultimately, it comes to trade-offs for both the manager and the investor. Investors need to ensure their investment is handled and executed according to their expectations. It is the manager's job to convince them of such an outcome.

Sponsored Funds

Sponsors need to use necessary controls to ensure internal dealings are compliant with not only the governing regulations but also with a fiduciary standard. The easiest and most acceptable solution is not to engage in internal dealings at all, such as transactions with the sponsoring parent and its affiliates. However, there could be occasions when these transactions are necessary. If so, these activities should be completely disclosed, and the sponsor should provide a written policy that not only talks about the process to be followed, but also the reasons for such decisions and the assurance that no transaction will be made that would be detrimental to investors.

The sponsoring entity can add value to the fund by mere association. For example, an Asian fund sponsored by a large private equity fund in the United States will benefit from the processes, IP, network, relationships, investor base, and experience of the sponsoring entity. This would help the fund and its portfolio companies to do better than if they were to go on their own. However, if the only contribution of the sponsoring entity is marketing acumen, it leads to questions of whether the relationship will last long term once the local team has built its own brand and can raise its own capital. The investing team would not want to unnecessarily give up economics to sponsors—something most investors also support to ensure a stable and sustainable team with very little disenchantment with the sponsor.

Over time, the sponsor and the local team may split up. There are many reasons why, and much of it is centered around control, value addition, and share of economics. A good example is the relationship between Westbridge Capital and Sequoia, the global venture capital firm.[3] Westbridge merged with Sequoia in 2006 after it had already raised and invested two funds. The merged entity, Sequoia India, raised five funds and rapidly scaled up both AUM and the team. However, six years after the merger, the original Westbridge team left Sequoia India to restart Westbridge Capital, this time to focus primarily on public market investing. Sequoia India continues to operate without the partners who left.

Governance of the fund could also become an issue. Does the sponsoring entity exert undue control over the fund that in turn relegates the interests of other investors? Managers need to ensure policies and procedures are not only fair but also provide for other investors to have reasonable oversight as they steward their allocation with the manager.

FUNDRAISING AMID MANAGEMENT CHANGE, SUCCESSION, OR OTHER TRANSITIONS

Fundraising during a transition, planned or unplanned among senior members of the team, can be a real challenge for most marketers, for good reason. That is why cordial and mutually acceptable transitions at most funds happen after the fundraise, with succession discussions occurring beforehand. Investors are not just underwriting the strategy, but also expect the team to faithfully execute the strategy and sustain the firm's accomplishments. When there is a change in the team, especially at the senior levels, questions about stability, continuity, and ability will arise—all of which can be serious obstacles for a fundraise. These hurdles decelerate momentum, invite skepticism and scrutiny, lengthen the process, and raise costs.

As the alternatives industry continues to mature, succession plans are becoming increasingly important especially as leadership at asset management firms enter their twilight years. Firms must communicate their succession plans with clarity and confidence prior to and during the fundraise, and they must do so as early as possible.

Focus on Development

Succession is not just about transitions occurring over a year or two; it is about strong development of the next generation of leaders throughout a firm, development of a strong culture based upon ownership, and equitable sharing of economics broadly across market cycles. This is a long-term game with effective transitions taking place over the life of multiple funds, and these plans are an important aspect of the success of any firm.

Start Early

In the years leading up to a fundraise where planned succession might take place, the partnership must map out the terms of succession over multiple funds with respective legal counsel in a formal memorandum of understanding (MOU) or legal document. You cannot go into a fundraise with any ambiguity. LPs will speak directly with you about it during their onsite due diligence sessions and will ask for clarity on the topic in RFPs and DDQs. Fund managers push CEOs of their respective portfolio companies to have clear succession plans in place, but many times do not focus on their own firm's succession plans.

Communicate Clarity of Terms

With the support of trained legal counsel, succession management must be clearly mapped out around the terms of ownership, management, and governance and communicated to the broad LP community and internally within the firm. At one private equity firm where the cofounders were well beyond retirement age, the succession terms around economics and governance among the executive team and cofounders for the next two funds were succinctly mapped out in one simple slide in the investor presentation for surprised LPs to see. This refreshingly transparent slide resonated well with LPs who were initially concerned about succession, but now could clearly see metrics around ownership, carry, and governance (number of seats on board, IC, and compensation committees) for the upcoming and then subsequent fund. They could see key decisions were to be made by the majority of votes, with appropriate minority protections, and how the CEO was responsible for day-to-day operational activities and when governance rights would cease for the founders.

Manage the Future and Control the Unexpected

Change and transition can be difficult. Retiring leaders often have their identity centered around their firms. Many have their names on the door and have built up their businesses over many decades. For them it can be hard to let go, even for these illustrious and dynamic leaders fast approaching retirement. Egos, personalities, and economics have strong influences on seamless succession and the unexpected can happen. In one case, despite mapping out succession, the founders nevertheless could not let go, exercised a loophole in the MOU, and the partnership fell apart a few weeks before the first close on a major fundraise—with the new executive leadership departing the firm.

CONCLUSION

Every fundraise is challenging in its own way. However, when some situations make it particularly difficult to fundraise, trying to figure out solutions in the middle of a frantic period is not practical. In most cases, lack of self-assessment to prepare for potential investor questions and concerns leads to unfavorable outcomes. Most marketers and fund managers who have successfully traversed difficult fundraising terrain often prepare themselves for the challenge much like a marathoner conditions themselves for a long race. Elements of the toolkit in this chapter can be an ideal starting point for managers and marketers to structure their response to their own situation to improve their chances for success. However, the implementation of any plan is dependent on organizational and investor buy-in. Fund managers would see positive outcomes when the communication effort is in line with the situation being addressed.

OTHER CONSIDERATIONS

CHAPTER 15

Technology in Alternatives Marketing

We live in a world where technology permeates every moment of the day and the alternatives world is no different. Several factors drive the use of technology in marketing alternatives: regulatory requirements to safeguard investors and ensure financial system stability, business efficiency, and investor demand. Traditionally, GPs have viewed technology as a cost center, but it is increasingly seen as a competitive advantage. Digitally savvy investment managers are already leveraging technology to change the competitive field.

Among alternatives, hedge funds have been the earliest adopters of technology. Some considered it part of their strategy, and others thought it led to better execution. Private equity and especially venture firms (even the ones who exclusively invest in technology companies) have been more reluctant and guarded. They prefer to rely on personal and professional relationships for deal flow, and the GPs depend on intuition to identify opportunities and add value to their portfolio companies.

While many private equity firms do promote tech adoption as a part of the value proposition for their investments, they themselves are restrained in this area. Secondaries funds, FoFs, and FoHFs show greater acceptance, using data analytics to identify the right opportunities before expending resources and effort to chase a deal.

Technology is becoming increasingly important for alternative funds. It enables a mobile and remote workforce, and improves operational efficiency (e.g., through the use of robotic process automation

[RPA]). Technology can harness data analytics to make better decisions and enhances investor communication and transparency through greater efficiency and a better user experience. It offers protections against cyberattacks and cybercrime, and protects confidential and proprietary information.

WHAT TECHNOLOGY SOLVES FOR THE MANAGER

One of the lasting effects of the Covid-19 pandemic on the industry is the wider acceptance of remote work by alternatives firms. This means firms now have to increase their focus on cybersecurity, privacy protection, data storage, and retention processes. Gone are the days when firms retained stacks of signed documentation for each investor. Now, contracts are completed online, speeding up the process and helping prevent errors from manual entries. The growing acceptance of videoconferencing has, at least partially, supplanted face-to-face communication. This lessens the need for business travel and enables more investor meetings per day—a benefit during fundraises and due diligence—and even accommodates meetings where LPs from different locations can participate.

Moving business interactions online saves money, is less stressful for managers, and leads to more involved interaction. Team members can opt to make short appearances, which was not possible in the old "traveling salesperson" model. Even for LPs, the availability of videoconferencing for in-person events is a boon. It allows some to "join in" or "listen in" when in-person attendance is not possible or practical. Another concept gaining traction is virtual due diligence. While it is too early to say this will be a permanent change in a post-pandemic world, it allows on-site meetings to be more focused and shorter. In-person interactions can deal with the most pressing issues, since routine questions have been answered earlier—virtually. The industry has largely accepted relationships cultivated online between LPs and GPs, rather than meeting in person or by phone.

An increasingly flexible workforce using mobile devices does risk greater security breaches—anywhere from an improperly secured home network to a transit hotspot to an attack on a mobile device at a coffee shop. However, there are further benefits for GPs and for LPs. GPs can parse actionable insights from the vast amounts of data available to make improved investment decisions and also to better know their investors. Technology can offer LPs a well-organized and easily navigable website to obtain all the information they need about their investment in the fund, including financial reports such as statements, tax records, and performance reports; manager communication such as newsletters, updates, portfolio performance, and capital calls; and a comprehensive data room to share confidential information.

SOCIAL MEDIA AND THE GROUP OF ONE

A social media presence is becoming a necessity. Some venture capitalists use social media to build an image of thought leadership and accessibility to attract founders seeking capital from the "right kind of venture capitalists," and investors who are looking for venture capitalists with an edge in attracting deal flow. Social media lets potential LPs get to know a manager's thought process and actions, while preserving the freedom to choose when and if they will interact with the GP.

While digitizing interactions is efficient, it does not have to be impersonal. Take the case of credit card issuer Capital One: the company changed the way card issuers looked at consumers by segmenting them into buckets that warranted differentiated terms, rather than applying a one-size-fits-all strategy—"mass customization." Today, technology allows customization for a "group of one." Any customer engagement (email, web, mail, account management, analytics, etc.) can be personalized to make it appear to be a bespoke interaction, as opposed to impersonal forms. As simple as it sounds, a personalized experience can make a client feel special. Some firms have deployed even more advanced technology to respond to things like RFPs, routine investor requests, DDQ questions, and even to update information in DDQ packets periodically.

User experience is being changed by technology especially in marketing and investor relations. We learned of funds that spent significant time and money building a system for investor communication and information-sharing, only to find out that investors were not using it; they preferred to reach out to the team for information. The interface was not easy to navigate, which was a hurdle for less tech-savvy investors. Firms should focus on ease of use first, rather than showing off the system.

ONE VIEW OF THE INVESTOR

Disparate systems used across the organization can mean information about the investor is siloed. Sales CRM systems disconnected from the customer access platforms translate to an incomplete understanding of the LP's experience with the fund. For example, has performance been above the relevant benchmarks since the LP's investment? Are there any issues still outstanding? Have there been customer complaints? GPs who have taken an integrative approach to get one view of the LP do benefit. Such single-point solutions can enable on-demand financial reporting and enhanced transparency—both of which are highly valued and demanded by LPs.

ARTIFICIAL INTELLIGENCE AND MACHINE LEARNING

In alternatives, artificial intelligence is transforming the landscape. It has become essential to the processing of the massive amounts of data crunched to predict discontinuities in pricing, forecast price paths, estimate supply and demand situations, optimize trading strategies by approximating market impact of trades, and improve execution efficiency (e.g., reducing unfilled trades).

There is already a crop of hedge funds that rely purely on AI platforms and machine learning algorithms. While technology has long given an edge to some of the largest funds, the game changer is the ability of these new systems to autonomously make changes to their algorithms without human intervention. However, the black-box nature of these AI-enabled strategies run against the expectations of investors, who do not have the same level of trust in such systems. Developers cannot explain what underlying factors compelled the AI-system to act the way it did and why it chose a certain path. This is where the evolution of Explainable AI, or systems in which the solutions can be explained to others, has found favor in investing and especially in alternatives.

TECHNOLOGY AND EFFICIENCY

Alternatives is a high-margin business, but that margin is shrinking as investors push for lower investment management costs. Technology is often used to lower costs without impacting performance. Operations is where efficiencies are most easily realized, by automating repetitive processes such as trade reconciliation. Digital technologies take it a step further: they create bespoke experiences for the LP while cutting costs.

Cost overruns and missed timelines are the most common complaints about implementing new technology solutions at alternatives firms. A large hedge fund invested more than $6 million over 18 months redesigning its entire IT infrastructure, only to abandon the project due to complexity and emergence of newer technologies.

Buying or building a technology platform is not the only solution. GPs need to develop new skill sets to derive the value offered by the technology and to create differentiation. An example of the inefficiency of these platforms is when GPs purchase databases of prospects from multiple sources and blanket them with solicitations. We have had discussions with marketers who rue an unproductive "list" that resulted in multiple calls without any real interest. This wastes resources and creates a negative brand image. Instead, it is more productive to analyze the database first, identifying prospects by looking at their prior investments in the asset class, and seeing whether they espouse a strategy similar to the GP's fund, prospect's asset size, and check size.

Another issue is low participation, dooming the solution. If information is not updated in the CRM technology after each interaction with an investor, it defeats the purpose of having a central repository of investor information and wastes the money spent.

One of the biggest obstacles to technology adoption is the existence of legacy systems that are difficult to manage and cause user inertia. These often create migration bottlenecks due to the complexity of the systems and the multiple interlinkages with other legacy systems. Cost of migration could range from tens of thousands to millions of dollars. Timelines even for simple migration takes several months of planning, installation, quality assurance, user acceptance testing, user training, migration, and post-migration problem-solving and support. Cloud migration is enabling many firms to cut their connection with legacy systems that had bogged down technology adoption, since it had enabled a piecemeal rather than an all-in-one-shot approach.

ROLE OF TECHNOLOGY IN MARKETING ALTERNATIVES

At a very basic level, the role of technology is to enable a more efficient and effective fundraising process. Yet, no amount of efficiency at prospecting is going to be useful if it does not turn into an allocation, and an initial allocation will not help build a lasting franchise if investors' expectations are not met. Technology's role is to meet investor expectations in how the fund is operated. For the GP, tech enables the fund to find LPs and convince them to allocate capital.

For most of the authors' careers, fundraising technology started and ended with a spreadsheet and an office productivity software bundle. With the adoption of advanced analytics and targeting tools, technology is taking fundraising to the next level. The primary technology used in fundraising is basic office software and a CRM system, which track data about investors and prospects, contains a repository of investor reports and performance benchmarks, holds consolidated data of investor attributes and experiences, offers data analytics tools, and enables scheduling platforms.

Some funds use marketing platforms with integrated marketing efficiency analytics to address a broader marketing effort. This could include outsourced marketing services that integrate into the firm's marketing outreach by combing broad database marketing with client-specific targeting (by investor type, region, etc.). These may include social media, LinkedIn or direct marketing solicitations to generate initial interest in the fund prior to actual sales. The first step for any GP who has procured a database of prospects is to analyze the information for accuracy and to identify prospects who will most likely be interested in the product. This process ranges from simple human judgment to advanced analytics and AI techniques for filtering and prioritizing leads.

Once an investor is interested, they will need access to confidential information and the opportunity to review and understand the fund's processes and manager's abilities. A good practice is to share such information using a secured system called a data room, which lets users control access to information, tracks NDAs, and reports who was given access to the data.

LPs want to ensure that the technology infrastructure can support the full execution of the intended strategy while being efficient and accurate. This includes the ability to communicate with systems used by service providers outside an organization. They also want to ensure their data is safe and has the necessary information to monitor the GP and investment performance. The systems shared with the LP may include trading platforms, trade reconciliation systems, ledgers, data analysis systems, information security, access controls, and cybersecurity.

At a minimum, marketers should educate themselves about the firm's technologies and be able to present that information to prospective LPs, including:

- Overall IT infrastructure, Information security
- Regulatory compliance, monitoring, and archival systems
- Redundant systems
- Backup and data retrieval processes and systems

- Intersystem connectivity and integration (or the lack thereof)
- Voice and internet access
- Information access control and tracking
- Secure communication and contact management
- Use of any innovative, emerging, and evolving technologies and trends: big data, robotic process automation, blockchain, AI, social media, machine learning, edge computing, cognitive computing, and others

Once an LP has decided to make an allocation, the documentation can be done entirely through electronic signature and workflow/process flow systems. These systems reduce errors, make retrieval of information easier, and reduce the regulatory compliance burden for updating information at regular intervals as mandated.

After the LP is accepted into a fund, investor relations steps in with communication and reporting. In addition to CRM systems tracking all investor touch points, there should be an effective communication platform in place that shares information with LPs. This may be a secure access platform that functions as a single source repository for all investor information, including financial statements, investor reports (including on-demand statements and reports), and investor communication.

CONCLUSION

Typically, a manager's objectives can be accomplished with a reasonable technology investment and without undue loss of efficiency or continuous oversight. Technology success requires an adherence to process. A disciplined approach yields better results than investing in a technology that does not find acceptance and use within the organization. However, despite all the advancements in technology, marketing alternatives remains at its heart a human endeavor.

CHAPTER 16

Legal and Regulatory

The fund counsel, either an internal official or an external hire, is one of the most important service providers for a fund, and especially for a new fund. They are involved with the drafting and finalizing of offering documents and negotiating on behalf of the fund with LPs who want special terms. Given the complexity of fund structures and their regulation by the SEC or state regulators, it is advisable to hire counsel with relevant industry experience. The counsel needs to understand legal and regulatory issues in key jurisdictions and they also need to know the investor landscape, and their concerns and sensitivities to help the fund negotiate effectively for a win-win solution.

A fund should focus on their service providers as much as the internal team. A team with a strong platform for operations, managed by experienced and competent staff and built for growth, is a necessity; LPs do not want to commit to managers whose strategy may be compelling but lack back-office capabilities. Important elements of those capabilities include strong legal processes, documentation, and operations. Imagine presenting documents to potential LPs where they question your adherence to regulatory requirements. Despite how favorable the LP was until that moment, they will have second thoughts, or worse, decide not to invest.

A law firm that has experience serving multiple funds for years will not only provide legal and regulatory advice, they are also another window into your competition, industry conditions, and best practices. They can help GPs or fund sponsors decide on the terms of the fund in line with market expectations for that asset class. This is critical because the economics of the fund is at stake—ask for too little, and your fund will not make enough money to attract necessary talent; ask for too much and the LPs will not take you seriously. It is a rarity for firms to successfully raise capital when their terms are not in line with the market.

A strong legal team with a good understanding of the LP landscape and in-depth knowledge of investor groups will have valuable experience dealing with demands from potential investors—and will help a GP sort out what is possible, what is without precedent and needs special scrutiny, and what is a potential trade-off or alternative solution that can be acceptable to the LP. A legal firm with experience will also be a source of referrals and references to other providers such as fund administrators, accountants, prime brokers, and custodians.

The primary roles of an alternatives fund counsel is to fully own or assist the fund managers on various matters, including:

1. **Formation of materials and structures**
   - Draft, develop, and maintain the fund's offering documents
   - Review pitchbook and other marketing materials
   - Review and confirm fund as well as individual track records
   - Review distribution and placement agent agreements
   - Fulfill regulatory filings such as broker-dealer or investment advisor filings, and advise on licensing requirements for the firm and its employees
   - Work with tax counsel to ensure the structure of firm and all its funds are compliant and tax-efficient

2. **Facilitate compliance and governance**
   - Ensure compliance with regulatory and legal requirements relating to marketing, investor relations (IR), investing activities, and fund management
   - Provide timely responses to regulatory queries, and represent the firm during regulatory examinations
   - Monitor and identify regulatory changes that impact the firm's business or its relationships
   - Create a corporate governance structure for the firm and all related entities

- Find other counsel to address ancillary issues such as employment, real estate, taxation, trade disputes, litigation
- Draft policies for know your client (KYC) and other regulatory issues, if they are also responsible for compliance

3. Conduct effective negotiations

- Review and negotiate terms and side-letter agreements with investors
- Create, review, and negotiate transaction documents, including term sheets, NDA/confidentiality, LOIs, ancillary agreements, contracts, and settlements
- Negotiate counterparty terms such as ISDAs, purchase agreements, trading terms, service-level agreements, and commitments
- Negotiate transactional terms with investee companies or bearers on issues such as restructurings, amendments, credit, and bankruptcy options
- Negotiate terms with vendors, prime brokers, clearinghouses, and all other service providers
- Address ad-hoc investor issues such as transfers of interest, missed capital calls, regulatory complaints, and compliance with agreed-upon side letters

In addition to legal qualifications, fund attorneys are expected to have in-depth knowledge of securities laws and regulations applicable to alternative fund managers. This includes expertise in matters related to private fund offerings, which encompasses all alternatives funds, like the Investment Company Act of 1940, Regulation D, and the Securities Act of 1933. Fund counsels can be expected to review, analyze, structure, negotiate, approve, litigate, and verify the legal validity of documents and business operations of the fund.

Beyond their role in providing legal protection to the fund, counsels can also act as champions of the fund. They can be sources of referral, deal flow, introductions, and information. Fund counsels well versed in the art of negotiations may be the ones who can protect your interests and create momentum for you without antagonizing the other party—be it a potential investor, vendor, regulator, or a counterparty.

Picking the fund counsel need not be tricky. In a situation where familiarity with regulations and their interpretations matter, counsels with experience working in similar situations is important. In addition to having the right experience, counsel must also be committed and available when needed, which will almost certainly be unpredictable. Furthermore, it is important for investors to ensure there is access to additional expertise in related areas within the law firm. Remember that good legal advice is not cheap; for emerging managers tempted to minimize legal costs now, the price of poor legal protection may be too high to pay later on.

CONCLUSION

Your law firm should have processes in place to ensure they are current on regulatory changes, while having the necessary experience to understand which direction interpretations will lean. The fund counsel typically becomes the primary source of legal advice for the fund, and it helps if a manager works with a firm that has relationships in countries and jurisdictions where the manager would have a presence.

CHAPTER 17

Fund Success
Through Diversity

D iversity is pivotal to a fund's long-term success. It can serve a key role in fundraising, in addition to fostering an inclusive workplace. GPs should prioritize employing a team whose members vary in terms of ethnicity, gender, religion, physical ability, and sexual orientation. Other dimensions of diversity include ownership, decision-making, and how the manager's economics are shared across these groups.

LPs are leading the way in promoting diversity in the alternatives investment industry, and GPs are beginning to follow suit. Why do LPs and GPs care? In the case of LPs, their stakeholders care, they gain access to unique management teams and deal flow, and diversity of views encourages better judgment and decision-making. GPs care not only because LPs care but also because younger generations of employees care and the war for talent is intense.

The alternatives industry has matured in the past 25 years. Exponential growth has been seen in a variety of strategies. Yet the industry has not progressed as much when it comes to diversity among fund managers—both as owners of asset management firms and as investment and operations staff. For example, as of 2019, only 17.9 percent of the employees in private equity funds globally were women, even though they fill 53 percent of IR positions and comprise 34 percent of IR leaders.[1] In the case of emerging managers, the asset class has historically been less diverse. Caught at the right point, the right ones actually outperform the median.

This lack of diversity extends beyond alternatives. It is a phenomenon observed across asset classes in the investment management industry. A 2021 report by Knight Foundation showed only 6.1 percent of US asset management firms were owned by minorities, even though they comprised 39.9 percent of the population.[2] The disparity is even more pronounced when considering AUM managed by minorities is a mere 0.7 percent. Minority managers are underrepresented and less successful at gathering AUM compared to their nonminority counterparts. Women fare worse. They are 50.8 percent of the population but own only 6.1 percent of firms and manage only 0.7 percent of AUM. These figures could be overly generous. Not all firms reporting as minority- or women-owned are 100 percent owned by them. However, alternatives managed to fare better than mutual funds where only 0.4 percent of AUM are managed by minorities and only 0.6 percent of AUM are managed by women.

What are the reasons why we are not already more diverse? Historically, limited diversity at the senior leadership levels and a challenging environment recruiting diverse talent has been a problem. Additionally, there is greater diversity at junior levels, which indicates they are not being appropriately retained, promoted, or mentored. Venture capital tends to have higher diversity than buyouts. This is partly because there are more smaller managers and also because venture managers value a wider range of backgrounds (e.g., operating, strategy) than the traditional private equity industry does, which looks for a more conventional background.

Yet there is no difference in performance from minority or female managers across asset classes, including alternatives. A common excuse about the lack of diversity is a scarcity of talent. This argument rings hollow. A large population of minorities, women, and other underrepresented groups have received the same education as nonminorities and worked at the same firms as the experts of the investment management industry.

We are in an age where society is pushing for change: inequality and lack of diversity are not sustainable. Even if it could be, it should not be acceptable. Asset allocators represent society, especially for pensions where the beneficiaries reflect the population at large and their members are demanding inclusion and diversity. Institutions are representatives of societal wealth and scrutinize fund managers for a lack of diversity in their ranks. Students are encouraging universities to make their endowment investments as equitable and diverse as their admissions.

In some instances, such as in venture capital, diversity improves performance.[3] A diverse group of investing partners have better performance than ones with shared ethnicity. The success rate for IPOs and acquisitions improves from 26 percent to 32 percent for a diverse group. In 2021, hedge funds with minorities and women in the management teams returned 29.6 and 21.6 percent, compared to the nondiversified hedge fund manager returns of 12.7 percent for the one-year period ending September 2021.[4]

Diversity in ranks is a selling proposition for managers. Some state laws require institutions like the University of California to report on its diversity strategy annually. Many public pensions and universities have active allocations to minority fund managers. Duke University publishes a report on diversity of its external investments,[5] while the Commonfund OCIO has a diversity office to engage in manager selection. For a fund manager, especially an emerging fund manager or a midsize fund manager, diversity might be the difference that can help land a desirable LP, which in turn propels the growth of the fund. Some engage in the Rooney rule of manager selection.[6] Managers are looking for ways to increase their team's diversity through initiatives such as talent development, opening up the recruitment funnel to a larger set of candidates and nontraditional profiles, and focused hiring that targets under-represented populations.

Diversity speaks to management's willingness to seek out a variety of perspectives and opinions necessary for a well-informed decision. LPs are no longer content with a nominal diversity face in the room. They want the person to have a say and be a real part of the investment process. They want to ensure that the firm is invested in the people who represent the broader population and are provided the opportunity to thrive.

As demographics change in the United States and other countries, an all-male cohort is not seen as an affirmation of investment prowess but a serious deficit in keeping up with the times. Lack of diversity ushers in the potential for a blind spot brought on by not understanding demographic shifts.

The alternatives industry should take steps to improve its track record in diversity. For example, firms could set up formal internal teams or structures with senior management participation to focus on the diversity discussion with appropriate metrics in place. Throughout the deal life cycle, from sourcing to execution, diversity discussions and metrics should be an integral part of the process.

Within the private equity portfolio companies, leaders should consider diversity strategies at the board level and across management teams. Such endeavors could lead to improved culture and performance, enhancing value creation. Additionally, an honest assessment of structural racism from corporate policies across the portfolio could be beneficial.

CONCLUSION

Overall, diversity is a long-term win-win for all stakeholders in the alternative industry. Displacement of entrenched mindsets and interests is difficult to overcome, but can reap positive dividends to those who persevere on the path least trodden upon.

CHAPTER 18

Advice for Aspiring Marketers

We both began our careers in marketing during the boom that preceded the financial crisis in 2008. Since then, we have each spent more than 15 years, much of our professional careers, trying to understand the art of marketing alternatives. We continue to learn more each day. Oftentimes, the experience was frustrating, having committed a mistake that in hindsight seemed entirely avoidable. In some instances, we spent too much time with an LP who was never going to commit, and other times we did not spend enough. We often had the benefit of learning from someone who had a better understanding of the process and possessed superior marketing skills than we did when we were learning the ropes. That helped us enjoy the sweet taste of success and achievement. But we can with faith say, it has been a fulfilling experience. While our experiences may not be true for everyone, we are certain they would not be unique.

We each came into marketing alternatives from different paths. One was steeped in numbers, a hard-core analyst whose career in marketing alternatives was an "accident," stepping into the role when there was a need due to a departure on the team. The other was a people-person, a management consultant who had built a phenomenal Rolodex and was encouraged to translate those relationships into the world of alternatives. This is reflective of the industry where marketing professionals come from all sorts of backgrounds: some are immersed in investment literature and experience, while others enter without any investing know how. Yet most find their own way to thrive in an industry that provides valuable opportunities.

Although backgrounds differ, the industry is much kinder to the ones with the "right pedigree"—where you went to school, who you went to school with, where you worked, and who is in your network. Pedigree helps open doors to opportunities. Your Rolodex or the ability to build one may be the minimum qualification for a marketing role. However, a lack of pedigree is not a disqualifier. Educational qualifications matter less as long as you can gain an intrinsic knowledge of the fund, the markets, and investors and are able to conduct yourself in a manner that empowers you to build strong relationships with prospective investors.

About the Job

Socializing and meeting people may be the glamorous part of the job, but very few succeed that way. A more certain path to success is following a thoughtful and disciplined process. Blanketing the potential market does not work well in marketing alternatives. You only end up tarnishing the brand.

You will get more rejections than you expected, even if you know that your offering is well suited for a prospect. You need patience and perseverance to find the right investor at the right time. Each refusal is also an opportunity to learn what could be done better—by you and your fund/ firm. By seeking feedback, whether the decision is favorable or not, you will find a way to learn how to do it better the next time. Your sincerity in learning the investors' perspective might build better relationships with ones who provide meaningful feedback. Fundraising is a marathon. Not every meeting will lead to a conversion. Not everyone who shows interest will sign a check. This results in the process always taking longer than either you or the LP would expect or hope for. Finding the reasons for an LP's reluctance to commit capital may pave the path to a "Yes."

Not every lead may be worth pursuing. Time spent on qualifying leads is a great ROI. In the first few months as an alternatives fundraiser, Hemali's manager reiterated, "You have hundreds of relationships and can keep on building new ones. But focus on your top 10 targets at any given time."

Cold-calling has a very low success rate. Not calling is worse. The choice is not difficult. You cannot be afraid of failure or not being heard.

At the same time, embrace the fact that we are in a trust-based business where people commit capital to those who they are familiar with and respect. Most people in the industry are no more than three degrees of separation away. Find ways to turn a potential cold call into a warm introduction. If nothing else, you will have an enjoyable conversation.

Consistency is more important than bursts of intensity in investor relations. Out of sight is usually out of mind, and it takes a lot to be truly back on the radar.

Ideally, do not join a firm in the middle of their fundraise. Building relationships takes time, but time is the biggest constraint during a fundraise. As a newcomer to the firm, you want to make a good first impression to help you succeed, but the odds are stacked against you. There is intense pressure to deliver results without being able to spend the time to fully learn about the firm and the fund. Time is limited from others on the team to share their knowledge and advice with you.

On Attitude, Personality, and Character

If you cannot deal with rejection, you will be better off finding a new career. Rejections and disappointments are common, and one needs to learn to compartmentalize and not bring them home. When things are not going well during a fundraise, eagerness to sell becomes an obstacle. But desperation to sell is a deal killer. You will see better success by being balanced and secure in your approach.

No matter what your plans are, marketing ultimately is a team sport. Ensure all players on the team know their roles and what is expected of them. Not all fundraisers will be gifted at marketing. It is your responsibility to listen to your team, get their buy-in, and coach them in areas of marketing where they may need help. At the same time learn from your partners what you do not know about the business. LPs do not expect you to be an expert at everything, but they certainly want you to be aware of and reasonably educated about the firm, people, strategy, and the market, in general.

Do not ever compromise on principles, fiduciary responsibilities, and ethics. LPs respect transparency, which is critical to maintaining trust. Shortcuts are enticing and might appear harmless while getting a deal done, but always play by the book. Do not idly sit by if you see anything out of the ordinary. Seek counsel. Any digression will not just impact your career and personal reputation, it may also result in legal consequences. Walk away if you cannot convince people to do the right thing.

On Relationships

Seek a mentor and build a circle of friends within the fundraising community. It is quite likely someone has dealt with the issues you are facing and can provide guidance. Investors are reasonable and thoughtful. The toughest investors can also be your greatest teachers and cheerleaders.

Good investor relations is not about responding after the investor reaches out to you, but anticipating investor needs and reaching out to them proactively. When the time comes for a decision, your service level will play a role. How you deliver on expectations may favorably bias them toward a re-up or a new allocation.

CONCLUSION

Fund performance and capital formation (investor relations and fundraising) are two important factors that determine an investor's experience and disposition toward a fund manager. The IR and fundraising professionals becomes the face of the firm to the investor. Therefore, firms strive to find the right people for these critical roles to ensure their own long-term success. While there is no single way to succeed in these roles, certain elements increase the probability of success: process orientation, right attitude and personality, and an affinity for building relationships. Success in marketing alternatives requires you to work hard consistently, develop the right skills, and cultivate the right attitude. The good news is that, other than a bit of luck that can be helpful, the rest are within the marketer's control.

APPENDIX

SAMPLE DATA ROOM (PRIVATE EQUITY)

Data rooms are essential technology tools that enable managers to share information in a confidential manner with prospective investors. Data rooms, with strong access controls, allow for sharing of confidential or proprietary information that would be necessary to convince an LP to allocate capital while simultaneously protecting them from wide dissemination or misuse. Some of the commonly included documents in a private equity data room are listed in the following table. While most of the elements are common between the two, there are some differences. If specific information is requested by more than one investor, we err on the side of adding it to the data room as a show of transparency to investors.

Fund Documents	• Fund PPM and supplements • Pitchbook • DDQ • Limited partnership agreement • Subscription agreement and packet • Management agreement • Fund structure
Registration and Legal	• Registration documents • Form ADV • Legal and tax opinions (if needed) • Insurance
Team	• Track record and attribution analysis • Audited financials and PPMs of previous funds • Organizational structure, biographies, and contact information • Senior advisors and their biographies • Redacted deals sheet by partner • Compensation agreements • References
Investment Strategy and Process	• Investment strategy • Deal flow log, pipeline (including passed deals) • Case studies and investment memos • Exit decisions and memos • Portfolio due diligence checklist/report • Investment committee notes • Value addition (100-day plans, etc.)
Policies	• Valuation • Responsible investing • Portfolio monitoring and engagement, internal dashboard • Portfolio company reporting requirements
Manuals	• Investment manual • Compliance—insider trading, AML, KYC • Information security • Data collection and privacy
Other	• Valuation and financials of unrealized portfolio • Distribution waterfall • Sample capital call notice • Sample capital distribution notice • Sample investor newsletters and communication • Firm infrastructure • IT infrastructure • Evidence of ILPA compliance • External and internal market reports

SAMPLE DATA ROOM (HEDGE FUNDS)

The data room for hedge funds are similar to private equity funds, but some strategy-specific elements (such as long and short attribution for long-short hedge funds) are required for completeness.

Fund Documents	• Fund OM/PPM and supplements • Pitchbook • DDQ • Limited partnership agreement • Subscription agreement and packet • Management agreement • Fund structure
Registration and Legal	• Registration documents • Form ADV • Legal and tax opinions (if needed) • Insurance
Team	• Track record, including short and long attribution • Individual attribution (as appropriate for the strategy) • Audited financials for previous years • Organizational structure and biographies • Compensation agreements • References
Investment Strategy and Process	• Investment strategy and value addition • Security selection and execution • Case studies and investment memos • Portfolio due diligence checklist/report • Investment committee notes
Policies	• Valuation • Responsible investing • Portfolio monitoring and engagement • Portfolio company reporting requirements
Manuals	• Compliance—insider trading, AML, KYC • Information security • Data collection and privacy
Other	• Order management and trade reconciliation • Valuation and financials of illiquid portfolio • Sample investor newsletters and communication • Firm infrastructure • IT infrastructure • Disaster recovery plan • Risk manual/matrix • External and internal market reports

NOTES

INTRODUCTION

1. David Swensen, "Letter to Fund Managers," *Yale Investments Office*, October 2, 2020, https://static1.squarespace.com/static/55db7b87e4b0dca22fba2438 /t/5f93366562f64e6fc88cab83/1603483237324/Manager+Diversity+and+ Inclusion+Letter.pdf.

2. Rose Horowitch, "Swensen Tells Money Managers to Increase Diversity if They Want to Work with Yale," *Yale News*, October 27, 2020, https:// yaledailynews.com/blog/2020/10/27/swensen-tells-money-managers-to -increase-diversity-if-they-want-to-work-with-yale/.

3. "2020 Preqin Global Private Equity and Venture Capital Report," Preqin, 2020, https://docs.preqin.com/samples/2020-Preqin-Global-Private-Equity -Venture-Capital-Report-Sample-Pages.pdf.

4. https://www.preqin.com/insights/global-reports/2021-preqin-global-private -equity-and-venture-capital-report and https://www.barclayhedge.com/insider /fund-flow-indicator-august-2021.

CHAPTER 1

1. Heather Long, "History of Charitable Endowment Giving," *Love to Know*, accessed January 19, 2022, https://charity.lovetoknow.com/history-charitable -endowment-giving.

2. "Glebe land," Diocese of Gloucester, accessed June 20, 2022, https://www .gloucester.anglican.org/support-services/housing/glebe-land/. https://www .oxford.anglican.org/support-services/glebe-land/; Islamic Relief World- wide, "WAQF (Endowment)," *Islamic Relief Worldwide*, accessed January 19, 2022, https://www.islamic-relief.org/category/strategic-business-units /islamic-social-finance-strategic-business-units/waqf-endowment/.

3. David Chambers, Elroy Dimson, and Justin Foo, "Keynes, Kings and Endow- ment Asset Management," *National Bureau of Economic Research*, Working Paper 20421 (2014)

4. National Association of College and University Business Officers, "NACUBO-TIAA Study of Endowments: Summary Results and Key Insights (2019)."

5. US Department of Education, "National Center for Education Statistics, 2021," US Department of Education, 2021, https://nces.ed.gov/fastfacts /display.asp?id=73.
6. National Association of College and University Business Officers, "NACUBO-TIAA Study of Endowments (2018)."
7. Harvard University, "Financial Report Fiscal Year 2021," Harvard University, 2021, https://finance.harvard.edu/files/fad/files/fy21_harvard_financial _report.pdf.
8. National Association of College and University Business Officers, "NACUBO-TIAA Study of Endowments: Summary Results and Key Insights (2019)."
9. Seth Alexander, and Ahron Herring, "Endowment Spending Policy at MIT," *MIT Faculty Newsletter*, May/June 2008, https://web.mit.edu/fnl/volume/205 /alexander_herring.html.
10. Foreword to the book by David Swensen, *Pioneering Portfolio Management: An Unconventional Approach to Institutional Investment* (New York: Free Press, 2009).
11. For a more in-depth discussion, see Chapter 12 on due diligence.
12. Nikolay Shevchenko, "Did Reagan Really Coin the Term 'Trust but Verify,' a proverb revived by HBO's Chernobyl?" *Russia Beyond*, June 17, 2019, https:// www.rbth.com/lifestyle/330521-reagan-trust-but-verify-chernobyl/.
13. Quote Investigator, accessed on November 18, 2021, https://quoteinvestigator .com/2011/07/22/keynes-change-mind/.
14. Most states have adopted UPMIFA or a modified version of the UPMIFA. Elaborating on the differences is beyond the purview and scope of this book. Please seek the advice of a regulatory authority or your legal counsel to understand the differences.
15. See "Spending Policies" section on page 7 for more details.
16. Andrew Carnegie, "The Gospel of Wealth," Carnegie Corporation of New York, accessed January 25, 2022, https://www.carnegie.org/about/our-history /gospelofwealth/.
17. "1969 Annual Report," Ford Foundation, December 31, 1969, https://www .fordfoundation.org/about/library/annual-reports/1969-annual-report/.
18. "Management of Institutional Funds Act," Uniform Law Commission, accessed November 18, 2021, https://www.uniformlaws.org /committees/community-home?CommunityKey=63a66841-533c-419d-8b26 -82152512c14f.
19. "Private Foundations," *Cause IQ*, accessed January 25, 2022, https://www .causeiq.com/directory/private-foundations-list/.
20. "Trustee Compensation: Should Your Foundation Pay?" *GMA Foundations*, accessed November 18, 2021, https://www.gmafoundations.com/trustee -compensation-private-foundation/.

21. See "Endowment Structure and Staffing" and "Asset Allocation and Manager Selection" in the Endowments section (pages XX–XX), as foundations have similar practices.

22. "Uniting and Strengthening America by Providing Appropriate Tools Required to Intercept and Obstruct Terrorism (USA Patriot Act) Act of 2001," US Congress, October 26, 2001, https://www.congress.gov/107/plaws /publ56/PLAW-107publ56.pdf.

23. "The Financial Action Task Force," *Financial Crimes Enforcement Network*, accessed November 18, 2021, https://www.fincen.gov/resources/international /financial-action-task-force.

24. David Moore and Douglas Rutzen, "Double Issue: Global Philanthropy," *International Center for Not-For-Profit Law*, April 2011, https://www .icnl.org/resources/research/ijnl/legal-framework-for-global-philanthropy -barriers-and-opportunities.

25. The 1 percent rate is applicable only in the year in which spending exceeds the prior 5-year average spend.

26. "Program-Related Investments," IRS, accessed November 18, 2021, https:// www.irs.gov/charities-non-profits/private-foundations/program-related -investments.

CHAPTER 2

1. Vauhini Vara, "The Real Reason for Pensions," *New Yorker*, December 4, 2013, https://www.newyorker.com/business/currency/the-real-reason-for -pensions.

2. "A Timeline of the Evolution of Retirement in the United States," Georgetown University Law Center, 2010, https://scholarship.law.georgetown.edu /cgi/viewcontent.cgi?article=1049&context=legal

3. "A Timeline of the Evolution of Retirement in the United States."

4. "A Timeline of the Evolution of Retirement in the United States."

5. Melissa Phipps, "The History of Pension Plans in the U.S," *The Balance*, October 14, 2021, https://www.thebalance.com/the-history-of-the-pension -plan-2894374

6. "Employee Benefits Security Administration, Private Pension Plan Bulletin Historical Tables and Graphs 1975–2019," US Department of Labor, September 2021, https://www.dol.gov/sites/dolgov/files/ebsa/researchers/statistics /retirement-bulletins/private-pension-plan-bulletin-historical-tables-and -graphs.pdf

7. "Global Pension Assets Study," Thinking Ahead Institute, September 7, 2021, https://www.willistowerswatson.com/en-US/News/2021/09/top-pension-fund -assets-rise-strongly-despite-pandemic-uncertainty.

8. "Top 100 Largest Corporate Pension Rankings by Total Assets," *Sovereign Wealth Fund Institute*, accessed on January 19, 2022, https://www .swfinstitute.org/fund-rankings/corporate-pension.

9. Final average salary, which is either the average of the highest annual earnings for a set number of years (usually 3 to 5 years) or the average salary during the final years (3 to 5 years, again) of service.

10. "NASRA Issue Brief: Public Pension Plan Investment Return Assumptions," National Association of State Retirement Administrators, last modified February 2021, https://www.nasra.org/files/Issue%20Briefs /NASRAInvReturnAssumptBrief.pdf.

11. "NASRA Issue Brief."

12. "NASRA Issue Brief."

13. Amy Whyte, "Public Pensions Pour More Money into Private Equity," *Institutional Investor*, January 31, 2019, https://www.institutionalinvestor .com/article/b1cy61jsl24097/Public-Pensions-Pour-More-Money-Into -Private-Equity.

14. Jean-Pierre Aubry and Caroline V. Crawford, "Impact of Public Sector Assumed Returns on Investment Choices," Center for Retirement Research at Boston College, State and Local Pension Plans no. 63 (2019), https://crr.bc .edu/wp-content/uploads/2019/01/SLP_63-1.pdf.

15. "Investment Company Fact Book, 59th edition," 2019, https://www.ici.org /system/files/attachments/pdf/2019_factbook.pdf.

16. *2020–21 Annual Comprehensive Financial Report*, calpers.ca.gov, accessed March 15, 2022, https://www.calpers.ca.gov/docs/board-agendas/202111 /financeadmin/item-7a-03_a.pdf.

17. *Release: Quarterly Retirement Market Data, Third Quarter 2021*, Investment Company Institute, December 16, 2021, https://www.ici.org/statistical -report/ret_21_q3

18. Please see the discussion on endowments in Chapter 1 for a detailed explanation.

19. N. Raymond and D. Ingram, "N.Y. Pension Fund Manager, Brokers Charged in Pay-to-Play Scheme," Reuters, December 21, 2016, https://www.reuters .com/article/us-new-york-corruption-pensionfund/n-y-pension-fund-manager -brokers-charged-in-pay-to-play-scheme-idUSKBN14A1M3.

20. "Employment Retirement Income Security Act (ERISA)," US Department of Labor, accessed on August 16, 2019, https://www.dol.gov/general/topic /retirement/erisa.

CHAPTER 3

1. James Beech, "Global Family Office Growth Soars, Manages $5.9 Trillion," *Campden Research*, July 19, 2019, https://www.campdenfb.com/article /global-family-office-growth-soars-manages-59-trillion.

2. "The Global Family Office Report," UBS, 2019, https://www.ubs.com/global /en/wealth-management/uhnw/global-family-office-report/global-family -office-report-2019.html.

3. "The Global Family Office Report."

4. "The 2020 Global Family Office Report," UBS and Campden Research, 2020, https://hkifoa.com/wp-content/uploads/2021/05/ubs-global-family-office-report-2020.pdf.
5. "The 2020 Global Family Office Report."
6. "The 2021 Global Family Office Report," UBS, 2021, https://www.ubs.com/global/en/global-family-office/reports/gfo-r-21-4-client.html.
7. "The 2020 Global Family Office Report," UBS, 2020, https://hkifoa.com/wp-content/uploads/2021/05/ubs-global-family-office-report-2020.pdf.
8. "The 2020 Global Family Office Report."

CHAPTER 4

1. Adrian Blundell-Wignall, Yu-Wei Hu, and Juan Yermo, "Sovereign Wealth and Pension Fund Issues," *OECD Working Papers on Insurance and Private Pensions*, no. 14 (2008).
2. *Appendix 3 Sovereign Wealth Funds—US Department of the Treasury*, accessed March 20, 2022, https://home.treasury.gov/system/files/206/2007_Appendix-3.pdf.
3. "We Are the World's First Sovereign Wealth Fund," Kuwait Investment Authority, accessed January 20, 2022, https://kia.gov.kw/about-kia/#maindate.
4. "Kiribati's Revenue Equalization Reserve Fund," PitchBook.com, accessed January 20, 2022, https://pitchbook.com/profiles/limited-partner/52324-93#overview.
5. "History," New Mexico State Investment Council, accessed December 4, 2021, https://www.sic.state.nm.us/about-the-sic/history/.
6. "Government of Singapore Investment Corporation Is Formed," Government of Singapore, last updated August 2019, https://eresources.nlb.gov.sg/history/events/13ca991b-fef6-4f87-a95a-40d360a66faa.
7. Diego Lopez and Daniel Brett, "Global SWF Annual Report," *Global SWF*, 2021, http://investmentnews.co.nz/wp-content/uploads/3-SWF-Annual-Report.pdf.
8. "Sovereign Wealth Funds Surpass $9 Trillion in Assets," Sovereign Wealth Fund Institute, September 9, 2021, https://www.swfinstitute.org/news/88265/sovereign-wealth-funds-surpass-9-trillion-in-assets.
9. *Crude Oil Prices—70 Year Historical Chart*, Macrotrends.com, accessed March 28, 2022, https://www.macrotrends.net/1369/crude-oil-price-history-chart.
10. H. Raymond, "Sovereign Wealth Funds as Domestic Investors of Last Resort During Crises," Économie Internationale, no. 123 (2010), 121–159, https://doi.org/10.3917/ecoi.123.0121.
11. "Sovereign Wealth Funds: IMF Global Financial Stability Report," International Monetary Fund, accessed December 4, 2021, https://www.imf.org/external/pubs/ft/gfsr/2007/02/pdf/annex12.pdf.

12. Christine Ebrahimzadeh, "Dutch Disease: Wealth Managed Wisely," *International Monetary Fund*, last updated February 24, 2020, https://www.imf.org/external/pubs/ft/fandd/basics/dutch.htm.

13. State Street Global Advisors, Sovereign Investment Trends, January 2018 and January 2020.

14. "Know Your Investor: Hedge Funds," ALTS Capital, 2019, https://www.altscapital.com/know-your-investor.

15. "Sovereign Wealth Funds in Motion," Preqin, May 2021

16. Christine Ebrahimzadeh, "Dutch Disease: Wealth Managed Wisely," *International Monetary Fund*, last updated February 24, 2020, https://www.imf.org/external/pubs/ft/fandd/basics/dutch.htm.

17. "Linaburg-Maduell Transparency Index (LMTI)," Sovereign Wealth Fund Institute, accessed December 4, 2021, https://www.swfinstitute.org/research/linaburg-maduell-transparency-index.

18. "Sovereign Wealth Funds Generally Accepted Principles and Practices 'Santiago Principles'," International Working Group of Sovereign Wealth Funds, October 2008, https://www.ifswf.org/sites/default/files/santiagoprinciples_0_0.pdf.

CHAPTER 5

1. "Insights Global Macro Trends: Dream Big," KKR, October 2021, https://www.kkr.com/sites/default/files/Dream_Big_20211006.pdf.

2. "Facts + Statistics: Industry Overview," Insurance Information Institute, accessed December 6, 2021, https://www.iii.org/fact-statistic/facts-statistics-industry-overview.

3. "Insights Global Macro Trends: Dream Big," KKR, October 2021, https://www.kkr.com/sites/default/files/Dream_Big_20211006.pdf.

4. "Natixis Insurance Survey: Rates, Liabilities and Regulation Put CIOs Between a Rock and a Hard Place," Natixis, November 25, 2019, https://www.im.natixis.com/us/research/insurance-survey-2019-regulatory-challenges.

5. "Insurance Markets in Figures," OECD, June 2021, https://www.oecd.org/daf/fin/insurance/Insurance-Markets-in-Figures-2021.pdf.

6. "Preqin Special Report: Private Equity Funds of Funds," Preqin, November 2017, https://docs.preqin.com/reports/Preqin-Special-Report-Private-Equity-Funds-of-Funds-November-2017.pdf.

7. Robert S. Harris, Tim Jenkinson, Steven Neil Kaplan, and Rüdiger Stucke, "Financial Intermediation in Private Equity: How Well Do Funds of Funds Perform?" Darden Business School, Working Paper No. 2620582 (2017).

8. Lawrence Calcano, Eileen Duff, Hannah Shaw Grove, John Imbriglia, Peter Montgomery, Ryan Van Geons, Dan Vene, and Nick Veronis, "Registered Investment Advisors and Private Equity," iCapital Network, June 2016, https://s3.amazonaws.com/icn-web/RIA_Whitepaper_RGB_060716_A.pdf.

9. "2020 RIA Sentiment Survey," TD Ameritrade Institutional, January 7, 2020, https://www.tdainstitutional.com/content/dam/institutional/resources /ria-sentiment-survey/presentation_2020_RIA_sentiment_survey_7Jan2020 _1271014.pdf.
10. "Registered Investment Advisors and Private Equity."
11. See Chapter 15, Technology in Alternatives Markets for a discussion on the technological advances to simplify subscriptions and processes.
12. Discussion on the characteristics and differences of these fund structures are beyond the scope of this discussion other than to state that they are essentially unlisted closed-end funds organized under the Investment Company Act of 1940 that allows investment into illiquid strategies. A good discussion is available at https://www.ultimusfundsolutions.com/the-need-for-yield-why -should-asset-managers-consider-launching-an-interval-or-tender-offer-fund -and-what-do-they-need-to-know/.
13. "Registered Investment Advisor ('RIA') Private Real Estate Survey," MLG Capital, accessed January 21, 2022, https://mlgcapital.com/news/registered -investment-advisor-private-real-estate-survey/.

CHAPTER 6

1. "ILPA Principles 3.0 (2019)," Institutional Limited Partners Association, accessed December 15, 2021, https://ilpa.org/ilpa-principles/.

CHAPTER 7

1. "First-Time Fund Managers," *Preqin*, February 2017, https://docs.preqin .com/newsletters/pe/Preqin-Private-Equity-and-Venture-Capital-Spotlight -February-2017.pdf.
2. "First-Time Funds in Emerging Markets," Global Private Capital Association, July 31, 2015, https://www.empea.org/research/empea-brief-first-time -funds-in-emerging-markets/.

CHAPTER 9

1. For a good discussion on benchmarks, please see CFA U.K.'s research and position paper at https://www.cfauk.org/-/media/files/pdf/pdf/5-professionalism /3-research-and-position-papers/benchmarks-and-indices.pdf.

CHAPTER 11

1. Amy Gallo, "The Value of Keeping the Right Customers," *Harvard Business Review*, 2014, https://hbr.org/2014/10/the-value-of-keeping-the-right-customers.

CHAPTER 12

1. "Due Diligence Questionnaire and Diversity Metrics Template," Institutional Limited Partners Association, accessed December 9, 2020, https://ilpa.org /due-diligence-questionnaire/.
2. "Due Diligence Questionnaires," Alternative Investment Management Association, accessed December 9, 2020, https://www.aima.org/sound-practices /due-diligence-questionnaires.html#?active=tab-ddq-for-investors.
3. "Sound Practices for Hedge Fund Managers," Appendix II, Managed Funds Association, accessed December 9, 2020, https://www.managedfunds.org /wp-content/uploads/2011/06/Final_2009_complete.pdf.
4. See Appendix 1 for a sample of the documents that are made available in a typical PE data room.
5. The data rooms of old are physical storage areas for confidential documents kept in the manager's office. Today, all data rooms are online platforms, although some managers might still have a couple of documents they would show only in person.
6. SEC.gov, accessed April 4, 2022, https://www.sec.gov/rules/final/2011/ia -3221-appc.pdf.
7. Chris Kundro, "The problem When Asset Allocators Don't Manage and Mitigate Operational Risks in Multi-Fund Portfolios," SS&C Technologies Inc., November 13, 2019, https://www.ssctech.com/blog/the-problem-when -asset-allocators-dont-manage-and-mitigate-operational-risks-in-multi-fund -portfolios-1.

CHAPTER 13

1. John Nofsinger, "Familiarity Bias Part 1: What Is It?" *Psychology Today*, July 25, 2008, https://www.psychologytoday.com/us/blog/mind-my-money /200807/familiarity-bias-part-i-what-is-it.
2. Gur Huberman, "Familiarity Breeds Investment," *Review of Financial Studies 14*, no. 3, Fall 2001, 659–680, http://rfs.oxfordjournals.org/.

CHAPTER 14

1. "Private Fund Strategies Report," *PitchBook.com*, accessed January 15, 2022, https://pitchbook.com/news/reports/q3-2021-private-fund-strategies -report.
2. "First Time Funds," Morse, January 16, 2018, https://www.morse.law/news /first-time-funds/.
3. "Westbridge Team Splits from Sequoia India; to Focus on Public Equity." VC Circle, January 18, 2021, https://www.vccircle.com/westbridge-team-splits -sequoia-india-focus-public-equity.

CHAPTER 17

1. "Women in Private Equity," Preqin, 2019, https://docs.preqin.com/reports/Preqin-Women-in-Private-Equity-February-2019.pdf.
2. "QuickFacts: United States," *US Census Bureau*, accessed February 10, 2022, https://www.census.gov/quickfacts/US.
3. Paul Gompers, Silpa Kovvali, "The Other Diversity Dividend," *Harvard Business Review*, July 9, 2018, https://hbr.org/2018/07/the-other-diversity-dividend
4. Alan Mirabella, "Hedge Funds Run by Women, Minorities Outperform Market Peers," *Bloomberg*, November 8, 2021, https://www.bloomberg.com/news/articles/2021-11-08/hedge-funds-run-by-women-minorities-outperform-market-peers.
5. "Diversity," DUMAC Inc., accessed February 10, 2022, https://dumac.duke.edu/diversity/.
6. "The Rooney Rule," NFL, accessed February 10, 2022, https://operations.nfl.com/inside-football-ops/diversity-inclusion/the-rooney-rule/.

INDEX

ABOUT THE AUTHORS

Hemali Dassani is a senior fundraiser and consultant to multiple private equity funds. She has two decades of experience raising capital for well-respected private equity, hedge funds, and other alternative asset managers. She has built strong relationships with some of the largest public and private pension funds, endowments and foundations, insurance companies, family offices, and FoFs. She has been a Managing Director with CapLink Securities, which connects alternative investment managers and select companies to institutional investors. She was Director of Investor Relations and Chief Compliance Officer at Argand Partners, a leading private equity fund. Previously, Hemali was Director of Investor Relations at Castle Harlan, where she helped lead global fundraising efforts. When she is not managing investor relations or raising funds, Hemali is active with the Harvard Business School Club of Greater New York where she previously served as the President and is currently a lifelong board member and served as Co-Chair of the Racial Equality Task Force.

Nandu Kuppuswamy, CFA, is an investment management professional with expertise as both an asset allocator and an investor relations professional. His career and professional experience spans investor relations, fundraising, asset allocation, due diligence, operations, analytics, research, and strategy. He has a track record of raising funds from institutional investors as well as HNIs. Currently, Kuppuswamy is the COO and Partner at 3Lines Venture Capital and the founder of Ambrosian Sun Advisors, an advisor to alternative fund managers. Previously, he has managed investor relations and fundraising for Sandstone Capital (hedge fund), Kotak Mahindra Inc. (multi-asset manager), and Zodius (growth PE). Earlier he was an asset allocator at Spider Management Company (University of Richmond's endowment) and managed credit risk for an $8 billion amortizing portfolio at CapitalOne.